A Glad Obedience

A GLAD OBEDIENCE

Why and What We Sing

Walter Brueggemann

WESTMINSTER
JOHN KNOX PRESS
LOUISVILLE · KENTUCKY

First edition
Published by Westminster John Knox Press
Louisville, Kentucky

19 20 21 22 23 24 25 26 27 28—10 9 8 7 6 5 4 3 2 1

Book design by Sharon Adams
Cover design by designpointinc.com

Library of Congress Cataloging-in-Publication Data

Names: Brueggemann, Walter, author.
Title: A glad obedience : why and what we sing / by Walter Brueggemann ; foreword by John Witvliet.
Description: Louisville, KY : Westminster John Knox Press, 2018. |
 Identifiers: LCCN 2018036441 (print) | LCCN 2018044015 (ebook) | ISBN 9781611648997 | ISBN 9780664264642 (pbk.)
Subjects: LCSH: Church music—Protestant churches. | Hymns, English—History and criticism.
Classification: LCC ML3100 (ebook) | LCC ML3100 .B82 2018 (print) | DDC 264/.23--dc23
LC record available at https://lccn.loc.gov/2018036441

PRINTED IN THE UNITED STATES OF AMERICA

♾ The paper used in this publication meets the minimum requirements of the American National Standard for Information Sciences—Permanence of Paper for Printed Library Materials, ANSI Z39.48-1992.

Most Westminster John Knox Press books are available at special quantity discounts when purchased in bulk by corporations, organizations, and special-interest groups. For more information, please e-mail SpecialSales@wjkbooks.com.

for
David Ellis
and
William West

Contents

Foreword

This book is a vocational summons offered to everyone baptized into Christ. Indeed, in our baptism we are "buried with him by baptism into death, so that, just as Christ was raised from the dead by the glory of the Father, so we too might walk in newness of life" (Rom. 6:4). That's why both ancient and recently renewed baptismal liturgies invite us to reject Satan and all of Satan's empty promises and to affirm our allegiance to Jesus as Lord, a subversive message worthy of the most robust texts for singing together. This book is a witness that the church's singing is an indispensable baptismal pedagogy, a school of joyful, revolutionary formation for all people who seek to live out their baptismal calling.

This calling is not only for pastors, theologians, and church musicians. It comes to each and every one of us. What remarkable opportunities we all have to live out our calling as we sing together—to frame our songs, following Professor Brueggemann's lead, as "script[s] for subversive activity," to sing in such a way that we relinquish "Promethean pretensions to management and control," to feel deeply the ways in which robust doxology "will propel us to engage on behalf of altered production, distribution, and consumption . . . altered toward neighborliness," and to embrace the life-giving conviction of the Heidelberg Confession that our only comfort is that we are "not [our] own, but belong— body and soul, in life and in death—to [our] faithful Savior, Jesus Christ."[1]

Brueggemann's work is a poignant call to stop singing on automatic pilot, to resist our long-standing habit of inattention to the words we sing. Like a master docent who awakens the imagination of otherwise beleaguered tourists on their too-hasty tours of art museums, Brueggemann here invites us to slow down and pay much deeper attention to the church's songs, alert to the stunning way they so often recast the world in which we live.

This high view of church song also blesses and sharpens the specific vocation of the church's lyricists and songwriters. Today's congregational song lyricists are called into a long-standing tradition of lyrical craft, in which artistry consists not in obscuring elusive and noncommittal responses to the world but rather in rendering profound spiritual mysteries and heart-achingly poignant confessions and sentiments in ways that are accessible on first encounter and that reward repeated exposure over time. It is a holy and mighty challenge indeed. What an affirmation it is to have one of the church's most prominent theologians pay sustained attention not only to theological treatises but also to hymn poems—to the poetry of Watts and Wesley, Washington Gladden and Civilla Durfee Martin, and to the anonymous words of prophetic freedom songs and folk hymns.

There is a particular blessing here for those who paraphrase or echo the prophetic poetry of Scripture—those who write less as an act of self-expression and more as an act of apprenticeship. Indeed, the ancient words, images, and genres of Scripture are truly still out ahead of us, beckoning us on toward deeper, richer communion with God, one another, and the world that God loves. How we need prophetic poets apprenticed by Scripture.

The more I immersed myself in this text, the more I thought of the thousands of people across the world who, each and every week, choose and lead the songs of God's people gathered for worship—people who need to be affirmed, thanked, called, challenged, and resourced. Alert congregational leaders reading this text could generate quite a job description for these important roles in church life:

- Frame songs as acts of joyful, life-giving resistance to idolatry. Teach us that songs are an antidote to exploitation and depersonalization.
- Learn to study the Scripture texts in, around, and under the songs you love.
- Do not become so attached to subversion for its own sake that you fail to recognize genuine, covenantal, Christ-shaped forms of subversion. Cultivate the radical theological imagination needed for that discernment.
- Teach us by example what it means to sing as gift and gifting—each song a gift, each singing of a song a gift, each song a witness to gift and giving, each singer a gift in the giving.
- Devote attention to songs that convey the weightiness and hope of *hesed*, God's tenacious, covenantal solidarity and loving-kindness.
- Rescue chestnuts from the dustbin of sentimentality. Resist kitsch.
- Pay attention to context—the unique context of each Scripture text, the unique context in which each song was born, the unique context in which it will be sung today.

- Choose not only songs that express what a community already experiences but also songs that will stretch a community toward ever deeper obedience to God, ever more vivid ways of imagining God's covenantal love and fidelity.

Oh, to have more job descriptions for pastoral musicians with instructions like these. What a powerful antidote this could be to the habit so many communities have, as Brueggemann might say, of taking world-upending, astonishment-inducing texts and then rendering them with music that is utterly conventional and ultimately sentimental.

Finally, this book offers a vocational call to those who live in the spiritually fraught world of "the worship industry." Songs are bought and sold in our world, including songs about God's covenantal fidelity. Ideally, this economy provides just compensation for those called to be poets, composers, arrangers, curators, publishers, and even professors who write books. Praise God for all who participate in this economy with justice-oriented integrity. Yet it is a spiritually dangerous world, ever tempted by the idolization of celebrity and the kind of totalitarian, depersonalized commodification that Brueggemann laments.

May everyone who participates in this economy heed the message of this book: Be vigilant to fight the commodification of the church's song. Resist anything that blunts the fullness of the Christian gospel. Do not squelch the dimly burning wicks of voices at the margins whose songs may not otherwise be heard. Resist cultural imperialism. Embrace ways of creating, curating, receiving, and singing songs that demonstrate the shalom of God's way in the world.

May God's Spirit use this book as a catalyst for this kind of faithful, baptismal witness—sung shalom to the glory of God.

John D. Witvliet
Calvin Institute of Christian Worship
Calvin College and Calvin Theological Seminary
Grand Rapids, Michigan

Preface

In 2013 the Presbyterian Church (U.S.A.) published a new hymnal, *Glory to God: Hymns, Psalms, and Spiritual Songs*.[1] In order to get the new hymnal before the congregations of the church, a series of regional "launches" was offered. Happily for me, I was invited to participate in the first of those launches, and later I shared in a celebration of the hymnal in one presbytery. The material that follows in this book consists, with considerable expansion, in the presentations I made at those events.

The subtitle of this new hymnal, "Hymns, Psalms, and Spiritual Songs," is a phrase quoted from Ephesians 5:19 and Colossians 3:16. That phrase, used in the two epistles, indicates both that the early church was committed to singing and that it understood itself to be in continuity with the singing of Judaism in the usage of the Psalter. In the usage in Ephesians, such singing is contrasted with drunkenness and debauchery; the writer urges the church to be "filled with the Spirit" (Eph. 5:18). The phrasing suggests an allusion to the Pentecost narrative wherein the earliest church participants were "filled with the Holy Spirit" (Acts 2:4) and were judged by observers to be "'filled with new wine'" (Acts 2:13). The contrast of "filled with the Spirit" with drunkenness ("'filled with new wine'") in both Acts and the epistle suggests that the singing of the church was robust and emotive. In the usage of the phrase in Colossians 3:16, commendation of "psalms, hymns, spiritual songs" is in the context of a holy life marked by forgiveness and thanks; this context suggests that the singing of the church was an act of emancipation from quid pro quo interactions (which were without forgiveness) and from self-sufficiency (which was without gratitude), marks of the world in which the church did its singing.

The entire paragraph in the Letter to the Colossians (3:12–17), with its reference to singing, suggests that singing, along with forgiveness and thanks, is indeed a countercultural activity that marks the participants of the church and that distinguishes it from its cultural context. Indeed, it is still so that congregational singing, along with forgiveness and thanks, marks the church as a very different community in the context of a culture that is, for the most part, unforgiving and ungrateful. As a result, we might consider this new wondrous hymnal as a script for subversive activity. It is for certain that congregational singing, judged by the norms of our market culture, is an absurd enterprise: a group of intrepid people eagerly lining out poetry filled with archaic images and metaphors reflective of a prescientific worldview and singing ancient memories, hopes, and mysteries that contradict the "reason of the age." Such singing, when done intentionally, is perfectly countercultural.

This new hymnal is a marvel and a wonder because it reflects in a quite fresh way the great diversity and scope of the church's singing around the world. The variety of hymns assembled here provides a serious script, out beyond any sectarian or ideological parochialism, for singing alongside Christians in many other cultures. The hymnal features, moreover, many new hymns that move beyond both traditional patriarchal imagination and uncritical triumphalism as the church accepts its new role in the world. My friend Bart Campolo has decided to be a "humanist" college chaplain seeking to evoke and form communities of spiritually alert students who are untouched by any conventional Christian faith claims but who embody a wide spiritual hunger and eagerness. Campolo comments that the formation of such a humanist community is difficult because "the church has all the good songs." This hymnal is compelling evidence of that claim. The church around the world does indeed have "all the good songs" and continues to generate good hymns around which church faith and church life can be gathered and voiced.

Given the subtitle of the new hymnal, "hymns, psalms, and spiritual songs," and given my own locus in Old Testament studies, it was inescapable that my presentations at the launch would concern the book of Psalms. For that occasion, I decided to take up four long psalms that come in canonical sequence and engage in different actions reflected in very different genres. My focus is on the question "Why do we sing?" It is a question not very often asked in the church, even though we sing often and regularly. I mean by that governing question to reflect on what it is we are doing when we sing hymns, psalms, and spiritual songs. The answer to that question I think is not abstract or theoretical. It is rather an answer given in the way we practice the songs themselves. Thus in the sequence of Psalms 104, 105, 106, and 107, we see the church after Israel, by way of sustained cadence and rich poetic imagery, performing and exhibiting human practices that belong peculiarly (but not exclusively) to the Christian community. The practices performed in these particular psalms, which recur in many church hymns, are definingly human when it is remembered that our humanness consists in our lives played out in the presence of God. We can thus see the following:

- In Psalm 104, we have a practice of wonder and awe that issues in exuberant praise.
- In Psalm 105 we have an act of remembering God's good actions that moves us to glad obedience.
- In Psalm 106, we have an act of remembering our own waywardness that situates us honestly in our need and hope for God's rescue.
- In Psalm 107 we have acts of gratitude that specifically name the occasions of God's transformative fidelity and our response with material gratitude.

The four liturgic actions—praise, readiness for obedience, readiness for rescue, and thanks (to which other like actions can be readily added)—together constitute a rendering of humanness as it is given in the biblical-evangelical tradition and as it may be performed in our worship.

After I had completed this exposition, I was fortunate to have access to a dissertation from the University of Gloucestershire by Peter C. Ho, who suggests that these four psalms constitute in the Psalter something of an intentional corpus.[2] Along with the obvious fact of their shared uncommon length, Ho observes a number of intertextual references in the psalms that together suggest some intentional coherence to the four. Such a judgment can only strengthen the case I have tried to make for the focus of discussion. The four psalms together provide ample testimony to why we sing.

These dimensions of humanness, which are embraced as they are performed, amount to "a world of gift" that refuses the more conventional and pervasive "world of commodity." The momentary departure from the world of commodity in worship requires a practice of imagination and emotional emancipation that together defy the tight calculus of market ideology. The contrast between the commodity world "out there" and the "gift world" in here in our singing is made clear in the following comment on a sermon by Charles Chauncy in 1747, "A Caveat against Enthusiasm."[3] Chauncy championed the "reasonableness" of Christian worship and warned against enthusiasm:

> That you can't reason with them [the enthusiasts] is the first sign, but interestingly enough, all the others have to do with their bodies: "it may be seen in their countenances," "a certain wildness . . . in their general look," "it strangely loosens their tongues," "throws them . . . into quakings and tremblings," and they are "really beside themselves, acting . . . by the blind impetus of a wide fancy." It is precisely the feeling that one's body has been entered by some "other" that Chauncy wishes to warn against.[4]

The alternative to "enthusiasm" is reasoned worship and reasoned talk that values analytic cognition operating through intellectual control and market exchanges. In such a world, worship is essentially "talk," the kind of reasoned talk in which Presbyterians and many other Christians are wont to engage in worship.

In contrast, singing is artistry that entails a kind of freedom that resists such analytic control. Lewis Hyde says of such a contrast:

> The ceremonies of enthusiastic religions tend to include the body, rather than talk. The celebrants dance and sing, they quake and tremble. But no one dances ecstatic dances in the church of the rich. Nor do they speak in tongues or raise their hands in the gesture of epiphany the way the Christian enthusiasts do. The rich would seem to sense that the more you feel the spirit move in the physical body on Sunday, the harder it will be to trade in cash on Monday. Better to sit in one's pew and listen to a talk.[5]

The contrast of course need not be complete, and certainly the hymnal committee did not intend to champion "enthusiasm." But the point of the contrast is worth noting. Singing is, by the way of the world, quite "unreasonable" and bears witness to an alternative reality.

The sum of the contrast can be seen in any singing congregation. There is an occasional break with bodily restraint as there is a break with closed reasoning into daring imagery beyond our explanatory capacity. People sometimes raise their hands or move their feet and sway a bit with the cadence. Thus an answer to "Why we sing?" is that in singing we may evidence and enact our God-given humanness, which is marked by bodily freedom, by uncensored articulation, and by full-person engagement. Israel, which has been dancing and singing since Miriam defied Pharaoh, has known this (see Exod. 15:20–21). The early church knew this in Pentecost, which made imperial magistrates nervous (see Acts 16:25–34). Martin Luther knew this as he exposited the grace of God that contradicted all human "law." He knew that such grace must be sung. Martin Luther King Jr., kneeling before sheriffs, knew that singing counters intimidation and evokes courage. And now with this new hymnal we know it in the late days of capitalism, which wants to cover over bodily humanity (with its wounds and possibilities) by the offer of religious kitsch. The singing church has always known better. The more the church forms its life outside the restraints of dominant values and outside economic necessity that insists on those values, the more its singing is an emancipatory practice of full-bodied selves in the image of God. To this end, the new hymnal is a compelling, inviting, accessible script of treasures new and old.

The second half of this book, titled "What We Sing," explores fifteen different hymns—some old chestnuts that no longer appear in some hymnals and others that are newer compositions—and asks the question "Why do we sing this particular song?" I conclude with a more recent presentation that I offered at Xavier University. The happy occasion for my presentation was the fact that the university has acquired a copy of the new St. John Bible, with its spectacular calligraphy and other artistic work. That occasion gave me opportunity, through the exposition of three other psalms, to draw out some implications of my original exploration in relation to the new hymnal.

I am grateful to David Dobson, David Maxwell, and a host of Louisville Presbyterians who included me in the hymnal launch. Beyond that I am glad to be able to salute my ancient Psalms teachers, Allen G. Wehrli and Samuel Terrien, and a goodly company of Presbyterian Psalms scholars, including Patrick Miller, William Brown, and Clint McCann.

I am glad to dedicate this book to my friends David Ellis and William West, who are among the most zealous, talented, and generous church singers I know. David from time to time offers solos in our worship. William, from the first pew, enables the congregation to find its doxological voice. Together they make a difference in the way we sing.

To know why we sing may bring to us a deeper delight in our singing and a strengthened resolve to sing without calculation before the God who is "enthroned on the praises of Israel" (Ps. 22:3).

PART ONE
WHY WE SING

What is the linkage between a hymnal and my work in the Old Testament? I propose that the interface or commonality is this: We have 150 psalms, and we only know and use six of them (Pss. 23, 46, 103, 121, and two more on special occasions in the church year: Ps. 22 on Good Friday and Ps. 51 on Ash Wednesday). That practice leaves us free to disregard all the other psalms.

When hymnal committees convene to choose the texts for their new collection, they have tough choices to make. Some hymns are obvious candidates for inclusion. Some will barely make it. Some will cause the hymnal committee no end of consternation, even long after they've made their particular decisions. But mostly we know, love, and are likely to sing about thirty-five of them, if that many, no matter what the particular hymnal committee had in mind. Thus we treat both collections, the Psalter and our hymnal, in the same way: as inventories of rich resources—in both of which we are highly selective and exclusionary in practice, sometimes militantly and defiantly so.

Thus I begin by considering the psalms along with the question, "Why do we sing hymns and psalms?" If one were an anthropologist and regarded a worshiping congregation as a primitive tribe (sometimes it is!) and observed its worship practice from the back of the room, congregational singing might appear odd indeed. It consists in a mighty effort, sometimes with the urging by the leader to do louder or better, sometimes poorly and inadequately rendered, and sometimes done well by paid professionals. But it is always a serious investment in a bodily enterprise that requires some energy and that at its best brings us into community. An anthropologist would readily see that we are engaged when we sing hymns in "world construction," the articulation of a world that is very different from the one we have regularly in front of us.[1]

Martin Luther, the great father of congregational singing, was of course no disciplined anthropologist. He was rather a bold energetic preacher, teacher, liturgist, and exegete who celebrated the notion of "evangelical" in order to assert that our ultimate trust is not in any humanly constructed world—not the Bible, the church, or the church's doctrine; not morality, liturgy, piety, or polity; and not the flag, the currency of the state, or the ideology of the corporation or the market. Instead, our ultimate trust is in the God of the gospel, who is out beyond our best reason, distorted as that reason is. Luther understood that congregational singing not only creates unity in the body but also offers a particular kind of unity, a shared act of rendering one's whole life before the mystery of God. That rendering, because it probes the emotional extremities of our existence, must perforce be done in a lyrical fashion that creates openings in our reasoning, that invites a kind of honest assertion and submission that is lacking in reasonable prose. We sing because life is God-given, God-sustained, and God-claimed. Our singing is our glad assent to that God-givenness and a refusal to have our lives be less than, more than, or other than that.

In the next four chapters I will consider four long psalms that come in sequence and are in the center of the Psalter (Pss. 104, 105, 106, 107), none of which makes "the big six" that we know and love. I will bring to each of these psalms in turn the question "Why do we sing?" I will ask it particularly of each psalm: "Why do we sing *this* psalm?" What are we doing when we sing it? What would we miss if we did not sing it? What do we miss because we mostly do not sing any of these four psalms? My comments will be quite text specific; as you read, however, I invite you to generate a list of hymns that would be linked to and reflective of particular psalms. You can work from your best thirty-five, but perhaps more than that will be given to you by the spirit. Or you can probe your own hymnal to find what you may have overlooked.

Thus we sing to render our lives in all of their rich complexity, in honesty, back to God. Gerhard von Rad has famously concluded that the psalms, along with the wisdom tradition, constitute a "response" to God, to who God is and to what God has done.[2] We do so as a part of a singing company that has been so rendering its life back to God since the tambourines of Miriam (Exod. 15:20–21), since the triumph of Deborah (Judg. 5:2–31), since the grief of David (2 Sam. 1:19–27), and since the defiant hope of Mary (Luke 1:46–55).

Chapter 1

Psalm 104

I begin with Psalm 104 because it is our best model for a "creation hymn," partly derived from Egyptian religion but now drawn close to YHWH, the God of covenant in Israel.[1] We sing it in order to situate our lives amid God's creation, locating ourselves among the many creatures, fully honest about our creatureliness, which is like all the other plethora of God's creatures but peculiar among them in our particular mode of feedback to the creator. Clearly other creatures all praise God, as the Psalms assume, each in its own appropriate mode.

We sing because we trust the structured generativity of creation that we receive with sacramental sensibility (vv. 1–24). The speaker, a glad creature of God, makes a quick self-identification at the outset: "O my soul . . . my God." But then it is all about YHWH, all about "you" in direct address. The divine name is uttered once in verse 1, and then not again until verse 24 (except for the incidental mention in verse 16). The hymn is direct address to "you," a known, named primal agent who has acted and who continues to act. This speaker knows that "you" must be addressed and dares to imagine that when "I" ("my soul") sings to YHWH, YHWH's glory, honor, and sovereignty are in mighty ways enhanced or, as we say, "magnified." As we have voice, so we declare ourselves to the creator God. This long inventory of twenty-three verses moves from the grand landscape of creation to the particulars of daily life, all held in God's purview.

The doxology begins with the ordering of all the creation, all the heavens, all the earth, all the clouds, all the wind (vv. 1–9).

- You are clothed.
- You are wrapped.
- You stretch out the heavens.
- You set the beams.
- You make the clouds.
- You ride on the wings.
- You make the winds.
- You set the earth.
- You cover it.
- You set a boundary.

The singer has no doubt that this seething mass of vitality is ordered and rebuked, tamed and limited, restrained by a God-authorized boundary that it will not cross (v. 9). The singer takes into full account the seething but knows about the sovereign voice that presides over it to cause safe living space. The chaos is contained and must submit to the will of the creator. Thus the very singing evokes a world in which the effect and threat of chaos are limited and contained. The poetry refuses any explanation; the song is about wonder, not explanation, about trust, not control.[2]

The song is sung in an arid climate, and we may sing it now as we come to the "water wars" in which water will be scarcer even than oil. Here in exuberance the singer chooses terms that "splash" with freshness:

> You make springs gush forth in the valleys;
>   they flow between the hills,
> giving drink to every wild animal;
>   the wild asses quench their thirst.
> By the streams the birds of the air have their habitation . . .
>   the earth is satisfied with the fruit of your work.
>
> vv. 10–13

Even in translation we get the concrete, life-giving goodness of the water: "gush" (v. 10), "quench" (v. 11), "satisfied" (v. 13). Human creatures have no privilege here; "all creatures of our God and king" are sustained. In the singing we may imagine ourselves "quenched" and "satisfied," like animals at an African watering hole along with wild asses and birds, all of them guaranteed in the earth. When we are quenched and satisfied, moreover, we may gain a bit of distance from our anxious consumerism, discerning that we are never quenched and satisfied by commodities but only by gifts given by the creator. That same water causes grass to grow:

> You cause the grass to grow for the cattle,
> and plants for people to use.
>
> v. 14

In a single verse the nonhuman and human creatures stand together before the life-giving gifts of God.

But then the lyric comes closer to us human creatures. Now the concern is for our "heart" and our "face" (v. 15), that is, full human health flourishing. Our face and our heart require the following:

- Wine to gladden
- Oil to shine
- Bread to strengthen

After all the big structure of heaven and earth, the real gift of the creator is *bread, wine, and oil.* This is the stuff of daily food without which we cannot live. It has, however, been transposed in our liturgical imagination into the stuff of sacrament, the gift making real the giver. So we pray,

> Gracious God, pour out your Holy Spirit upon us
> and upon these your gifts of bread and wine,
> that the bread we break and the cup we bless
> may be the communion of the body and blood of Christ.[3]

It is an audacious albeit familiar prayer. It is, however, an audacity that is rooted in the deep sense already voiced by the psalmist, who saw that such food is more than biological sustenance, though it is that. It is a holy gift that "gladdens" and "makes shine," that vivifies "humanness." Daily food is sacramental! These daily elements witness to the truth of gift, giving, and giver; we, we creatures, are on the glad receiving end of olive oil from trees that we did not grow, bread we did not bake, and grapes we did not produce: wine, oil, bread! These are gifts that bespeak life given; they cannot be owned, possessed, stored up, confiscated, or monopolized. They are for all human creatures who yearn to have glad hearts and shining faces.

The creatures all sing of this amazement concerning the very flow of life too readily taken for granted. That life is made possible and assured by the generous gift of water, wine, oil, bread, and grass, appropriate for each creature, for each creature can digest the generous gift.

> The trees of the LORD are watered abundantly,
> the cedars of Lebanon that he planted.
> In them the birds build their nests;

> the stork has its home in the fir trees.
> The high mountains are for the wild goats;
>   the rocks are a refuge for the coneys.
> You have made the moon to mark the seasons;
>   the sun knows its time for setting.
>
>   vv. 16–19

The cedar trees stand tall in praise (v. 16). The birds nest confidently (v. 17). The storks settle gratefully; the goats climb securely (v. 18); the coneys (rabbits) twitch their noses; the moon shines; the sun rises (v. 19); and all creatures are busy with their joyous vocations. All creation works in an ordered way. All have food. All have water. All have time.

There is time for hungry animals:

> You make darkness, and it is night,
>   when all the animals of the forest come creeping out.
> The young lions roar for their prey,
>   seeking their food from God.
> When the sun rises, they withdraw
>   and lie down in their dens.
> People go out to their work
>   and to their labor until the evening.
>
>   vv. 20–23

There is a time for everything, a time to work and a time to rest, a time to prowl and a time to hide! The night is occupied by young lions who rove in their hungry roar, knowing that they are on the receiving end of God's food. But they are not, however, creatures that work 24/7. They know when to stop . . . at dawn. They make way for a new set of creatures, human persons who have been sleeping and now go out to work (v. 23). But these day-time human creatures are also not 24/7 creatures. They will yield in due course to "lion-time" when the sun sets. The singer sketches from the big canvas of heaven and earth, ruled by God who presides over all that is, seen and unseen. But the doxology from there draws close to food and sleep, knowing that

> ". . . life [is] more than food, and the body [is] more than clothing."
> (Matt. 6:25)

The singer finds that life in its dailiness is from God and so yields it back to God.

The singer has withheld the name of the creator until verse 24. All the data is collected, enough data to make scientific probes, enough material out of which to imagine evolution. But then the name of the creator bursts into the song: "O Lord" (v. 24), O YHWH, O wow! It is your works, your wisdom, your creatures. It all you! And we have received it. We receive it every day. We live every day on the terms you give; we receive, we along with rabbits and lions and birds and cedar trees, all living, all receiving. YHWH is the daily reliable giver. O my!

We sing because we know about the rumble of chaos and are glad for its domestication by YHWH (vv. 25–26). Chaos is there; we do not deny it. It is the chaos present before time, *tohu wabohu* (Gen. 1:1). It is the chaos of disordered politics when "there was no king in Israel" (Judg. 19:1; 21:25). It is the chaos of surging waters when Jesus slept in the boat and finally awakened enough to call that it should shut up (Mark 4:35–41). It is the chaos of a family distressed, a failed marriage, an unwanted pregnancy, an unwelcome diagnosis. It is chaos in a society bent on violence, a world of hate, guns, and terrorism, a government that can host torture, a rapacious corporation that devours, an economy that leaves too many behind, a deeply felt disorder that makes us weary and edgy.

So we sing, "Yonder is the sea, great and wide " (Ps. 104:25). We see the whitecaps of confusion and hear the surging waters with ships tossed about. We know this seething, which is bottomless and endless, relentless in its devastating power. But we also know better. In our singing we also know about that old authoritative voice that commands chaos into obedience:

> I placed the sand as a boundary for the sea,
>   a perpetual barrier that it cannot pass;
> though the waves toss, they cannot prevail,
>   though they roar, they cannot pass over it.
>   Jer. 5:22

From the outset we have had this stately liturgy that prevailed over chaos: "God saw that it was good . . . very good," and God rested with no anxiety (Gen. 1:1–2:4). We anticipate an ending to such chaos with a new heaven and new earth and no more sea, no surging deathly force against us any longer (Rev. 21:1; see Isa. 65:17–25). Our lives are suspended between that initial "goodness" and that anticipated banishment of chaos. And we, midway between ending and beginning, can succumb in anxiety and fear. We can submit to surging chaos and act out our own chaotic antineighborliness.

But then we take a second look. We remember that he said to the waters, "'Peace! Be still!'" (Mark 4:39). That he said to the raging chaos, "'Be still, and know that I am God!" (Ps. 46:10). We watch and notice that the ships manage. It must have been fearful for the first Vikings and fearful of late for a cruise ship that lost its power. But they go! They travel all the way from Phoenicia to Tarshish and back again. They keep a schedule. The claim is vouched for me just now: out my window I see a regatta of seven geese in our pond, swimming single file. They do not hurry. They exhibit no anxiety. As much as I can tell, they accept the world given them and settle for an orderliness in their own lives. The ones on the ships from Tarshish back to Phoenicia record the stars and measure the winds. We can trace a direct line from ancient Vikings to our own present mates at Hubble. We have learned that even chaos has an order and a structure. We remember that even the monsters of the deep have limit and order and sense. They have enough intentionality, like birds that migrate, about proper coming and going (see Isa. 1:3a; Jer. 8:7). And we remember the dictum in the wake of the primal flood:

> As long as the earth endures,
>   seedtime and harvest, cold and heat,
> summer and winter, day and night,
>   shall not cease.
>   Gen. 8:22

We sing to celebrate that chaos is ordered:

> There go the ships,
>   and Leviathan that you formed to sport in it.
>   Ps. 104:26

It is God who intended the sea monster to have fun in the water. And you, you mighty creator, in your playfulness, perhaps enjoy a dolphin performance or the sea monster for entertainment; you treat them like toys. Jon Levenson refers to the sea monster as "God's rubber duckey."[4] You enjoy them; you, in your sovereign power, laugh at them in delight, and all the creatures find their best life in conformity to your will. Our singing reassures us, not in denial of vexed reality but in acknowledgment that you finally are Lord of lords, Lord of all creatures, even the odd ones who risk a bit of disobedience to you. With bold articulation, we sense that even our own chaos, so present to us, is not "on the loose." It is contained because your rule will not be outflanked. It all belongs to the creator:

> It is he who made the earth by his power,
>   who established the world by his wisdom,
>   and by his understanding stretched out the heavens.
> When he utters his voice, there is a tumult of waters in the heavens,
>   and he makes the mist rise from the ends of the earth.
> He makes lightnings for the rain,
>   and he brings out the wind from his storehouses.
>   Jer. 10:12–13

We in our supporting role yield the stage to you, you in your wonder that outruns our sense, you in your wisdom that outruns our anxiety, you with your creation that you cherish. We find ourselves being cherished and sustained, and all the others alongside us as well.

It is no wonder that YHWH teased our brother Job about Leviathan. When Job, like us, imagined his moral supremacy, YHWH reminded him of his modest creatureliness:

"Can you draw out Leviathan with a fishhook,
> or press down its tongue with a cord?
Can you put a rope in its nose,
> or pierce its jaw with a hook?
Will it make many supplications to you?
> Will it speak soft words to you?
Will it make a covenant with you
> to be taken as your servant forever?
Will you play with it as with a bird,
> or will you put it on leash for your girls?"
>> Job 41:1–5

Will you be able to treat chaos as toy, as do I? No, you will not press its tongue. No, you will not rope its nose. No, you will not pierce its jaw. No, he will not address petition to you. No, he will not make a covenant with you. No, you will not put it on a leash. No, the power of chaos will not be managed by you. It will be managed, however, by YHWH, who makes this enormous chaos for entertainment. No wonder we sing!

We sing because we know our secure place in the food chain that is sustained by divine watchfulness and generosity (vv. 27–28):

These all look to you
> to give them their food in due season;
when you give it to them, they gather it up;
> when you open your hand, they are filled with good things.
>> See Ps. 145:15–16

When we forget the dependence of other creatures on God's generosity and imagine that we are lords of the food chain, we scramble to produce more and possess more and consume more. We build bigger barns. We build storehouse cities as Pharaoh did, and, like Pharaoh, we build them with cheap labor. We maintain engines of force to control food supplies, oil deposits, chemical resources, and cheap labor. We are propelled by our anxiety.

And then comes the voice that guarantees the food supply: "'Do not worry, saying, "What will we eat?"'" Because, said our rabbi in gender-exclusive language: "'Your heavenly Father knows that you need all these things'" (Matt. 6:31–32). It is to the "Father who art in heaven" that we pray for daily bread. We have been praying for daily bread since that first daily bread was given us in the wilderness. We were warned then not to accumulate or hoard, and now we watch while our surpluses get worms and smell and melt (Exod. 16:20–21). But we know better; we have known better since the first surprise of bread in a place where there seemed at first to be no bread. For good reason Jesus wondered aloud to his disciples, "'Why are you talking about having no bread?'" (Mark 8:17).[5]

We look back at the birds and the lilies and the rabbits (coneys!) and chipmunks and the geese and the deer. And we know that they have been feeding forever. It all works! It yields food! Creation is the gift that keeps giving! We along with the other creatures are situated in a food supply that is reliable. We all are situated there by virtue of our status as creatures. They look to thee. We look to thee. We all look to thee! Where else should we look? Certainly not to the ideologies of market capitalism or communism. None of those ideologies is finally generous to creatures who neither toil nor spin.

> You give in due season;
> You give and they gather;
> You open your hand; they are filled.
>   Ps. 104:27–28, au. trans.

You give, and you open; we gather, and we are filled. Food starts with you. On the receiving end they (and we) gather and are filled: "Some gather[ed] more, some less . . . those who gathered much had nothing over, and those who gathered little had no shortage; they gathered as much as each of them needed" (Exod. 16:17–18).

We say our little table prayers. We mumble them, or do not have time for them. We now know how to produce our own food. We now have lab-produced food laden with preservatives . . . and obesity. When we imagine that we may have food on our own without the mysterious giving of creation, we eat too much, or we eat the wrong things. We eat what we want, even after we are warned about the consequences for our health. We eat what belongs to our neighbor. We imagine that we can have bread that is not broken and that it will nourish us. We imagine that we can drink wine to satiation without its being poured out in forgiveness.

But the sight of our fellow creatures stops us short. They do not gather more than they need. They do not hoard. Who ever saw a hummingbird that is overweight? But that very bird has enough! When and if we remove food from our anxiety zone, we will be sated. Because life is more than food, we eat daily bread. We do it in peaceableness. We do it in anticipation of the heavenly banquet when all will be fed. Food is the great zone of anxiety among us. And now in our singing, it becomes a zone of trust and gratitude and neighborliness . . . filled with good things!! Our singing leads us to both confidence and awareness. Amid the doxologies of abundance we learn more, if we are discerning, about the scarcity all around us. It is scarcity that contradicts the creator—scarcity produced by anxiety, greed, and violence. And we expect, when we are alert, that our doxologies will propel us to engage on behalf of altered production, distribution, and consumption. Without doxology, it is certain that these practices will not be altered toward neighborliness.

We sing because we have breath (vv. 29–30). Lessons in singing are much about breathing properly. Singing is a way to measure and appreciate the gift of breath. It is a rule of life that we must inhale before we exhale. It is a rule of life that we receive before we give. It is a rule that we cannot live without oxygen, for without it we would soon have brain damage. We must have it; we must receive it. But we cannot hold it, not for very long. We cannot hold it, possess it, store it up, sell it, buy it, or trade it. It is a gift that keeps on giving, and we keep receiving until we cannot any longer.

Because we can breathe, we must sing. When we live in a context of fear, greed, and violence, however, we cannot breathe freely, and we cannot sing. We know about the terrified cry of racism: "I can't breathe." When we are bondaged, coerced, and driven long enough, none of us can breathe. And we surely cannot sing in such life-damaging circumstances. But sing we must. To sing, we must breathe freely. And to breathe freely, our bodies must be freed; our lives must be freed from threat. So the psalmist ponders free breath and all that free breath means for a good life.

We sing in order to conduct a quick seminar on *ruah*, "wind, force, breath, spirit." We remember that when we catch our breath, we can function again; but we must stop to catch it. We notice that God's good *ruah* caused creation. It was that breath that hovered over the chaos and evoked life (Gen. 1:2). When God authorizes another breath, we live. When God breathes on plants, they grow. When God breathes on animals, they prosper. We are all creatures of the breath. But it is also the case that God's breath, taken as hot wind, can cause grass to dry up:

> The grass withers, the flower fades,
>> when the breath of the LORD blows upon it;
>> surely the people are grass.
> The grass withers, the flower fades.
>> Isa. 40:7–8

We sing of God's breath to remember that we are drastically penultimate, dependent on that gift of breath.

With God's breath comes God. God's own lordly presence must be hosted. When God is not welcomed, we may find an absence. Call it exhaustion. Call it depression. Call it despair; or call it pride, the attempt to be self-created, self-sufficient, self-possessed, "selved" to security. Without the breath, we are indeed reduced to "selfies." We fence out new life; we imagine that the breath will not penetrate our vaults, our gated communities, our "whole life centers," our closed moral systems, our preferred economic arrangements, our fixed ideologies, or our flattened worlds. And then we die!

> We die in dismay when you hide your face.
> We die in shriveling when you give no *ruah*.
>> Ps. 104:29, au. trans.

We die in pride with unsustainable self-sufficiency. We die, and the body politic dies.

In the face of such death Jesus came as the Easter lord, and he breathed on them (John 20:22). And they lived. No wonder we sing! Because we have been breathed on!

We die on our own without you. But that is why the positive of verse 30 follows the negative of verse 29:

> When you send forth your spirit, they are created;
> and you renew the face of the ground.
>
> v. 30

The hard truth of our singing is that we are not on our own. The good truth of our song is that we live from this divine iron lung who renews us instant by instant, who gives to us breath in our weariness, who enlivens us when we fail.

We sing because our lives are God-occupied (vv. 31–35). Now we have again the divine name; we heard it in verse 1 ("O Lord"), incidentally in verse 16 ("the trees of the Lord"), and then bursting out in verse 24 ("O Lord, how manifold . . ."). Until now those are the only times the speaker mentions the creator's name! Otherwise it is all "you," all "thee," just a pronoun—until verse 31. But then verses 31–35 gather it all together with an avalanche of soundings of the divine name (au. trans.):

- "May the glory of YHWH endure forever" (v. 31)
- "May YHWH rejoice in his works" (v. 31)
- "I will sing to YHWH as long as I live" (v. 33)
- "I will sing to my God while I have being" (v. 33)
- "I will rejoice in YHWH" (v. 34)
- "Bless YHWH, O my soul" (v. 35)
- "Praise YHWH" (v. 35)

It is now all YHWH! Karl Barth thought we could not move with religious initiative from the world to God; he insisted that the move is in the other direction. But John Calvin knew that we can work it in either direction, from God to world or from world to God.

> In the first place, we cannot look upon ourselves without immediately turning our thoughts to the contemplation of God, in whom we "live and move." The knowledge of ourselves not only arouses us to seek God but also, as it were, leads us by the hand to find him.[6]

> Here it is from creation to creator, culminating in the name
> that is above every name,
> that is in, with, and under all,
> who is the Lord of chaos,
> who is the guarantor of food,
> who is the source of breath.

We sing the name laden with generosity, because we cannot do else wise. The world, gospel practiced, leads us there.

> So we say with the Psalmist, "Glory to YHWH";
> as it was in the beginning, is now and shall be forever.
> So we sing with the Psalmist that we "rejoice in YHWH":
> Joy to the world, the Lord is come!

This God has mightily to do with the world: This is the one

> who looks on the earth and it trembles,
> who touches the mountains and they smoke.
>
> Ps. 104:32

The earth trembles in obedience; the mountains smoke in acknowledgment. This God impinges upon, calls to account, assures, waters, and forgives. And when we attend to this impingement and notice and acknowledge, what else will we do but sing?

> I will sing as long as I live
> because it is the focus of my life;
> I will praise while I have being
> because my being is situated in my praise.
> I will sing; I will rejoice!
>
> Ps. 104:33, au. trans.

We sing because we acknowledge, in gladness, that we are penultimate. When we do not sing, when we imagine ourselves ultimate, we will end in self-serving hubris or self-destructive despair. We will end devoured, in pride or in defeat, by ourselves. It is our singing that guards against too much diminishment or too much enhancement. It is our singing that reminds us of limit and vocation and purpose. It is our singing that assures us that no good can come from our self-funding arrogance or our self-denying impotence. We are safe from chaos (vv. 24–26); we are fed to satiation (vv. 27–28); we are breathed on (vv. 29–30). My life, our life together, has no other purpose than to glorify and enjoy God. So we say at the outset and at the end:

> Bless the LORD, O my soul.
> Ps. 104:1, 35

Enhance the Lord, O myself; that is my beginning and the end of our song.

We sing because there is a sticky footnote of sternness at the end of this song. It is a little notice in verse 35 that we will never sing in church (also see Ps. 145:20):

> Let sinners be consumed from the earth,
> and let the wicked be no more.

It is an odd reference to "sinners" and "the wicked." They have no staying power. They will be consumed until they are no more. Who are they? They are the ones who do not sing. They are the ones who do not bless, who do not acknowledge, and who end up having no "soul." They are the ones who think they will manage chaos on their own. They are the ones who think they can have their own food supply. They are the ones who think they can hold their breath and sell it as a commodity if they train hard enough. They are the ones who imagine they are not creatures but have themselves created. They have no future!

We sing our penultimacy as an act of resistance and as a proposal of alternative. The resistance performed by this singing is against the reduction of creation to a series of commodity transactions because it is all gift. It is thus a resistance against market ideology that seeks to buy and sell and trade and own everything. It is resistance against scientism (notice that I do not say "science"!) that tries its best to explain and thereby control everything. Singing has no conflict with science that is grounded in wonder nor any need to dispute evolution. But this singing does resist our Promethean pretensions to management and control. This singing is an act of alternative to the rat race grounded in an ideology of scarcity. It is the affirmation that we live in a generous context of abundance in which there is enough for all of God's creatures. Such abundance requires, as the ancient singers surely knew, discipline and generosity and a readiness to forgo every luxury and convenience for the sake of the neighborhood. Thus this singing is inherently subversive; it is lining out a subversion of reality that gives our lives back in wonder to God in acknowledgment of a governance other than our own.

So imagine: we sing our penultimacy. We sing our derivative quality. We reach our lives back to the creator, glad enough to be creatures alongside rabbits and lions and birds, especially hummingbirds! Glad to be penultimate. In Hebrew the last words of the psalm, "Praise the Lord," are "Hallelu-Yah," a combination of "praise" (*hallal*) and the name of the creator, *Yah*.

We know about singing "hallelujah" to the creator since the ancient cadences of St. Francis:

> All creatures of our God and King,
> lift up your voice and with us sing.
> Alleluia! Alleluia!
> O brother sun with golden beam,
> O sister moon with silver gleam,
> sing praises! Alleluia!
> Alleluia! Alleluia! Alleluia![7]

Francis sings directly from the Psalter into a world preoccupied with control and certitude. He sings resistance and alternative.

We also know "hallelujah" in new singing. In the new Presbyterian hymnal *Glory to God* we get fresh resistance and alternative in an all-new doxology:

> Hallelujah! Sing praise to your Creator,
> sun, moon, and stars and angels above.
> Praise the Lord, whose word established the heavens,
> who upholds all the earth in power and love.
> God reigns on high, let the heavens rejoice!
> God reigns on high, let the heavens rejoice!
>
> Praise the Lord, all mountains and oceans,
> rolling thunder and wind and storm clouds on high.
> Praise the Lord, your Maker,
> all living creatures, all the beasts in the fields and birds in the sky.
> Both young and old, come and join in the song!
> Both young and old, come and join in the song!
>
> Give to God all glory and honor.
> From the depths to the heights let praises resound to the Lord,
> the source of strength and salvation
> for all people on whom God's favor is found.
> Praise God, you saints who are claimed as God's own!
> Praise God, you saints who are claimed as God's own.[8]

In both ancient cadence and contemporary beauty, the people of God sing because we are called to live in an alternative world that requires constant reiteration. It is a world of *order* amid palpable chaos, of *food* for all creatures, and of *breath* given reliably and sovereignly withheld. It is no wonder that we continue, even in our frightened context, to sing exuberantly to the God of life who dwells beyond all our explanations.

Chapter 2

Psalm 107

Psalm 107 provides a welcome counterpoint to Psalm 104 because it is as specific as Psalm 104 is generalizing. Whereas Psalm 104 is *praise* as an act of exuberant self-abandonment, Psalm 107 is a *song of thanksgiving* with all the particularity of blessings counted and gifts named. These gifts and blessings invite gratitude and evoke verbal and material response. We tend to conflate praise and thanks, and sometimes the same conflation occurs in the Psalter. We would do well, however, to make a clear distinction between the two, because they emerge differently, they function differently, and they imply different actions and practices.

Harvey Guthrie has provided a helpful, acute sociological analysis of thanks and praise. He judges that temple worship of the city-state in the ancient world (for Israel it was Jerusalem) took over the generic hymns of praise from other high cultures. The hymns of praise celebrated the cosmic sovereignty of God and by derivation affirmed the cosmic authority of the king of a city-state:

> From the temple-palace complex at the highest place in the kingdom,
> the place nearest to heaven, the order and security ensured by the cosmic

sovereign flowed out into the city within whose walls people were safe under the protection of the king, the vice-regent of the cosmic sovereign. Likewise, order and security flowed outward from the city to the city's cultivated and protected territories in which the king's plows and police held chaos in check.[1]

The authority of the king via the temple was sustained by hymns that affirmed the legitimacy of the established order.

By contrast, outside the domain of the city-state and "outside the cosmos" existed a peasant economy that depended on the specific gifts of God. This community rendered thanks for specific acts of deliverance and prosperity. In contrast to the cosmic God of establishment hymns, the God of the peasant community was a personal God, intimately linked to the life-and-death crises of a relatively impotent class of people. This class distinction between the powerful and the vulnerable and their songs is in sync with the study of Erhard Gerstenberger, who has shown how more vulnerable communities articulate God in more intimate personal terms.[2] This study illuminates the preferred practice of the lyrics of what we might call frontier religion with its more romantic casting in such familiar hymns as "The Old Rugged Cross," "I Come to the Garden Alone," and "I Need Thee Every Hour." The powerful do not need to "cling to the cross" and surely do not need God "every hour." These thanksgiving songs of which Guthrie and Gerstenberger write are quite in contrast to "praise hymns" of both stately cathedrals and contemporary megachurches, in which the singing lacks almost all specificity. In the cathedrals the hymns of cosmic order are impressively regal. In many megachurches they are singularly vacuous, with no story to tell.

The great Psalms scholar Claus Westermann sees the matter in a very different way, a point noted by Guthrie. Westermann regards thanks as subordinate to praise in the Psalms and as characteristically offering less-adequate theology because it "can become a duty," is private and concerns "no one except the one thanking," and can be "something required."[3] Thus thanks, in Westermann's purview, runs in the direction of bargaining: "I thank you because you did this for me." There is no doubt that the practice of thanks can function in that way. I would judge, however, that such practice constitutes a betrayal of authentic thanks, because genuine gratitude is not a requirement or duty, nor is it private. It is rather an overflow of appreciation for blessings that can be counted one by one. Thus I conclude that Guthrie is right to suggest that thanks functions with a particularity that draws faith close to lived experience, whereas praise can float off into a vacuous generic enterprise without the embarrassment of the particular. Granted, the two genres and practices of thanks and praise are merged and have coalesced in the Psalms, but it is important with reference to specific psalms to notice and pay attention to the distinction.

I thus ask of Psalm 107, why do we sing it? Why do we not sing it? What is lost when we do not sing it? My answer is that we sing it because we must attest to our gratitude; we do not sing thanks, I hypothesize, because such thanks is a demanding engagement and requires too much embarrassing awareness that we are on the receiving end of gifts that we must have to live, but do not merit. When we do not sing thanks, we curb our gratitude and keep it private and unexpressed without transformative currency among us. We may thus deceive ourselves into an illusion of self-sufficiency.

The structure of Psalm 107 begins with a more generalizing introduction (vv. 1–3). This is matched by a double conclusion at the end. In verses 33–36, we have thanks voiced for the work of the *creator*, thus showing some affinity to Psalm 104; in verses 39–42 we have rumination on the work of the *redeemer*. Together these two conclusions acknowledge YHWH as creator (vv. 33–36) and redeemer (vv. 39–42), the one who presides over the order of the cosmos and the one who intervenes in the processes of history.[4] Every zone of reality is credited to the one to whom thanks is rendered. Between this introduction and these two conclusions we have, in verses 4–32, four specific case studies that provide the grounds for gratitude and the enactment of thanksgiving. The generalized introduction and the conclusions depend for their verification on the concreteness of the named blessings and recognized gifts that are credited to YHWH, the giver of all good gifts in the verses in between.

In verses 1–3 we are addressed with an abrupt, plural imperative: "Give thanks!" The verb in Hebrew is *yadah*, which becomes the noun *todah*, "thanks." The verb *yadah* means to verbally acknowledge, to attest, to confess, to recite the narrative. The noun *todah* means to match the verbal with a material act, thus "thank offering." The imperative at the outset of the introduction is followed by a double motivation for giving thanks:

• Because YHWH is good
• Because YHWH's covenantal fidelity lasts forever

The congregation, the plural company addressed by the imperative, is invited to speak out, to "say so." Thus thanks involves narrative reportage on that for which we are grateful.[5] The same imperative invitation is more fully expressed in Psalm 118:

> Let Israel say,
>   "His steadfast love endures forever."
> Let the house of Aaron say,
>   "His steadfast love endures forever."
> Let those who fear the LORD say,
>   "His steadfast live endures forever."
>   Ps. 118:2–4

The address in Psalm 118 is triple: to Israel, to the priestly order of Aaron, and to the ones who fear YHWH. The point in each summons is the same. It concerns YHWH's *hesed*, YHWH's abiding fidelity that is acted out and made manifest in a particular way. In what follows in our psalm, we will see that the body of the psalm consists precisely in testimony about specific exhibits of divine fidelity. Thanks is "saying so." We sing because we must "say so."

The ones who are summoned to speech are the ones redeemed. The rhetoric identifies the responders in two ways. The "redeemed" are those who have been "bought out" of slavery from which they could not extricate themselves. That same language is used of the exodus, in which YHWH is said to have paid for the freedom of Israel. On the other hand, the "redeemer-avenger" is a next of kin who has intervened to maintain the honor, dignity, and well-being of a vulnerable member of the family. We sing along with and after the emancipated slaves and the protected vulnerable members of the family. That is us! That is why we sing! These emancipated selves and protected family members bear witness, and we bear witness with them, that YHWH, in fidelity, has brought them (and us) to a place of well-being to which they could not have arrived themselves. We sing because we are the emancipated; we sing because we are the protected vulnerable. We are the ones brought to a safe place.

The second act for which thanks is rendered is that YHWH has intervened to "gather." This is a preferred term for bringing exiles home, the ones who have been "scattered" in vulnerability. Thus Isaiah can say concerning eunuchs and foreigners, two categories of the "severely disqualified" from belonging,

> Thus says the Lord God,
>   who *gathers* the outcasts of Israel,
> I will *gather* others to them
>   besides those already *gathered.*
>   Isa. 56:8, emphasis added

Or in a text that rejoices in the anticipated ingathering:

> Do not fear, for I am with you;
>   I will bring your offspring from the east,
>   and from the west I will *gather* you;
> I will say to the north, "Give them up,"
>   and to the south, "Do not withhold;
> bring my sons from far away
>   and my daughters from the end of the earth—
> everyone who is called by my name,
>   whom I created for my glory,
>   whom I formed and made."
>   Isa. 43:5–7, emphasis added

What we likely have in Psalm 107, then, is thanks for rescue by those who have been displaced and who can remember their vulnerability and the risk of that exile. That same formula of gathering is used in my church, the United Church of Christ, as a summons to the Eucharist:

This is the joyful feast of the people of God. Men and women, youth and children, come from the east and the west, from the north and the south, and gather about Christ's table.[6]

Our thanks is for the great *ingathering* of the *scattered* to the God who gathers! The geography of homecoming has been transposed into the liturgy of homecoming. It is all of a piece. Thanks grows out of lament. And lament characteristically is about loss, displacement, isolation, helplessness, and abandonment. Israel will give voice to its deep need, and so Israel now is compelled to give voice to its newly received well-being that is grounded in God's *hesed*. Thanks requires that we have available in our memory and imagination a "before" of misery or need and an "after" of well-being, and that we acknowledge the agency of YHWH, who brings us from the "before" to the "after." This is this same before-after that is voiced by the father in our best-loved parable:

"'But we had to celebrate and rejoice, because this brother of yours was dead and has come to life; he was lost and has been found.'" (Luke 15:32)

In the same gospel Jesus offers an inventory of the ways in which he has moved "before" to "after":

"The blind receive their sight, the lame walk, the lepers are cleansed, the deaf hear, the dead are raised, the poor have good news brought to them." (Luke 7:22)

We do not often enough render the before of lament or the after of thanks for the agent of the transformation. That agent who is good and steadfast is front and center in Israel's thanks. It is YHWH, who has done for us what we could not do for ourselves. That is why we sing.

With that introduction, the psalm plunges into four concrete testimonies. In these verses those redeemed and gathered do indeed "say so." They have witnessed that the world is open to and impinged upon by the good resolve of the faithful God. Thus thanks attest God as active agent moved by need. This attestation is contrary to the progressives who are embarrassed about an "interventionist God" and is contrary to fundamentalists who have reduced God to a cardboard proposition so bound in pure perfection that there can be none of the adrenaline of compassion. This attestation of thanks yields a world *in need of gifts* and *in receipt of gifts* that, in first-person witness, will not be explained away. Such testimony is always against establishment epistemology that assumes that no new gifts will be given.[7] The witnesses are not embarrassed by their gratitude and are not intimidated by more "reasonable realities." The witnesses step up to give an account of a transformation credited to YHWH. These witnesses attest to an ancient transformation, but their characterization of that ancient transformation is open enough that we can take their characterization and see that it applies to our own lives as well. We give thanks, as do they, for the same wondrous turns from "before" to "after." We sing that inexplicable movement from death to life.

We sing because we can vividly remember that we were rescued from hopeless wandering in the desert (vv. 4–9). We sing because we must bear witness to that wonder performed by YHWH for us. As we will see in these four cases, these articulations of thanks are highly stylized. The patterned speech consists in four recurring elements: characterization of the trouble, a turning to YHWH, YHWH's response, and giving thanks.

First, there is *a characterization of the trouble* to which YHWH responds (vv. 4–5). In this case it is wandering aimlessly in the wilderness before there was MapQuest. This is perhaps the experience of caravan traders who were lost between oases without resources. Their condition was one of weakness from lack of food and water, a slow sentence of death. In Israel's canonical recital, such an experience is the wilderness sojourn wherein Israel regularly and abrasively disputed the inadequate leadership of Moses and the inadequate food supply from YHWH (Exod. 16–17). In our own contemporary experience, that threatening dislocation may take many forms of lack of resources: perhaps the strange new world of rapid communication, mobile finance, and the disappearance of a neighborly infrastructure. We know, as did the psalmist, about being in a context without adequate resources and an inability to cope in a user-unfriendly environment.

Second, those lost in the desert know what to do. *They turned to the Lord* (v. 6). They engaged in lament, protest, and complaint to YHWH, who should have made better provision for them. In Israel's initial complaint in the Exodus narrative, the matter is different. There they only "cried out," not addressing anyone in particular, simply raw bodily distress (Exod. 2:23). But by now Israel knows better. It knows now whom to address in extremity. As a result, even their cry of need is an act of faith. The cry is focused on YHWH, the one who invites engagement and has promised attentiveness. Thus the cry of weakness is a summons that YHWH should enact covenantal fidelity.

The cry is followed promptly by a third element: *YHWH delivered* (vv. 6–7). The line does not even say that YHWH "heard." YHWH went immediately to transformative action. He "snatched" them out of danger. He plucked them up. He led them back to a safe habitat. This cry of Israel in need and this response of YHWH with succor together constitute the most elemental features of faith. It is no wonder that Karl Barth can say that prayer consists in "simply asking."[8] In this case, the "ask" is heard and answered. The cry evokes YHWH's restorative activity.

The fourth element is *thanks* (vv. 8–9). It is the same verb here as the initial imperative of verse 1. Thanks is to give concrete verbal attestation, to "say so," to tell aloud what YHWH has done. The subject of thanks is divine *hesed*. The ground of human gratitude is active divine fidelity that is long-lasting and far-reaching, even into the desert. Thanks for *hesed* as covenantal fidelity in verse

8 is parallel to a second theme of thanks, namely, "wonderful works." The phrase bespeaks an inexplicable turn, a hard thing that human agents could not perform, an impossible action that defies our expectation. It is a turn for which our best term is "miracle," that is, a show of divine power that refuses all explanatory calculus. Notice, I do not say that it violates natural law. Such a formula is to situate YHWH's action in our reasonableness. Rather, the act of rescue is an exhibit of YHWH's capacity to override intractable circumstances in order to create a new possibility for life. Martin Buber judges that such a divine act is one marked by "abiding astonishment," an event that becomes a defining memory to which the community bears continuing witness.[9] Verse 9 is a reprise that reiterates the specificity of the miracle (au. trans.):

- "YHWH satisfies the thirsty."
- "YHWH fills the hungry with good things."

YHWH acts to override life-threatening scarcity with life-enhancing abundance. This quenching of thirst and this satiation of hunger together sound like the famous sheep of Psalm 23, who receive good pastures and still waters; it is a drama that recalls the ancient miracles of water and food in the wilderness (Exod. 16:13–14; 17:6) and anticipates the revolutionary expectations of Mary:

> He has filled the hungry with good things,
>   and sent the rich away empty.
> > Luke 1:53

The drama of thanksgiving is a wondrous move from *a zone of death* to *a new zone of life*. The move is regularly and paradigmatically enacted in these terse lines (au. trans.):

- "They cried to YHWH" (v. 6)
- "Let them thank YHWH" (v. 8)

YHWH dwells in the midst of crises. It is divine action that is the antidote to crisis. Thanks is not rendered for what is owed and paid. It is not rendered for what is expected. It is rendered in fullness for gifts given beyond merit or expectation. The one who shows up on the lips of Israel is the one who is able to "accomplish abundantly far more than all we can ask or imagine" (Eph. 3:20).

We sing because we remember how our prison cells were opened, and we must tell the tale of our emancipation (vv. 10–16). The second episode of gratitude enacts the same four rhetorical elements seen in verses 4–9. The only difference is that the text lingers longer over the initial description of trouble (vv. 10–12). It is prison. The theological reason for imprisonment in verse 11 is that they "rebelled against the words of God," defying the guidance of the Most High. But such a verdict should not be taken at face value, for such a theological affront did not, in ancient Israel, merit prison. We may guess, reasoning backward, that prison was a fate for those who defied established authority, who did not pay taxes or bills, who did not show up for work, who defied settled order. Prison is for those who refuse conformity and the expectations of the political economy. In our season of "mass incarceration," this episode in the psalm is particularly poignant, given the shabby unbearable condition of our prison system.[10] These prisoners in the psalm get "hard labor" (v. 12). When I read that phrase I thought of Nelson Mandela on Robbin Island. He got hard labor. And no doubt the regime would have said that he defied the law of God. But what they meant is that he refused to conform to apartheid, which seemed, for some, to be God's will. In any case, the ones who speak had "no one to help" (v. 12). That is how it often is with those who end up in prison.

Second, Israel in its helplessness knew an overriding agent of help (v. 13). They cried to the Lord. They were helpless and bowed down in their misery. Even there, however, they remembered that YHWH is the one who hears and saves. So they cried in protest and petition.

YHWH then saved them (vv. 13–14)! YHWH saved from prison. YHWH brought them out. YHWH broke their bonds asunder. The action echoes the exodus when YHWH brought the Israelites out of Egypt. The attestation of deliverance is like the poetry in which the poet declares:

> For the LORD hears the needy,
>   and does not despise his own that are *in bonds*.
>   Ps. 69:33, emphasis added

> He has sent me to bring good news to the oppressed,
>   to bind up the brokenhearted,
> to proclaim liberty to the captives,
>   and release to the prisoners.
>   Isa. 61:1, emphasis added

YHWH here and often is on the side of the prisoners against the imprisoning establishment. The opening of the prison is given narrative celebration in the book of Acts:

> Suddenly there was an earthquake, so violent that the foundations of the prison were shaken; and immediately all the doors were opened and everyone's chains were unfastened. (Acts 16:26; see 12:6–11)

This God is remembered as having acted against incarceration!

Well, you now know what the first response to the wonder will be: thank YHWH (v. 15)! Thank YHWH for *hesed*; thank YHWH for the inexplicable wonder of fidelity that exhibits YHWH's power. The response of verse 16 reiterates the wonder in concrete terms: doors shattered, bars cut in two, the force of God stronger than bronze and iron. It could not have happened, but the witnesses "say so." They say they walked out, saved. The singing is thanks whereby the wonder of YHWH is enhanced and continued with abiding astonishment.

We sing because we remember our illness from which we were healed, and we must tell about the recovery (vv. 17–22). First, the description of the trouble is graphic (vv. 17–18). We were near death, having lost our appetites and refusing to eat. This commentary insists yet again on the old quid pro quo of sin/punishment that sin causes illness.[11] Indeed, even Jesus linked illness and sin so that he could talk and act about healing or about forgiveness; either way the situation is desperate, and the need for restoration is urgent (Mark 2:9). We, of course, think we know better than that; nonetheless we often continue to parse our ailments in that way along with Job's friends. What counts for these witnesses is not the cause of the illness; what matters is the divine response of healing.

The second element is the same as in the preceding narratives, again quite terse (v. 19). They cried out to YHWH as their only source of help and comfort; what else could they do? By now we know the force and immediacy of the divine response (vv. 19–20). YHWH is ultimately attentive to the cries of need and pain. YHWH saved! The laments of Israel evoke divine engagement. Israel knows that and so cries out not only in urgency but with confidence. YHWH saves; YHWH heals; YHWH rescues from total obliteration. The final element of the sequence is now expected by us: thank YHWH (vv. 21–22)! Thank YHWH for active *hesed;* thank YHWH for miracles. Thank YHWH for an act of sovereignty whereby the negations of death are nullified. That move has now become routinized in this patterned speech.

In this third episode, however, there is a significant variation from the first two cases. In verse 9 in the first episode the conclusion was a reiteration of the rescue:

> For he satisfies the thirsty,
> and the hungry he fills with good things.

In verse 16 in the second episode, the conclusion is again a reiteration of rescue:

> For he shatters the doors of bronze,
> and cuts in two the bars of iron.

But not here! If we had followed the pattern of the first two episodes, verse 22 would have said,

> [He] forgives all your iniquities;
> [he] heals all your diseases;
> [he] redeems your life from the Pit.
> Ps. 103:3–4

But we have an alternative in this third conclusion. Now the invitation to thank in verse 21 is instruction to *offer* and to *tell* in verse 22 (emphasis added):

> And let them *offer* thanksgiving sacrifices,
>   and *tell* of his deeds with songs of joy.

The "offer" is a material presentation. On the thank offering, see Leviticus 7:11–18, included in the inventory of Israel's sacrifices. In that inventory the term is *todah*; but the *todah* of offering is not completed without the telling, without the narrative that traces the drama from need to well-being, from cry to being heard.

Harvey Guthrie, following Gerhard von Rad, has seen that the *todah* becomes, in the reiterative practice of Israel, a normative recital.

> It is probably evident by now . . . , that the cultic roots of the process [of credo recital] undoubtedly lay in *todah*.[12]

Thanksgiving becomes settled and routinized enough to become credo. But Guthrie goes even further:

> We must finally understand, if we are to understand the Old Testament at all, that contact with God is made as a people lives a *todah* life, not as the finally true, abstract dogma is apprehended by the human mind.[13]

For good reason, Guthrie eventually is able to trace a line from *todah* to Eucharist, as Eucharist is not only a freighted rite but a way of living in gratitude. These psalm speakers, through the wonder of their healing by God, were inducted into such an alternative life of gratitude, a life given sacral specificity by the offering rendered. I remember, do you not, as a child when we had a "thank-offering box" from church. In it we put pennies to do good. But this *todah* is not about pennies. It concerns a material offering of significant commodity value. So in Psalm 116 one can sense the gladness of serious giving:

> What shall I return to the LORD
>   for all his bounty to me?
> I will lift up the cup of salvation
>   and call on the name of the LORD,
> I will pay my vows to the LORD
>   in the presence of all his people.
> Precious in the sight of the LORD
>   is the death of his faithful ones. . . .
>
> I will offer to you *a thanksgiving sacrifice*
>   and call on the name of the LORD.
> I will pay my vows to the LORD
>   in the presence of all his people,

in the courts of the house of the Lord,
in your midst, O Jerusalem.
Praise the Lord!
Ps. 116:12–15, 17–19, emphasis added

In verse 15 the term "precious" is used for the life and death of the faithful in the eyes of the Lord. The term means "rare" or "weighty" as a gem, or splendid. As the faithful are *precious* to YHWH, so the offering back to YHWH must be *precious*. Thanks cannot be nickel-and-dime. Thus Micah muses about an appropriate offering:

"With what shall I come before the Lord,
and bow myself before God on high?
Shall I come before him with burnt offerings,
with calves a year old?
Will the Lord be pleased with thousands of rams,
with ten thousands of rivers of oil?
Shall I give my firstborn for my transgression,
the fruit of my body for the sin of my soul?"
He has told you, O mortal, what is good;
and what does the Lord require of you
but to do to justice, and to love kindness,
and to walk humbly with your God?
Mic. 6:6–8

We of course know this text. But we have not, I think, taken it as a question about how to render thanks, how to quantify gratitude. Micah's conclusion, beyond commodities, is that God will have all:

Were the whole realm of nature mine,
that were a present far too small;
love so amazing, so divine,
demands my soul, my life, my all.[14]

Or as we used to sing at youth rallies,

Give of your best to the Master;
Give of the strength of your youth;
Throw your soul's fresh, glowing ardor
Into the battle for truth.[15]

Thanks is giving back what is precious along with talk. Thanks requires the best in response. We miss the richness of thanks when our gift is parsimonious or when it is given without talking. It is the force of our commodity society, opposed to gratitude as it is, that has shrunk our thanks to embarrassing modesty. Commodity ideology does thanks on the cheap, without a narrative, for narrative specificity about shipwrecks and illness violates the symmetry of the market, in which there is no free lunch from anyone, not even from God. Serious *todah*—generous materiality and testimonial narrative—is a defiance of commodity ideology, an acknowledgment that our lives are situated in a different zone from the predominant zone of scarcity, greed, and anxiety.

It does not take very long to forget our ailment or shipwreck or emancipation from prison. It does not take much time for us to accept our new status of well-being and imagine that it is not a gift but simply a legitimate status that we ourselves have produced. It does not take long to conclude, "My power and the might of my own hand have gotten me this wealth" (Deut. 8:17). But gratitude, practiced as material generosity and narrative concreteness, keeps us from forgetting the gift of generous restoration. George Stroup specifies the distinctiveness of Christian gratitude:

> Gratitude, or human thanksgiving, is never a fully adequate response to the prior giving of God. . . . There is no giving in human experience that is parallel or analogous to God's grace in Jesus Christ. Because Christian gratitude is a response to the prior giving of God, it is different in kind from all other forms of gratitude. To claim that gratitude is the creaturely counterpart to God's grace is to claim that gratitude to God is shaped by the grace, the divine favor, the good will that calls into being and makes it possible. Gratitude, therefore, that is appropriate to God is a thanksgiving that reflects the surprising, costly, free gift that is its source and object.[16]

We sing because we know the threat of chaotic water, because we sense the waters of chaos that lash at our zones of safety and security (vv. 23–32). We sing because we have been exposed to the waters of chaos, and we did not drown. We did not drown because we found the faithfulness of YHWH able to curb and contain the violent threat. And we must "say so."

This characterization of the storm at sea is longer even than the narrative of sickness healed (vv. 23–27). The speaker knows fully about the "mighty waters," the surge of chaos, and dares, in retrospect, to identify even surging chaos as an action of YHWH, as a "wondrous work" (v. 24). There is no doubt here that even the tsunami that threatens gives evidence of the mighty power of YHWH so that the storm evokes "How Great Thou Art." The verbs in these verses exhibit the actions of three agents:

- YHWH commanded and raised.
- The stormy wind lifted up, mounted.
- "They" melted their courage, reeled, staggered . . . like drunkards.

The collage of disturbing verbs—"commanded," "raised," "lifted," "mounted," "melted," "reeled," "staggered"—betray massive upheaval and helplessness.

The outcome is that they "were at their wits' end" (v. 27). More literally, "All their wisdom was swallowed up!" Their wisdom, their rational capacity, their common-sense management had failed. Everything is out of control.

But at wit's end, given failed wisdom, they take one more action: "They cried out to YHWH" (v. 28, au. trans.). They cried out to the *storm maker* who may yet be the *storm stiller*. Such a petition is not an act of wisdom. It is an act of instinct for those schooled, as were these Israelites, in the ways of YHWH. This urgent petition is a fallback in trust beyond all management skills or conventional rationality.

And, says this resolved evangelical witness, "He brought them out" (v. 28). The verb is the primary Exodus term. This is the God who has been managing the surging waters since Pharaoh died:

> The LORD drove the sea back by a strong east wind all night, and turned the sea into dry land; and the waters were divided. The Israelites went into the sea on dry ground, the waters forming a wall for them on their right and on their left. (Exod. 14:21–22)

Chaos is no match for this sovereign creator who is the emancipator. It is no wonder that they said in Mark 4:41, "'Who then is this, that even the wind and the sea obey him?'"

The psalmist anticipates the evangelist in testimony:

> He made the storm be still,
>   and the waves of the sea were hushed.
>   v. 29

The outcome, the alternative to chaos, is quiet and safe harbor:

> Then they were glad because they had quiet,
>   and he brought them to their desired haven.
>   v. 30

The God who stirs up chaos is the God who stills chaos and creates safe space for life.

What could they do but thank (v. 31)? What could they do but give narrative account and affirm it with a serious material gesture? We thank, yet one more time, for divine *hesed,* one more time for "wonderful works." The wonderful work is safe harbor that trumps the preceding wonderful work of the storm. He has got the whole world in his hands! And then, as in the third episode, verse 32 as a conclusion for the fourth episode also offers a variation. Now, instead of a reprise of the restoration that has concluded earlier episodes, we have a surge of gladness that ends with hallelu-jah. And since it is performed by the congregation amid the elders, this surely is a Presbyterian action! It takes a village to give thanks! It requires many, many voices to express adequately the conviction that the world is safely held by the Lord of chaos, king of kings and lord of lords . . . hallelu-jah!

We sing in the retrospect of this psalm in its two conclusions (vv. 33–42). We sing because we have now witnessed the creator who redeems, who makes and then remakes, who saves and rescues and heals and emancipates. We sing because this awesome, reliable agent deeply redefines the world. A flimsy world is for anxious management. But this world of deep trust requires not simply management; it evokes voiced active gratitude.

We sing the first conclusion of verses 33–35 because we see the wondrous power of God. Global warming causes deathliness and requires reparation. But hidden in these processes is the creator God who turns rivers into deserts (we see that!) and who turns deserts into good arable land. This is the God who presides over the agricultural enterprise of sowing, planting, reaping, and harvest. This conclusion alludes, does it not, to the cadences of the Genesis creation. It concerns "blessing" and "multiply":

> God blessed them, saying, "Be fruitful and multiply and fill the waters in the seas, and let birds multiply on the earth." (Gen. 1:22)

The world teems with sustenance!

We sing the second conclusion of verses 39–42 because we know about economic disparity and the endless contrast between haves and have nots. The God who presides over creation, it turns out, is the Lord of the economy. Right in our face—and in our singing—are the diminished, the lowly, those who live in oppression, trouble, and sorrow. And in an anticipation of social upheaval, the powerful are to be given over to contempt. So the psalm anticipates Mary in her song of social inversion, an inversion that comes for the benefit of the marginalized:

> He raises up the needy out of distress,
>   and makes their families like flocks.
>   v. 41

The inversion of the economy is not everywhere welcome. The "wicked" who were out of sync in Psalm 104 are the ones who are stunned (v. 42). But those allied with torah, the upright, are glad and know the inversion is coming. The one who stills the storm is the one who provides means for those without.

The final verse of the psalm is a reader's guide added by a librarian (v. 43). Don't be stupid! Get wise! Notice . . . pay attention. When we notice and pay attention, we can everywhere see YHWH's *hesed*:

- YHWH's *hesed* for those lost in the desert
- YHWH's *hesed* for those held in prison
- YHWH's *hesed* for those sick to death
- YHWH's *hesed* for those storm-tossed in chaos

The world is a vast arena for divine *hesed*. It is no wonder that that world constitutes a venue for thanks rendered as narrative and as generous materiality. Thanks voices divine *hesed*. Where there is no thanks, God's *hesed* will be unnoticed.

From the old precious inheritance of the church, we get a grateful response of thanks at the end of the devastating Thirty Years War. I treasure it with peculiar passion because it became the anthem of my tradition of evangelical German pietism:

> Now thank we all our God with heart and hands and voices,
> who wondrous things hath done, in whom this world rejoices;
> who, from our mothers' arms, hath blessed us on our way
> with countless gifts of love, and still is ours today.
>
> O may this bounteous God through all our life be near us,
> with ever joyful hearts and blessed peace to cheer us;
> and keep us in God's grace, and guide us when perplexed,
> and free us from all ills in this world and the next.
>
> All praise and thanks to God, who reigns in highest heaven,
> to Father and to Son and Spirit now be given:
> the one eternal God, whom heaven and earth adore,
> the God who was, and is, and shall be evermore.[17]

For ample reason this thank song was evoked at the end of the war with a horizon of thanks and gratitude as large as creation and as deep as the triune God. It is matched by a new hymn that paraphrases Psalm 111:

> A grateful heart is what I bring,
> a song of praise, my offering.
> Among the saints I lift my voice;
> in you, O God, I will rejoice.
>
> Your name is known in all the lands.
> You feed the poor with gentle hands.
> Your word is true, your works are just;
> in you, O God, the faithful trust.
>
> With saving love you set us free,
> and still you dwell in mystery
> with wisdom none can comprehend.
> Your praise, O God, will never end.[18]

This hymn, to be sure, mixes thanks and praise. In that it is faithful to the tendency in the Psalter. It has enough specificity, however, that we may count it as a voice of thanks. It is titled "A Grateful Heart," an act that resists and subverts the primary claims for the self-sufficiency of commoditization, reason enough to sing it! A grateful heart is an alternative to the "hard heart" that a thankless culture will inevitably evoke.

Chapter 3

Psalm 105

In 1938 Gerhard von Rad wrote a quite remarkable and most influential article.[1] He was at that time young and not much known, but he was destined to become the most important and influential theological interpreter of the Christian Old Testament in the twentieth century. The year of publication, 1938, was of defining importance. Von Rad was a pastor and a member of the Confessing Church in Germany. He wrote in the wake of the Barmen Declaration of the Confessing Church during the most acute years of the ominous rise of the National Socialist government in Germany. The Confessing Church sought, in those years, to stake out claims for a confessional position that would give it a place to stand in resistance to and as an alternative to National Socialism and the "German Christians" (*Deutsche Christi*) who supported the regime.[2]

In his article of 1938 von Rad famously delineated Deuteronomy 26:5–9 as an (if not *the*) early credo of ancient Israel. By "credo" he meant a *normative narrative recital*. All three terms in this formulation are crucial. The text of Deuteronomy 26 is a *narrative*; it features an action, and it presents YHWH as an active character who is able to do in narrative what a God formulated in proposition could never do. The narrative is *normative*, for it functioned as bottom-line articulation of the faith of Israel. Von Rad understood its function to be to articulate an Israelite identity that was distinct from the environment of Canaanite religion in which it flourished. The subtext for von Rad in his context of jeopardy was that the normative narrative recital would serve the Confessing Church in Germany as it served the Israelites in Canaan. *Mutatis mutandis,* as Israel appealed to its credo in order to withstand "Canaanite religion," so the Confessing Church would appeal to its normative recital in order to withstand the threat of National Socialism. The credo, according to von Rad's influential hypothesis, was designed for regular public *recital* through successive generations at periodic liturgical events. By the repeated recital of the normative narrative, Israelites in many different times, places, and circumstances could appropriate and participate in that same covenantal identity that celebrated the sustained fidelity of YHWH, the God of the covenant, and that summoned Israel to engage in obedience to that covenantal God.

That normative narrative recital of Deuteronomy 26:5–9, in the context of an offering before a priest, affirmed (a) that *Jacob, the Aramean ancestor of Israel,* was "perishing," that is, was in great jeopardy, (b) that the community derived from Jacob was *delivered from Egyptian* slavery by YHWH, and (c) that this community was *brought to the promised land* flowing with milk and honey. Thus the credo as normative narrative recital revolved around the historical memories that came subsequently to shape the canonical sequence of the early traditions of Israel in the Pentateuch. The first theme of Jacob became in expanded form the ancestral narratives in Genesis 12–50 wherein each generation of ancestors is narrated as at risk and perishing and then rescued and sustained by the faithfulness of God. The deliverance from Egypt became the extended narrative of emancipation in Exodus 1–15 that culminates in the singing of Miriam and the other women (see Exod. 15:20–21); and the entry into the land of promise became the forcible conquest narrative of the book of Joshua. Von Rad saw the canonical architecture of the "Hexateuch" (the first six books, thus the title of his article) as an arc from *the promise of God to Abraham* in Genesis 12:1–3 to the *completion and fulfillment of the promise* in Joshua 21:43–45:

> Thus the LORD gave to Israel all the land that he swore to their ancestors that he would give them; and having taken possession of it, they settled there. And the LORD gave them rest on every side just as he had sworn to their ancestors; not one of all their enemies had withstood them, for the LORD had given all their enemies into their hands. Not one of all the good promises that the LORD had made to the house of Israel had failed; all came to pass.

What became extended normative literature had its beginning, in this hypothesis, in a cultic recital of credo.

It is necessary to acknowledge that in subsequent scholarship von Rad's historical-critical assumptions concerning the date and function of the credo have not been sustained. Most scholars, against von Rad, no longer believe this material to be at all early; rather it was formulated much later. The loss of those critical judgments, however, does not vitiate the theological substance of the credo text nor, I think, the decisive claim of the text in its communal use. Von Rad's great insight that persists is that Israel's faith depended on narrative recital that features YHWH and that could be taken as standing ground in dynamic ways over time. Israel's faith is cast as a story, a story remembered, told, and retold so that belated tellers and hearers of the story can, in imaginative ways, situate themselves as participants in that same story. Thus the narrative is recurringly contemporary for new generations in new circumstances. One can observe the same contemporaneity in Christian narrative in the way in which the church celebrates Christmas and Easter as contemporary happenings in which we sing,

> Good Christian friends, rejoice with heart and soul and voice;
> give ye heed to what we say: Jesus Christ is born *today*.[3]

> "Christ the Lord is risen *today*!" Alleluia!
> All creation, join to say: Alleluia![4]

At both Christmas and Easter the church intends that the "today" of the songs is now, in this contemporary moment of liturgical performance. And of course the Eucharist depends on the "here and now" of the normative recital that is received as immediately contemporary in its present reiteration. This is true in the communing community even though the church has long disputed how, in what way, and by what means that "real presence" is mediated here and now. It is important to see that such a narrative recital does not claim and is not subject to the criteria of modern positivistic history. Von Rad is clear that the credo is *Geschichte*, a tale told that does not offer the proof of modern rational *Historie:*

> Historical investigation searches for a critically assured minimum—the kerygmatic picture tends toward a theological maximum. . . . No doubt historical investigation has a great deal that is true to say about the growth of this picture of the history which the faith of Israel painted; but the phenomenon of faith itself, which speaks now of salvation, now of judgment, is beyond its power to explain.[5]

In the Bible we are dealing with "kerygmatic" (that is "preached") theological maximums. Credos can make claims that do not parse into rational formulation, statements like the following:

- "God from God, light from light, true God from true God. . . ." (from the Nicene Creed)

- "He shall come in glory to judge the living and the dead." (from the Nicene Creed)
- "Christ has died, Christ is risen, Christ will come again." (from the Eucharistic Prayer)

These are all narrative affirmations that do not accommodate the reason of this age. They are for us in the community normative and regularly recited. The faith of the church, in such narrative affirmations, stands rooted in the testimony of the Bible. It is the case that so much critical study of Scripture has tried to impose upon the biblical text the criteria of modern positivistic history. But, in fact, Scripture taken seriously will not tolerate that kind of "reasonableness," try as we might. Thus entry into Scripture in general, and specifically into psalms like 105, requires the suspension of such critical reason and the embrace of another narrative practice. In his appreciation of the nature of such narrative, von Rad understood this quite well.

Now, the reason I take so long with this work from von Rad is that after von Rad delineates the credo of Deuteronomy 26, he traces further literary-liturgical derivatives from the credo. Among these literary-liturgical derivatives is our Psalm 105, which stands in the wake of the normative narrative recital of von Rad's credo. I shall consider, in what follows, the fact that when we sing these songs, we participate in the ancient practice of performing a normative narrative that yields for us a contemporary identification with that ancient community. That identity both bespeaks assurance that sustains in circumstances of risk and summons to a life in the world that evokes risk. As both assurance and summons, the credo tradition that we have in these psalms constitutes a risk that lives in tension with a culture that will not and cannot sing these songs. Thus we sing Psalm 105 in order to participate in an alternative act of imagination in which the person and purpose of God are taken as decisive for our life in the world. We sing this psalm because the world given us by Enlightenment rationality and its produce of consumerism and scientism does not ring true; we know an alternative that revolves around this Character who inhabits the story we sing.

Psalm 105 is framed by an introduction (vv. 1–6) and a terse conclusion (verse 45) that provides an important clue about why we sing this hymn. Between introduction and conclusion, the body of the psalm consists in a normative narrative recital concerning Abraham (vv. 7–15), Joseph (vv. 16–22), Israel in Egypt (vv. 23–25), Moses and the exodus (vv. 26–36), departure from Egypt into the wilderness (vv. 37–42), and arrival in the new land (vv. 43–44). The plot and sequence are familiar to us from the outline of the early books of the Old Testament canon that are, in von Rad's hypothesis, derived from liturgical recital.

We sing the introduction to this hymn because we are summoned to situate our lives before YHWH (vv. 1–6). After a long series of imperative summons, the psalm is addressed to the heirs of Abraham and Jacob (v. 6). That status as "heir" pertains to all the successive generations of Israel. In Christian confession, moreover, the church understands itself to be such an heir as well (see Gal. 4:1–7). Thus we sing rootage in this ancient narrative; each time we sing it, we engage that ancient rootage. These verses culminate with the claim of the heirs as "his chosen ones" (v. 6). This refers first of all to Jews, but Christians have taken the claim as their own as well.

The heirs are addressed with a sustained summons that features the following torrent of imperatives: "give thanks" (a beginning quite like that of Psalm 107), "call," "make known," "sing," "sing" (again), "tell," "glory in," "rejoice" (as a jussive), "seek," "seek" (again), and "remember." All these imperatives in sum constitute a call to situate life with reference to YHWH and YHWH's wondrous actions. Thus there is reference to YHWH's "name," "deeds," "wonderful works," "name" (again), "strength," "presence," "wonderful works" (again), "miracles," and "judgments." This torrent of words intends to saturate the imagination of the singer with claims that outrun any conventional reason. This inventory of references suggests the manifold ways in which Israel in the past has known YHWH, so that the entire narrative legacy of Israel is made immediately available in the singing.

In what follows in the psalm we will find a recital of "wonderful works," "wonderful works" (again), and "miracles" that defy every reasonable explanation; they are nonetheless disclosures of YHWH's "surplus" of faithful generosity toward Israel that sustains Israel through the generations. This is no ordinary memory; YHWH is no ordinary God; and Israel is no ordinary people. The singing of this song is to give thanks for and remember these inexplicable acts that exhibit YHWH in the world. The psalm is a script for an exhibit of YHWH in all of YHWH's incomparable power and fidelity. The summons to tell and declare does not identify an audience for such testimony. We may assume it means to declare to other nations. But quite practically it is likely first of all a witness to Israel itself in order to sustain its distinct identity and a witness to Israel's young to inculcate them into this community of memory, doxology, and obedience. The substance of the claim made for YHWH in this declaration is constituted by concrete memories that follow in the body of the psalm.

We sing the memory of Abraham and Sarah with God because the force of God's fidelity to them persists in our own faith (vv. 7–15). These verses quickly summarize the ancestral narratives of Genesis, including not only Abraham but also Isaac and Jacob. The ancestral narratives concern the way in which YHWH's faithfulness persists through the generations, each time at the last moment assuring continuity into the next generation by a new inexplicable birth. Three times these verses refer to "covenant" (vv. 8, 9, 10), twice with the modifier "forever," once to connect the covenant to the divine promise of land (v. 9; see verse 11). In the memory of Genesis the covenant is enacted by YHWH twice to Abraham, in Genesis 15 and then reperformed in Genesis 17:

> On that day the LORD made a covenant with Abram, saying, "To your
> descendants I give this land." (Gen. 15:18)

> "I will establish my covenant between me and you, and your offspring
> after you throughout their generations, for an everlasting covenant, to be
> God to you and to your offspring after you. And I give to you, and to your
> offspring after you, the land where you are now an alien, all the land of
> Canaan, for a perpetual holding; and I will be their God." (Gen. 17:7–8)

The covenant each time concerns land. En route to the land, the divine
promise assures safe passage. God is faithful. In Christian interpretation much
has been made since Martin Luther of Genesis 15:6, in which Abraham's trust
in God's promises is taken as the key mark of his life of faith. It is that trust in
God that is celebrated in Christian rendering:

> By faith Abraham obeyed when he was called to set out for a place that
> he was to receive as an inheritance. . . . By faith he stayed for a time in
> the land that he had been promised, as in a foreign land. . . . By faith he
> received power of procreation, even though he was too old. . . . Therefore
> from one person, and this one as good as dead, descendants were born.
> (Heb. 11:8–12)

This promise of course is fuel for much contemporary Jewish preoccupation
with and occupation of the land. The claim of "promised land" is of course
vexed and contested, which is inescapable when the promise is linked to violent power as it was in the ancient story of Joshua and as it is in contemporary
Zionism.[6]

For Christians the case is not as straightforward, as we do not imagine a
promise of land. But of course the Christian tradition has its own sorry story
of coercion and violence in the service of its singular claim to God's truth.
We Christians do, out of this lyrical affirmation, understand that we are heirs
through hope for a better country. It is from Abraham and Sarah, with the
messianic notion of verse 15 in the psalm, that Christians are positioned as
hopers and are open to the futures that God will yet give. Gerhard von Rad has
carefully considered the notion of land as "rest" that God promises and gives
to God's people. He calls attention to the ominous warning of Psalm 95:11 as
an outcome of forty years of disobedience in the wilderness:

> Therefore in my anger I swore,
>   "They shall not enter my rest."

The term "rest," as in Joshua 21:43–45, refers to safe, settled, undisturbed,
peaceable territory. Von Rad then notices that this text is the basis of Christian hope and expectation in Hebrews 3–4. Thus Psalm 95:7b–11 is quoted
in Hebrews 3:7–11 and 4:3. The upshot of Psalm 95 and its use in Hebrews is

that the land is given faithfully and generously but then is held conditionally, conditioned by adherence to God. The Christian propensity is to spiritualize the promise of land, against which von Rad warns. In yet another rendition of the land promise after the practice of Judaism and Christianity, there is no doubt that U.S. exceptionalism has latched on to the promise and has treated "the new land" with its limitless horizon as a promise made to the European founders of the United States. Thus it is "land that I love" "from sea to shining sea." The promise lingers for Jews, for Christians, and for Americans with immense impact; it is, however, taken with critical awareness in the tradition itself. We sing this psalm because we know that the future is open and presided over by God's good promises. If we did not sing this song, we would find, eventually, that the future is closed off, and we would be fated to a closed present tense. This song is a bottom-line antidote to despair that besets the modern world as an outcome of secular rationality. It is openness to the future that permits space for humanness in the present tense.

We sing the narrative of Joseph as a way to find our place amid the hostile requirements of empire (vv. 16–22). It is peculiar indeed for Joseph to be given as much air time in Israel's singing as he receives in this psalm. In the characteristic recurring formula in the tradition concerning the patriarchs, the usual sequence is "Abraham, Isaac, and Jacob," but not Joseph. Here it is very different. Joseph was wrongly imprisoned by Pharaoh, but in the end Pharaoh could not do without Joseph. In the acute food crisis faced by Pharaoh in the Genesis narrative, the great king needed an interpreter of his dream and then an administrator of his new predatory food policy. When he found no adequate interpreter in his intelligence community and no reliable administrator among his bureaucrats, he turned finally to this Jew, even a Jew in prison (Gen. 41:12–27). Jews, as the story goes, possess uncommon wisdom, rooted as they are in God's own life.

The narrative of Joseph concerns the one *humiliated* who becomes the one *exalted*. The king sent and released Joseph, so the king thought. But the song knows better. The song says that God "sent a man ahead of them" (Ps. 105:17). No one knew, in the plot of his brothers, that God was sending him ahead of them. No one knew, but in retrospect the narrative attests the providential working of God. It was indeed the case that the brothers meant it for evil, but God meant it for good (Gen. 50:20)!

Here the problem of the relationship between human intentions and the divine control of events is still more keenly felt: God has all the threads firmly in his hands even when humans are least aware of it. . . . The purposes of God and humanity are set over against each other, and the purposes of God prevail. It is only in singing that we can bear witness to this alternative purpose that is so elusive and yet so urgent for the life of Israel.

The story of Joseph thus is a story of radical social inversion, an account of how a prisoner of the state is made

> . . . lord of his house,
>   and ruler of all his possessions,
>   to instruct his officials at his pleasure,
>   and to teach his elders wisdom.
>   Ps. 105:21–22

The story tells what cannot be explained, because the providential presence of God remains hidden. Jewish hope, taken up by Christians, is always about inversion, always about the last becoming first, about the humble being exalted, the hungry fed, the dead raised.

It has required no acute imagination to find in Joseph an anticipation of the work of Jesus, the one sent ahead of them, the one subject to Friday humiliation as an enemy of the state, and raised to power on Sunday.

> And being found in human form,
>   he *humbled* himself
>   and became obedient to the point of death—
>   even death on a cross.
> Therefore God also highly *exalted* him.
>   Phil. 2:7–9, emphasis added

In the wake of Joseph and in the narrative of Jesus, we sing because we know that God's future is open to radical inversion; that is why we pray and wait and hope that God's rule will come fully on earth as it is in heaven. If we did not sing this song, we might eventually judge that no historical inversion is possible, that we are all fated to a closed, fixed future. Thus the Joseph narrative we sing attests that well beyond the reign of Pharaoh (and every contemporary Pharaoh!) there is another governance that will not be deterred for very long. Thus Martin Luther King Jr. could attest that another governance would prevail, though he knew not how:

> How long will prejudice blind the vision of men, darken their understanding, and drive bright-eyed wisdom from her sacred throne? . . . When will wounded justice, lying prostrate on the streets of Selma and Birmingham and communities all over the South, be lifted from this dust of shame to reign supreme among the children of men? . . . How long will justice be crucified, and truth bear it? I come to say to you this afternoon, however difficult the moment, however frustrating the hour, it will not be long, because "truth crushed to earth will rise again." How long? Not long, because no lie can live forever. How long? Not long, because "You shall reap what you sow." How long? Not long, because the arc of the moral universe is long, but it bends toward justice.[7]

Martin knew the long reach of the Joseph narrative; he knew that Pharaoh (then or now) cannot prevail because God meant it for good. We sing in insistence and confidence.

We sing the exodus because we do not doubt the emancipatory capacity

of YHWH in the world (vv. 23–36). We sing of our sojourn in Egypt, because Egypt becomes a figure for every alien place where faith puts us. Pharaoh becomes a figure for every exploitative regime that takes advantage of the vulnerable, in public or private sector. We sing to remember a momentary prosperity in Egypt when God's power for life caused fruitfulness and well-being (vv. 23–24). Even in Egypt the power of the creator God is decisive! We know about life in Egypt. We know about living in an economy of extraction that depends on cheap labor. Like our ancestors we sing, for we know about high interest rates, wage theft, exploitative credit arrangements, regressive taxation, and unmanageable debt. We know about predation that leaves us in despair.

We sing because we know that a prosperity system managed by cynical power and blessed by privileged priests will cause harm and hurt. It does immense harm and hurt in a world of fear, anxiety, and greed. We sing because God has made a decisive response to the harm of anxiety, the hurt of greed, and the force of violence. God heeds, we know, the cries of the wretched. God's response to those cries is new human agency. Out of the bush Moses and his brother Aaron are empowered in the face of the empire. They are dispatched to say in the face of Pharaoh, "Let my people go." They are summoned and authorized to enact signs and wonders (miracles!) that bamboozle the intelligence community of the empire and that outrun the astrological capacity of the kingdom of Pharaoh. So impressive are these signs and wonders (humanly enacted) that we sing them over and over, one by one, in great detail; we relish these inscrutable acts that defy and subvert the empire. We have just enough fingers to finger the ten wonders of emancipation that are beyond explanation. We know the list, and finger it slowly over and over in wonder and gladness:

- Water to blood
- Frogs
- Gnats
- Flies
- Livestock diseased
- Boils
- Hail and thunder
- Locust
- Darkness
- Death of the firstborn

The list cannot be summarized. It must be detailed. It must be performed with specificity. Each new act is yet another evidence that the empire of Pharaoh and all such combines of ruthless power are penultimate. They are not to be ultimately trusted, served, feared, or obeyed. The world is other than Pharaoh says it is! The wonders come from the world-changing God who lets us know God's own name. Before this it seemed like Pharaoh had the whole world in his hands. But then we knew: it is this God who has the whole world in his hands. He has not only you and me, brother and sister, in his hands. He has not only little bitty babies in his hands. He has Pharaoh and every predatory system in his hands. It is YHWH, the Lord of emancipation, who will govern and who will, soon or late, terminate the pretensions of every Pharaoh.

For that reason we sing of departure and sustenance (vv. 37–42). God is always emancipating, and we are always departing. It belongs to our covenantal DNA to be departing the empire of greed and violence, marked as we are by an alternative identity, "sealed as Christ's own forever." We recall from that old narrative that we did not leave empty-handed; we took enough provision from them for the journey (v. 37). We noticed that at long last it was a sense a relief even to the empire to have us go (v. 38). In that instant we are beyond the reach of Pharaoh, but without bread for the journey. Miriam and the other women sang our freedom (Exod. 15:20–21). But we were very soon hungry.

In that moment of departure when it seemed we were in free fall without resources, we were astonished by divine accompaniment. We were led and protected so that the sun did not smite us on the way by day, nor the moon by night. We received meat just when we were hungry (Ps. 105:40). We recall that bread was given when we were unglued in worry. We got quail just when we were short on protein. We were quenched with water from rock when thirsty (v. 41). The wilderness turned out to be a viable habitat for us, and we did not need to submit again to Pharaoh. We remember being in the wilderness where loaves abound, completely outside the economic zone of Pharaoh's cheap labor and aggressive production quotas that we had to meet. We discovered in our emancipated retrospect that Pharaoh's domain was the venue for *scarcity*. By contrast, the wilderness that seemed void of resources turned out to be an *abundance*. The spheres of scarcity and abundance were exactly other than we had been taught. Our delusion about Pharaoh's abundance was exposed as scarcity; the presumed scarcity of the wilderness became our habitat of abundance. The wilderness is the wonder of which the later poet spoke:

> You that have no money,
>   come, buy and eat!
> Come, buy wine and milk
>   without money and without price.
> Isa. 55:1

Then the poet asked us,

> Why do you spend your money for that which is not bread,
>   and your labor for that which does not satisfy?
> Isa. 55:2

We knew that we had labored too long for Pharaoh in way that did not and could not satisfy. So we left, and ate and drank abundantly. And then we sang!

We sing because the story ends as was promised at the outset (vv. 43–44). Land was promised, and now land is given! Safe place is provided. In this moment of elation over a safe land, it did not disturb us that we were forcibly displacing other peoples to whom the land already belongs. The reality of our own displacing violence did not even occur to us then. It would vex us later; much later it would vex us greatly. But not now, not in this singing moment, because the promise of God has been kept. That fulfilled promise however is like the entire story . . . against all odds!

So we sing the whole story. We do not skip over any episode because it all hangs together as our one story of identity and vocation. It is a story of wonder and fidelity; it is a story of risk and jeopardy; it is a story of departure and arrival. It is a story of obedience and recalcitrance. We sing it all. We sing the unexpected promise to Abraham and Sarah (vv. 7–14); we sing the unlikely elevation of Joseph (vv. 16–22); we sing the emancipatory courage of Moses (vv. 23–28); we sing the inexplicable resources that surprised us in the wilderness (vv. 38–41); and we sing God's promises kept (vv. 43–44). In our singing we become freshly aware that the world is other than we had thought. It is other than Pharaoh had pretended. It is other because the God of fidelity dwells within it and presides over it. We sing, and for an instant we are unencumbered by the pressures of Pharaoh. We are unencumbered enough to imagine that we are free at last, thank God almighty, free at last:

> "Sing to the LORD, for he has triumphed gloriously;
> horse and rider he has thrown into the sea."
>
> Exod. 15:21

But then, we take a deep breath, and we sing the terse conclusion of verse 45, the point toward which the entire song has been headed from the beginning. It is all "so that." The purpose of the story sung for forty-four verses is that it will lead to an embrace of torah:

> That they might keep his statutes
> and obey his commandments.
> Hallelujah!
>
> v. 45, au. trans.

The song places us in the zone of YHWH's sustaining providential care and protection. That venue, however, is not simply for our enjoyment or for self-indulgence or self-congratulations. It is in order to bring our practice of life into sync with the purposes of the God of the covenant that have been articulated in the Torah. **Thus we sing in order that we may be obedient to torah.**

This concluding verse of the psalm (which is the destination of the entire hymn) is quite terse. It does not give any specific substance to the twin terms "statutes" and "commandments." It is likely, however, that such terminology in the psalm refers specifically to the demands of the book of Deuteronomy, the most dynamic articulation of covenantal requirements. As Patrick Miller has shown, there is a particular affinity between the tradition of Deuteronomy and the claims of the Psalter. The statutes and commandments of Deuteronomy include attention to both *religious purity* and *social justice*, but the heavy weight of Deuteronomy is on the latter. Thus the concluding verse of the psalm suggests that the accent of the verse concerning covenantal expectation is on neighborly justice.[8]

The singing provides the narrative that sustains the commandments. Thus even the Ten Commandments of Sinai are framed by a narrative that sounds familiar from the cadences of Miriam: "I am the LORD your God, who brought you out of the land of Egypt, out of the house of slavery" (Exod. 20:1; Deut. 5:6). Without the narrative of God's mighty fidelity the commandments lack energy and foundation. But with the story sung, the emancipation remembered and embraced, the commandments flow in relentless, compelling authority. We may appreciate the force of this singing if we ponder what happens when we sing different songs: different songs produce different obediences. The singing of television commercials produces consumers who are readily branded. The singing of romantic love songs produces self-indulgent folk who never notice neighbors. The singing of harsh rap and rock music results in the potential for violence. The singing of patriotic songs produces citizens who may be drawn to chauvinism. So for us, the singing of this narrative produces this specific obedience that has widows, orphans, and immigrants in purview. The Torah persistently names the powerless and vulnerable in our society (Deut. 10:18; 14:29; 16:11, 14; 24:10–13, 14–15, 17–18, 19–22). The singing situates us, on behalf of God, in the midst of the vulnerable and powerless. The singing summons us, in our final verse, to a life of justice and neighborly righteousness, the life of those who "fear the LORD, who greatly delight in his commandments" (Ps. 112:1):

> They rise in the darkness as a light for the upright;
>   they are gracious, merciful, and righteous.
> It is well with those who deal generously and lend,
>   who conduct their affairs with justice. . . .
>
> They are not afraid of evil tidings;
>   their hearts are firm, secure in the LORD. . . .
>
> They have distributed freely, they have given to the poor;
>   their righteousness endures forever.
> Ps. 112:4–5, 7, 9

That is why we sing! We are reminded by our singing of who we are, where we have been, and to whom we will answer. The song is about awe and gratitude for wondrous works. Awe and gratitude are not simply verbal or liturgical acts. They constitute a way of life. Gratitude is coded in the tradition of

Deuteronomy as neighborly attentiveness, a daily "coming before God" with gestures of gratitude.[9] Awe is coded in priestly tradition as we stand at a distance before God's holiness. See Exodus 19:10–15 and more "primitively" 1 Samuel 6:19 and 2 Samuel 6:6–7. Out of this psalm the church, alongside the synagogue, sings a very different song. It is a song that we love to sing, and it defies all other easier songs of the world, the pop songs of love, the branding songs of television, and the power songs of patriotism. Given such awe and gratitude, it is no wonder that the church sings,

> I love to tell the story of unseen things above,
> of Jesus and his glory, of Jesus and his love.
> I love to tell the story because I know 'tis true,
> it satisfies my longings as nothing else could do.
>
> *Refrain:*
> I love to tell the story; 'twill be my theme in glory
> to tell the old, old story of Jesus and his love.
>
> I love to tell the story; 'tis pleasant to repeat
> what seems, each time I tell it, more wonderfully sweet!
> I love to tell the story, for some have never heard
> the message of salvation from God's own holy Word. (*Refrain*)
>
> I love to tell the story, for those who know it best
> seem hungering and thirsting to hear it, like the rest.
> And when, in scenes of glory, I sing the new, new song,
> 'twill be the old, old story that I have loved so long. (*Refrain*)[10]

We love this story because it has better futures than any other story we can imagine. Every time we sing this old story, it becomes a new song, fresh with wonder and urgent with imperative. It is no wonder we sing; and beyond the plotline it is no wonder that our psalm ends finally with a vigorous hallelu-yah, hallelu-Yah! Praise Yah; praise the Lord . . . none other (v. 45)!

"Hallelu-Yah" leads to exuberant abandonment before the Lord. It also leads to glad obedience to the commandments of this God that displace our wayward idolatries. So we sing in a newer version that we take as an exposition of the final verse of our psalm:

> I long for your commandments; your judgments all are just.
> Within yours words is wisdom, your teachings understood
> are comfort to my spirit's need and in the night my solace.
> Your statutes are my song.
>
> Without your lamp to guide me I wander from the way.
> Without your laws and precepts I stumble in the dark.

Your understandings are my hope that I may run in freedom.
Your ways are my release.

O God, I love your knowledge, more precious than pure gold.
It satisfies like honey, a sweetness on my tongue.
It leads me to salvation's door where you have spread your table.
O, lead me to your home.[11]

This remarkable new hymn focuses, in uncharacteristic fashion for Christians, on the final verse of our psalm. It affirms that singing this old story leads to glad obedience. Such a conclusion, long drawn by faithful Jews, is an urgent one in a self-indulgent culture that imagines us invited to a comfort zone that is without norms for our life in the world. The entire recital of our story, the old, old one, points to a mandate that is alternative to the toxic way of our present world.

Chapter 4

Psalm 106

Psalm 106 is a companion piece to Psalm 105, undoubtedly intentionally put back-to-back with it in canonical sequence. It is roughly the same length and traverses much of the same legacy of Israel, reciting the past with YHWH in narrative form. It does, to be sure, cite some different material and mark different accents and voices these differences because it has a very different intention with its testimony. Psalm 105 is a grand recital of the *inexplicable, inscrutable miracles of YHWH* that constitute Israel's narrative memory and that lead to obedience to torah. To that recital Psalm 106 offers a counternarrative. It focuses on *Israel's recalcitrant response to YHWH*, its defiance of torah, and its refusal to live faithfully in covenant.

We sing, along with Israel, the opening verses of joy (vv. 1–3). Address to YHWH evokes a glad sense of well-being, voiced as "hallelujah" ("Praise the LORD!") at the very outset, reinforced by a summons to thank. Thanks and praise! These gestures constitute a glad response to God's abiding steadfast love, made manifest in acts of transformative power. That doxology, however, immediately segues to the body of the psalm in verse 3; it celebrates those who enact "justice" and "righteousness," those who pursue neighborly torah. Thus the initial doxology is promptly turned toward Israel's covenantal obligations that are so well sounded by the prophets and with which the end of Psalm 105 is concerned: "that they might keep his statutes and observe his laws" (Ps. 105:45).

The two word pairs of "justice" and "righteousness" and "statutes" and "ordinances" together put us on notice that the agenda of this psalm is covenantal obedience. The only ones who can be "happy" with this wonder-performing God are those who act out the will of the wonder doer. With this positive assertion, the psalmist looks to the acknowledgments to come in the body of the psalm that Israel has not done justice and righteousness, has "sinned," "committed iniquity," and "rebelled" (vv. 6–7), and so has not been "happy" and cannot be "happy" (v. 3). The speaker of the psalm is caught up short, I suspect, by the intrusion of justice and righteousness into the doxology. YHWH might be eagerly praised and thanked, but such glad gestures are never distant from intense covenantal requirements that sober praise and thanks.

As a result, in verse 4 we have a first-person singular petition, "Remember me." This is one voice in Israel craving notice from God. We sing it along with this psalmist because we also want to be remembered. "'Remember me when you come into your kingdom'" (Luke 23:42). It is the prayer of all those who yearn to have God reach to them in their distress. It is the prayer of this psalmist in exile. It is the prayer of the other One to be executed by Rome at Calvary. It may be our prayer when we ponder the depth of our own lives. Even Nehemiah, that strong agent of Jewish recovery, could end his book and his testimony in the same tone:

> Remember me, O my God, for good.
> Neh. 13:31

In our verses the speaker anticipates that God will show favor, deliver, and give prosperity to Israel (vv. 4–5). But it is a personal, even intimate petition, dominated by first-person pronouns. This speaker is aware not only of the failed life of Israel; he is aware that he himself is deeply implicated in that failure. This is community history deeply felt by the individual speaker. The prayer of confession that follows in the body of the psalm is communal and at the same time intensely personal. The failure is palpable to the speaker. This psalmist reflects on the abyss of exile that is the consequence of the sins now to be confessed in the body of the psalm.

We sing it now in our own free fall of failure and despair, knowing that we, like Israel, have squandered the gifts of God. Now the truth must be told. **We sing precisely because the truth must be told about us**, about our historical antecedents, about the entire sweep of our communal history. We sing because we will not engage in denial. Only truth telling positions us for receiving the mercy and goodness of God. We may, for that reason, take this psalm as powerfully countercultural. The psalmist, like us, no doubt lived in a society of denial that was going through all the motions of religiosity, a theme frequently recited by the prophets. But religiosity and its shameless mantras cannot cover over the failed life that has been lived, then and now. So we sing to defy this seduction of denial as did the psalmist. The psalmist is one who knows that no secret can be hid from God and so must be brought to speech. Notice in Psalm 32:3–5 that sin brought to speech evokes ready forgiveness.

We sing the body of this psalm because it narrates the life of Israel and the life we live (vv. 6–46). It narrates Israel's failure (vv. 6–7) and the astonishing "yet" of YHWH's rescue (vv. 8–12). And then it does it over again, only more so, with an extensive narrative exposition of failure (vv. 13–43), again followed by YHWH's "Nevertheless" (vv. 44–46). The psalm pivots on the "Yet" of verse 8 and the "Nevertheless" of verse 44. These disjunctions bind Israel and YHWH in a deep contradiction, even as we are bound to the God of the gospel even in contradiction of God's will. The contradiction between our conduct and God's response is compelling evidence of divine freedom; YHWH is not encased in our disobedience. God can and does freely act out of God's own goodness, even our ungoodness notwithstanding. But the disjunction of inexplicable grace cannot be sounded in Israel's life until Israel voices a broad and deep wholesale acknowledgment of disobedience. So consider Israel's *two-fold refusal of YHWH* (vv. 6–7, 13–43) and *YHWH's two-fold disjunctive response* (vv. 8–12, 44–46), all of which we sing because our unhealth stands exposed, articulated, and then resolved before the health-giving God. This single "I" who speaks in verses 4–6 takes as a personal burden the entire sweep of Israel's life and faith. The speaker is not preoccupied with private or trivial matters of piety or morality. Rather the scope here concerns Israel's big national performance of hard-heartedness.

We sing the opening confession that mostly lacks particulars (vv. 6–7). We are like that; we prefer confessions without particulars. We can utilize a full vocabulary of contradiction: *sin, iniquity, wickedness, rebellion.* The only particular is "at the Red Sea" (which the footnote of historical criticism has demoted to "the Sea of Reeds"). The indictment refers to the fear and doubt Israel voiced just at the brink of deliverance:

> "Was it because there were no graves in Egypt that you have taken us away to die in the wilderness? What have you done to us, bringing us out of Egypt? Is this not the very thing we told you in Egypt, 'Let us alone and let us serve the Egyptians'? For it would have been better for us to serve the Egyptians than to die in the wilderness." (Exod. 14:11–12)

Israel discovered, amid its deliverance from Pharaoh by YHWH, that the risks of faith are immense. They asked why they had ever trusted YHWH and why they had ever followed Moses. And of course their complaint before the wonder of the terrifying waters is reiterated on the other side of the waters as they entered the wilderness:

"If only we had died by the hand of the LORD in the land of Egypt, when we sat by the fleshpots and ate our fill of bread; for you have brought us out into this wilderness to kill this whole assembly with hunger." (Exod. 16:3)

They wished they had never taken up the alternative world of YHWH and the alternative possibility of life outside Pharaoh's oppressive production system. They wished they had played it safe and conformed to the brick quotas, because the alternative freedom of the gospel was more than they could bear.

The recalcitrance of Israel voiced in these verses is followed by an affirmation of YHWH's "wonderful works," a phrase that here refers to the exodus deliverance (v. 7). That deliverance is an act of steadfast love. But the divine act and self-exhibit did not seem adequate for the threat posed by Pharaoh. Here in this single verse we have the juxtaposition of God's steadfast love and Israel's rebellion, the juxtaposition that according to this psalm characterizes the entire history of Israel. It was of course like that in the early Easter church. As Matthew comes to the end of his Gospel, just before the ringing missional affirmation "'All authority . . . go therefore and make disciples of all the nations'" (Matt. 28:18–19), he writes, "When they saw him, they worshiped him; but some doubted" (v. 17).

The Gospel ends with worship of the risen Christ, an exhibit of this God's effective power for life against the deathliness of Rome. Matthew adds tersely, "but some doubted." Well, yes, that's us! In Matthew the continuing obtuseness of the disciples throughout the narrative culminates in this verdict. Some doubted, cringing at their departure from the empire; some doubted and took refuge in Enlightenment rationality. Some doubted and stayed busy with Pharaoh's production schedule. Some doubted and could not risk the vocation concerning peace or justice or holiness. We know all about that. And so we enter the psalm and can sing, "Remember me." Remember me; I am the guy who lacked courage when we walked up to the waters of freedom. I am the gal who flinched at the thought of wilderness bread. We are among those who doubted and who acted short of the newness God would give. Remember me!

Having said that, we sing the great "yet" of God because that "yet" is our only source of hope given honest truth telling about our rebellion (vv. 8–12). Yet he saved!

- He rebuked the chaotic waters.
- He led through the desert, through the valley of the shadow of death.
- He saved from the hand of the foe.
- He delivered them from the enemy.

YHWH did all of that, resistance notwithstanding. YHWH did that not out of love for Israel but "for his name's sake." YHWH did that to exhibit divine power, to enhance divine reputation, to underscore the divine name (see Ezek. 36:22–33). Israel is the beneficiary of YHWH's self-regard.

YHWH is like a parent who endures, even with a recalcitrant child. Maybe out of love. Maybe not. Maybe just because it is who I am and what I do, at worst to keep up appearances, just for "my name's sake," my reputation. What "I" do is save and lead and deliver and rebuke. I do that. And I will not retreat from it, even because of your obtuseness. And then, for an instant the psalmist can say, and we can sing,

> Then they believed his words;
> they sang his praise.
> v. 12

Their believing may be not unlike the Easter disciples. Though some doubted, in sum they believed and trusted YHWH. Hold that! Hold that forever! Moses, back in Exodus 4:1, had asked YHWH concerning his mandate, "'But suppose they do not believe me?" And YHWH had answered, "Watch me." They were persuaded in that instant. Moses is trusted by the Hebrew slaves. Except that they have no staying power. In our psalm their trust only lasts one verse! On many days it was like that in the early church . . . and in the church since.

So they believed, but only for a moment. Soon after that we sing the long refusal of verses 13–43. The trust of Israel evaporated. The miracle does not abide for them . . . or for us. This long exposition is a refusal to abide in the afterglow of the miracle. Now we are back to flat-earth, one-dimensional resistance. This time the exposition goes on and on because there is so much that needs to be said of communal failure: "They soon forgot" (v. 13)! They forgot God their savior who did wondrous works (v. 20). They had been too well taught by Pharaoh. They had "wanton craving" (v. 14) in the image of Pharaoh, who is the godfather of all wanton craving. Like him, they wanted more. They wanted more land, more goods, more control, more natural resources, more security, more certitude, more of the things that imitated Pharaoh, more of the goods provided by Rome, more of the commodities on offer by the National Security State.

So they made a calf (v. 19)! Well, it was a bull, because they were bullish on their own terms. The bull is a sign and an act of fertility, of the capacity to generate one's own future, as we say, "When the time is right." The bull calls to mind the bull situated by the New York Stock Exchange. They thought they could secure their own future, so they manufactured idols of self-sufficiency and images of commodity. They worshiped them and coveted them and obeyed them . . . and forgot! A plenitude of commodities causes amnesia concerning the reality of life-giving relationships. This linkage between *commodity and amnesia* was clearly recognized by Deuteronomy via the mouth of Moses:

> The LORD your God is bringing you into a good land, a land with flowing streams, with springs and underground waters welling up in valleys and hills, a land of wheat and barley, of vines and fig trees and pomegranates, a land of olive trees and honey, a land where you may eat bread without scarcity, where you will lack nothing. . . . Take care that you do not forget the LORD your God, by failing to keep his commandments, his ordinances, and his statutes. (Deut. 8:7–11)

They forgot "great things," "wondrous works," and "awesome deeds" (vv. 21–22). Commodity seemed more reliable, as it always does, than such inexplicable, uncontrollable actions by the God whom they cannot command. They would have perished just then before God's holiness except for the intervention of Moses, who more than once talked God out of God's savage resolve. They were saved, but only by inestimable courage that averted the divine resolve.

They came to the good land (v. 24), but they did not respect the land. They thought they had to kill the indigenous population. They thought they could make it more productive with more might and more control and more pollution, but they made it inhospitable. They signed on with the Baal, the good god of self-invention and self-production (v. 28). Baal functions (in the polemical rhetoric and imagination of Israel) as the point person (or icon) for an entire system of land management that specializes in exploitative production at the expense of both land and neighbor. Engagement with that system of land management is only possible when YHWH, the giver of covenant, has been forgotten (see Hos. 2:13).

Somewhere in all this critical feedback on Israel we Christians sing (as they did not) of "original sin." Not the mythological kind that is passed on by semen but the original sin of having our own way ultimately by a refusal of covenantal responsiveness. Without any such rubric, Israel reads its entire history as a sustained act of disobedience. If you were doing this exposition, how would you translate this psalm among us in order to identify with the original sin of our community? Some certainly say the original sin among us is racism;[1] some might say it is the endless pursuit of commodity. Some would focus on military adventurism. Some would fix on violence of a hundred kinds. But it is all of a piece! My pastor says, "Original sin means that we are all screwed up." In this psalm Israel (and we) looks the systemic screwup in the face without qualification. One does not need to believe in sperm transmission or mythology to see that. All their life in the land was one of cheating on neighborliness and scarring the environment. Life in the land, that land, our land, is all about greed, anxiety, control, and expansionism. Verses 13–43 are surely more than we can take. So we never sing them. We reduce the specificity of the recital to generalized, stylized phrasing that allows ample wiggle room.

Except that we know the specificities to be true. Of late we have generated a recital of the names of vulnerable black persons who have been wantonly killed by officially approved violence, so much so that we are not far removed from "the lynching tree."[2] We know the violations to be true enough that something like divine dismay comes among us; and we are visited, as in verse 15, with "a wasting disease" or in the reduction of cities to jungle wilderness as in verse 26, or economic displacement and military damage as in verse 27 with the scattering of identity. We have not yet, moreover, even thought about assembling a roster of the names of those anonymous persons who have been killed by our wholesale drone program, which mostly remains unrecognized among us so that we practice a quiet killing field. Divine anger is not a popular subject, not even among Presbyterians; it does not go down well alongside the goodness of God. As a result we say it in a more palatable way: the world is morally ordered, and we cannot finally escape the consequences of foolish choices. The choices, says the psalmist, have been foolish among us for a very long time.

The original sin of Israel is upped in verses 35–39 to mixing ("they mingled"), imitating other modes of life that are incompatible with one's identity . . . sacrificing sons and daughters in policies and actions of insanity, pouring out innocent blood in economic expansionism, making idols of commodities, ending with a polluted land, becoming "unclean" enough that the holiness of God cannot dwell in such a place. We would not countenance child sacrifice and are appalled by any such prospect; but we do not flinch dispatching sons and daughters into harm's way for the sake of national imagination. It seems on occasion, as it did in ancient Israel, wholly proper and necessary to take such actions that violate and sacrifice what we treasure most deeply. Like old Israel, we have ready euphemisms to justify.

The concern here with mixing is not an obsession with purity. The alternative is not to be a withdrawn sect with the wagons in a circle. Rather the summons is to be clear about identity, loyalty, and obedience. Short of withdrawn sectarianism we sing about the result of contradicting the givenness of God's intent:

> He gave them into the hand of the nations,
>   so that those who hated them ruled over them.
> Their enemies oppressed them,
>   and they were brought into subjection under their power.
>   vv. 41–42

Until brought low (v. 42)! Brought low by the Assyrians and by the Babylonians and by the Persians and by Rome. And now, we . . . brought low in fear! Our anxious preoccupation with "security" may be an echo of the old curse:

> The sound of a driven leaf shall put them to flight, and they shall flee as one flees from the sword, and they shall fall though no one pursues. They shall stumble over one another, as if to escape a sword, though no one pursues. (Lev. 26:36–37)

The curse anticipates a context of inordinate anxiety evoked by a disordered common life. We sing that! And then we sing, "Jesus, Remember Me"

on that dread Friday along with the thief when the empire seemed to prevail
(Luke 23:42):

> Jesus, remember me when you come into your kingdom.
> Jesus, remember me when you come into your kingdom.[3]

We sing, "Remember me" as an act of relentless hope; we do not doubt, even
given this sorry truth of our life, that we may be well remembered by God.

**We keep singing. We sing right through verses 13–43 until we arrive
at verse 44, and we sing out beyond ourselves and our history, "Nevertheless."** In that very moment of being brought low, we come to acknowledge that the truth of our tradition is not about our failure. The truth
of our common life is that the "nevertheless" of God may override our
self-destructiveness.

After we sing in honesty, we sing in hope. We sing about the God who acts
in self-regard to salvage his reputation. This God with self-regard is focused
not on our failure but on our distress. This God is not mired in anger because

> The LORD is merciful and gracious,
>   slow to anger and abounding in steadfast love.
> He will not always accuse,
>   nor will he keep his anger forever.
> He does not deal with us according to our sins,
>   nor repay us according to our iniquities.
> For as the heavens are high above the earth,
>   so great is his steadfast love toward those who fear him;
> as far as the east is from the west,
>   so far he removes our transgressions from us.
> As a father has compassion for his children,
>   so the LORD has compassion for those who fear him.
> For he knows how we were made;
>   he remembers that we are dust.
>
> Ps. 103:8–14

This God remembers our status as creatures. We are the ones who forget.
But this God remembers back behind our recalcitrance to God's covenant.
That is how it was at the beginning with our initial cry of distress. God heard,
God saw, God knew, God remembered (Exod. 2:24)! God remembered God's
covenant, God's initial commitment made to father Abraham and mother
Sarah. This is the memory about which Mary will later sing:

> He has helped his servant Israel,
>   in remembrance of his mercy,
> according to the promise he made to our ancestors,
>   to Abraham and to his descendants forever.
>
> Luke 1:54–55

Finally in Psalm 106:45, we get the great triad, "covenant, compassion, steadfast love."

"God repented" (v. 46, au. trans.). The NRSV does not have that right and has erroneously emended the text. But the Hebrew is clear. God repented. God changed God's mind. The soft translation of the NRSV does not fully acknowledge that God has reversed field from previous anger. Thus Terence Fretheim can conclude that there are "two dimensions of repentance; the [divine] turning itself and the love which occasions the turning."[4] God moved past anger. That move is made possible by God's steadfast love that turned out to be bottomless. God has made a covenant commitment and not even the golden calf could void it. That is surely clear in Exodus 34 just after the golden calf; Moses intercedes, and God answers:

> I hereby make a covenant. Before all your people I will perform marvels, such as have not been performed in all the earth or in any nation; and all the people among whom you live shall see the work of the LORD; for it is an awesome thing that I will do with you. (Exod. 34:10)

God is always remaking and reperforming the covenant that persists through many violations: He shows them compassion and pity. He remembers. He reaches to them with a mercy that would be enacted for "all who held them captive" (v. 46). So Jeremiah can say to the Jews held in Babylon:

> "Do not be afraid of the king of Babylon, as you have been; do not be afraid of him, says the LORD, for I am with you, to save you and to rescue you from his hand. I will grant you mercy, and he will have mercy on you and restore you to your native soil." (Jer. 42:11–12)

This is an astonishing declaration. Not only will God have mercy on God's people, but the hostile regime, at the behest of God, will also have mercy . . . as became evident with the Persians. This God does indeed have the whole world in his hands:

- He's got the Jews in Babylon in his hands.
- He's got Babylon in his hands.
- He's got the church in his hands.
- He's got the United States in his hands.
- He's got the Islamic culture in his hands.
- He's got friends and adversaries in his hands.

God's hands work mercy. In the end, it is God, not us, not them—it is God and God's mercy. We sing that truth in defiance. **We sing when the truth can only be told by our singing.** The singing is about the bottom-line God who does not linger over our self-destructive foolishness. The psalm lingers many verses over failure because we need to linger there. But God does not finally linger with our recalcitrance but speaks the "nevertheless" that is grounded in God's own resolve!

Finally we arrive at verse 47, and we sing it. The entire psalm has been moving toward this one verse. It is a petition. It is an imperative addressed to God. Israel has positioned itself to issue an imperative to God by its long season of honesty. The address here is to "the LORD our God." Not even all the disobedience has changed that. You are still our God; we are still your people! We address you because it belongs to our DNA to turn to you. So we sing a double petition: "Save us . . . and gather us"! We dare speak a hope-filled imperative to God. We have used "save" in verse 8. We remembered the past saving of us at the Red Sea. And now one more time we ask God to perform God's quintessential wonder in the face of tribulation that we cannot manage ourselves. We say "gather" because we have been scattered, exiled to Babylon, rendered helpless and hopeless.

We sing these two imperatives because we have no alternative:

- We now know that our consumer economy will not save us.
- We now know that our military power will not make us safe.
- We now know that white privilege is nothing for us.
- We now know that our advantage and our entitlement and our superiority have reached their limits, and we are not saved.

We are not saved by any of that. We have seen how our socioeconomic self-regard has now scattered us in vulnerability and devouring anxiety. As a result we reach in our singing behind our recent seductions to a more elemental reality. That elemental reality is the fidelity of God, who invites us to an alternative way in the world.

In uttering this petition, we can anticipate its outcome. Such rescue will end in *praise, not in self-sufficiency.* Such gathering will end in *thanks, not in self-congratulations* (v. 47). *Rescue and gathering* will end in *praise and thanks.* And we will come down where we ought to be, unafraid, ready for new obedience, past our amnesia, ready for the wonder of emancipation, the bread of wilderness, and the good land to be honored and shared.

We sing this long hymn because there is so much about which to sing. There is the entire *recital of our failure* that will be acknowledged, and there is the *divine contradiction of that failure,* the majestic "yet" of the exodus (v. 8) and the great "nevertheless" (v. 44) whereby God refuses to be trapped in our zero-sum game and moves past our ignoble performance *to save and to gather,* the favorite work of the God of compassion. The great imperative prayer of verse 47 has been anticipated by the more modest petition of verse 4: "Remember me." The news is that God is the great rememberer in the face of our amnesia. And what God remembers God enacts. So we sing,

Just as I am without one plea
but that thy blood was shed for me,
and that thou biddest me come to thee,
O Lamb of God, I come; I come!

Just as I am, thou wilt receive,
wilt welcome, pardon, cleanse, relieve;
because thy promise I believe,
O Lamb of God, I come; I come![5]

Or in a contemporary hymn that remembers recalcitrance with Israelite specificity:

Our rebel forebears rarely grasped your mercy or your might;
we need your mercy, just like them: we, too, do wrong not right.

Before a golden calf they bowed—an idol in your place!—
until, by Moses' faithful prayer, you drew them back to grace.

But when they spurned the promised land, you made your anger plain:
they wandered long on desert paths, and served the Baals again.

Yet those whom once you sold in wrath, in mercy you restored;
may we, like them, be gathered in to thank and praise you, Lord.[6]

This hymn, like our psalm, pivots on the "yet" of God's mercy. The psalmist has no plea, no leverage, no case to make. What counts is coming home to evangelical reality. And in coming, we find the compassionate one waiting out beyond anger, out beyond our self-hatred with abundant steadfast love.

CONCLUDING REMARKS

My modest effort in these last few chapters has been to expand the repertoire of the psalms that we know and use and, by implication, to expand the rich, working repertoire of our hymnals, remembering that all music was once new music.

Thus, to summarize, we sing Psalm 104 and the wonder of creation and are left in wonder, awe, and praise. We sing of our utter, glad dependence on the goodness of God, who creates us, tames chaos, and gives us bread. We sing because we refuse the reductionist calculus of control:

All creatures of our God and King,
lift up your voice and with us sing,
Alleluia! Alleluia!
O brother sun with golden beam,

O sister moon with silver gleam,
Sing praises! Alleluia!
Alleluia! Alleluia! Alleluia![7]

When we do not sing Psalm 104, the world shrinks to our management. It may shrink in pride as we grow our own tomatoes, or it may shrink in defeat, mindful as we are that we cannot finally manage the processes of life. So we sing!

We sing Psalm 107 because our best life is a life of gratitude. This is our proper posture before the mystery of life. The gifts of life and transformation simply come to us and are not of our own making. We can name the blessings, the inexplicable wonder of rescue and newness, and we respond in thanks of testimony and thank offering. So we sing,

Now thank we all our God, with heart and hands and voices,
who wondrous things hath done, in whom this world rejoices;
who, from our mothers' arms, hath blessed us on our way
with countless gifts of love, and still is ours today.[8]

Gratitude belongs at the heart of our humanity and our faith because we live on the receiving end of all that matters. George Stroup thus writes,

Gratitude, or human thanksgiving, is never a fully adequate response to the prior giving of God. . . . Because Christian gratitude is a response to the prior giving of God, it is different in kind from all other forms of gratitude. To claim that gratitude is the creaturely counterpart to God's grace is to claim that gratitude to God is shaped by the grace, the divine favor, and the good will that calls it into being and makes it possible. Gratitude, therefore, that is appropriate to God is a thanksgiving that reflects the surprising, costly free gift that is its source and object.[9]

When we do not sing Psalm 107, we fall into ingratitude. The outcome of that is self-preoccupation that issues in parsimony, resentment, and self-regard that may result in inappropriate self-exaltation or finally in unbearable self-loathing. Such a life chokes generosity and precludes neighborliness. Stroup can say of such an alternative,

Ingratitude is a holding back, a refusal to give appropriate thanks for what has been given. . . . Ingratitude asserts that one does not live before God and neighbor at all or is only partially turned toward them. . . . Ingratitude is a denial of the giftedness of what has been given . . . [now] a new possession, personal property one now owns that must be grasped, guarded, defended, and never relinquished.[10]

So we sing!

We sing Psalm 105 in order that the miracle-infested reality of our life may come to glad obedience. The outcome of this memory well recited is that we come to know, in always fresh ways, that we live in a world of generous transformative miracles to which we want to respond. It is for that reason that Israel can speak of the joy of Torah, the love and gladness and restorative power of Torah. Because the commandments are the true shape of a life well lived. It is the story that undergirds the ethic.

When we do not tell the story, we fall out of it. We may fall out into other stories that are false, that seduce and mislead and eventually betray, among them the master narratives of Marx, Darwin, Adam Smith, or Freud. We can learn from each of these competing narratives, but not one of them is itself adequate for our life. Or we may end with no narrative at all, no tradition, no community, no deeply based identity, and so be on a path to despair and self-destruction. So we sing Psalm 105.

We sing Psalm 106 so that we do not forget where we have been and how much we have contradicted the life to which God has called us. "If we say that we have no sin, we deceive ourselves, and the truth is not in us" (1 John 1:8). We sing in order that we may not deceive ourselves. We sing so that we may, in a stance of honesty, be in a position to pray a serious petition to God. We know that the sacrifice that pleases God is truth telling:

> The sacrifice acceptable to God is a broken spirit;
>   a broken and contrite heart, O God, you will not despise.
> Ps. 51:17

We sing this song because we know we are not despised by God.

When we do not sing this psalm, we pale from honesty into self-deception and denial. We are forced to live a covert life of denial that eventually breaks out in violence toward self or toward neighbor. So we sing without one plea. The hymnal, like the Psalter, is our script for this life.

- We sing *wonder* to defeat self-groundedness (Ps. 104).
- We sing *thanks* to resist parsimony (Ps. 107).
- We sing *miracles* to fend off disobedience (Ps. 105).
- We sing *honesty* in order to refuse denial (Ps. 106).

There are many riches in our hymnals. Every time we use them, we sing along with older generations who sang before us. Every time we use them, we join the large song sounded by many tribes, nations, and tongues. Every time we use them, we enter into his courts with praise and candor. Every time we use them, we declare for ourselves and to our children that another way in the world is possible and is here embraced. We refuse the governance of death. We sing to the God of life, the one who wills life in a world of abundance.

PART TWO
WHAT WE SING

The repertoire of hymns available in most denominational hymnals is quite remarkable in its wording. The lyrics not only reflect poetic sensibility but also bring to speech important theological substance (unlike so-called "praise hymns" that are largely content free). Such theological substance variously reflects the assurances and summonses of the life of Jesus, great doctrinal themes, accents of the church year, and often great poetic surges concerning the deep "myths" that fuel and undergird great doctrinal affirmations.[1] Such hymns make possible both glad liturgical assertion and affirmation and winsome pedagogy as a school for the faithful.

My impression, however, is that, for the most part, singing congregations pay very little attention to the wording of hymns. On the one hand, great singable hymns that are familiar to us invite gusto in singing without attentiveness to the words. On the other hand, hymns that are unfamiliar and "difficult" to sing often require effort just to "get through," so attention to the claims of the lyrics is often not possible. (My further impression is that Episcopalians have the largest number of unsingable hymns!) Either way, I believe congregations pay little attention to what we sing.

For that reason I have decided to supplement my core argument concerning *why* we sing with some exposition of *what* we sing. The hymns that follow have been largely chosen at random. Some are old favorites while others are more contemporary. I have sought simply to exposit the words that I find rich and suggestive in order to exhibit the varied treasure of affirmation that is on offer in the tradition. I have done so for two reasons. First, I wanted to slow down and relish the words, phrases, and images that lie deep in our faith tradition. My intent is to show how these particular hymns may indeed be sense making for the faithful who have not succumbed to dominant ideology in our society; they articulate a quite alternative sphere of life for the faithful in which the claims of the gospel may be taken in serious ways. Attentiveness to the lyrics will suggest to a singing congregation the bold ways in which our hymnody contradicts and countermands the too-easily assumed dominant world among us. But second, I hope that my exposition of these particular hymns may invite a continuation of such work by church leaders (pastors, teachers, musicians) to slow down enough to exposit many other hymn words as well, so that our congregational singing might be more attentive and mindful.

I suggest that hymn singing is not unlike watching a film. We can (and often do) sing a hymn without critical reflection in the same way that we can view a film without critical awareness. In both cases we can participate in and enjoy the hymn or film to some great extent, as we should not underplay the rich emotive dimension of such participation. But the more we pay attention to the craft and intention of film making and hymn writing, the more we are able to appreciate and invest in the art form and the thick claims that are made. The "why" of our hymn singing is enhanced by the "what" of our singing. Hymnals are amazing treasures of many generative, imaginative generations of the faithful. How remarkable that we may join their singing! We are recipients and heirs of this singing tradition as we stand alongside many faithful singers who before us have engaged the lyrical world of that craft, sometimes with an awareness that led to deeper trust and joyous risk-taking obedience.

BLEST BE THE TIE THAT BINDS

John Fawcett, 1782

1 Blessed be the tie that binds
  our hearts in Christian love.
  The fellowship of kindred minds
  is like to that above.

2 Before our Father's throne
  we pour our ardent prayers.
  Our fears, our hopes, our aims are one,
  our comforts and our cares.

3 We share our mutual woes;
  our mutual burdens bear.
  And often for each other flows
  the sympathizing tear.

4 When we are called to part,
  it gives us inward pain;
  but we shall still be joined in heart,
  and hope to meet again.

5 From sorrow, toil, and pain,
  and sin we shall be free;
  and perfect love and friendship reign
  through all eternity.

Glory to God (2013), no. 306

Chapter 5

Blest Be the Tie That Binds

This well-loved hymn is a celebration of the intimacy and solidarity of a local congregation, reason enough to sing it. Its origin is in the work of John Fawcett, who during his lifetime wrote a legion of hymns. This particular one was evoked because he was called to leave his small Baptist congregation in Yorkshire for a congregation in London. But he could not do it! He was unable and unwilling to depart the congregation that he loved so well. The hymn voices his devotion to that congregation and offers both practical and theological reasons for his treasuring the congregation. We continue to sing it because we find the same gift of faithful social reality in many subsequent congregations.

Verse 1 voices the conviction that this particular congregation (and many alongside it) embodies qualities of covenantal fidelity that reflect and actualize the ultimate fidelity "above": the kingdom of God. Thus the local congregation at its best is a "foretaste" of the heavenly reality where God's will prevails without qualification. The accent is on "the tie," the way in which members of the congregation are intentionally and intensely linked to one another. The word "tie" is a one-syllable articulation of covenant in which mutual promises and responsibilities are readily embraced. Such mutuality is a disclosure of the will and purpose of God, a will and purpose that take place concretely among real human persons.

The second and third verses voice the specificity of such ties of mutuality. The congregation is a venue for honest prayer in which the whole life of the members of the congregation is given full expression without reservation or concealment. That prayer is "before our Father's throne"; thus it claims its access to the sovereignty of God, who is "more ready to hear than we are to pray."[1] One could anticipate that in Fawcett's congregation there were no stylized or rote prayers, and likely none with exaggerated oratory, but simple articulation of human reality addressed to God.

Verse 2 offers an inventory of human reality that becomes the proper subject of prayer:

"Our fears": It belongs to human reality to live in a world that is well beyond our control. The very act of voicing fear is already to anticipate an evangelical response of assurance:

> Do not fear, for I have redeemed you;
>   I have called you by name, you are mine. . . .
> Do not fear, for I am with you.
>   Isa. 43:1, 5

"Our hopes": Prayer is an opportunity to anticipate from God gifts that we cannot conjure for ourselves but that we desperately need for the living of our days. Hope is the ground for petition, of requests that must be congruent with the will and purpose of God. Thus Jesus instructed his disciples that they should "ask, . . . search, . . . and knock," and receive bread and not stones (Matt. 7:7–11). For good reason Karl Barth can assert,

> In the first instance, it [prayer] is an asking, a seeking, and a knocking directed toward God; a wishing, a desiring and a requesting presented to God. The man who prays . . . cannot come before God without also worshipping God, without giving him praise and thanksgiving, and without spreading out before him his own wretchedness. . . . Prayer is simply asking.[2]

"Our aims": Prayer in the congregation consists in declaring our resolve before God that our life should not be "one thing after another" or "a tale told by an idiot." Instead it should cohere with a purpose larger than ourselves, a calling in accordance with God's own life.

"Our comforts": In the congregation there can be honest recognition that there really are gifts given and resources extended. These comforts very often come through the initiatives of other members of the congregation. But they can indeed be named and identified as gifts from God, because all good gifts are sent from heaven above!

"Our cares": The congregation on occasion bubbles with worry, need, and anxiety because human life is vexed. The linkage of "our comforts and our cares" acknowledges the ambiguous ways we constantly live with blessing and woe, and how that ambiguity is shared with all because these realities of fear, hope, care, and comfort are "one," that is, are common to us all. No one has a monopoly on the good stuff; no one is exempt from the negatives. For that reason there need be no denial or concealment; what preoccupies us, we may be sure, preoccupies our neighbor as well.

This human inventory is rich and deep. One notices that omitted here is a sharing of "sin," because pastoral sensibility could fully discern that guilt is not a primary mark of honest community. Guilt is a secondary reality and so does not come first in this congregation of human reality.

The third verse presses deeper into the sharing of the congregation and focuses on woes and burdens. There are gifts, wonders, and blessings to be shared in the congregation, but the overriding agenda in the life of a congregation is trouble, for which we seek support and solidarity. The rhetoric of the verse evokes notice of two allusions to Paul. First, in Galatians 6:2 Paul admonishes the church, "Bear one another's burdens, and in this way you will fulfill the law of Christ." No member of the community can be abandoned in need. That is the "law of Christ." And just before, Paul asserts, "For the whole law is summed up in a single commandment, 'You shall love your neighbor as yourself'" (Gal. 5:14).

The congregation celebrated in the hymn embodies the intention of Paul. In a second reference Paul articulates this communal solidarity: "If one member suffers, all suffer together with it; if one member is honored, all rejoice together with it" (1 Cor. 12:26). This assertion of Paul is precisely reflected in verse 3 of the hymn; the members of the congregation are ready with empathy, sympathy, and compassion expressed as "tears." One can sense that the writer of these lines was a pastor who entered deeply into the personal lives of the members and helped them to connect to one another, not simply in liturgical articulation but in actual concrete engagement.

In verses 4–5 the hymn picks up the theme of hope from verse 2. It faces into the reality of pain. It may be that these lines concerning "when we are called to part" reflect the pastoral call to London and away from the congregation. That, however, is a small thing contrasted to the "call to part" at death. Death is real, and such loss causes "inward pain."

Death is recognized in the fifth verse as a relief from life's deep vexations: "sorrow, toil, and pain, and sin." Death may indeed be an emancipation: "We shall be free!" And for all the inward pain, the verse finishes with fervent Christian hope that echoes the phrasing of the creeds, of "life beyond death," of "the resurrection of the body and the life everlasting." One may judge that for this pastor and congregation the "inward pain" of death was situated in deep conviction that the God of life and death is fully committed in "perfect love and friendship" that is profoundly immediate, intimate, and personal.

So why do we sing this hymn? Well, because it testifies, celebrates, and summons us to a life together that is possible only because our common life is situated in the narrative of God's sustaining, transformative love. We can notice that other than the one usage of "Christian love" there is no mention of Christ. But reference to "our Father" in verse 2 clearly alludes to the defining reality of the Son who showed us in his common life the eternal love of the Father.

As we sing this narrative of that Father's love, we notice that what is celebrated here contradicts the assumptions and practices of the modern world of consumer capitalism. We sing because concrete awareness of this *contradiction* and the evidence of an *alternative life* are crucial to our well-being and identity. Too much slovenly ecclesiology comes to easy terms with the dominant culture; this hymn, however, for all its sentimental casting, sketches out an alternative that sharply challenges and rejects ordinary dominant values.

Thus, we sing this hymn because it affirms by appeal to "that above" that our life is in the presence of treasured mystery that cannot be decoded or commoditized. The phrase alludes to the rule of God, the kingdom that has already come in heaven. That affirmation contradicts the easy assumption of rational scientific modernity that there is no "above," no transcendent mystery, no will or purpose beyond our own, and no agency that can work good other than our will and resolve. Every time the Christian congregation meets, it affirms and celebrates the reality of that "other world," which is not an escape from "this world" but an alternative world that constantly impinges upon this world in transformative ways. Thus our worship is always an entry into that mystery where we live and move and have our being.

The readiness in verse 2 to "pour out our ardent prayers" is readiness and capacity to speak the truth honestly in the presence of God and in the midst of the congregation. The verse goes on to itemize that about which we are ardent: "fears," "hopes," "aims," "comforts," "cares." That act of honesty contradicts the propensity of ordinary culture to engage in immense denial about the reality of "the human predicament." The denial in the church may take the form of excessive guilt, as though if we acted better we would not be so vexed. In secular culture, denial is forcibly expressed in advertising that generates a false world of youth, beauty, and happiness, all on offer with the right product. Denial in the public sphere includes, on the one hand, the dismissal of our environmental crisis as a hoax and, on the other hand, imaginative euphemisms that misrepresent both the barbarism of war and the barbarism of policies committed against the vulnerable and the left behind.

Congregational prayer refuses such cover-up. It not only tells the truth about our life; beyond that in the practice of intercession it keeps before God the truth of many beyond the congregation (known and unknown) who suffer and are in great need. Such truth-telling prayer is a defiance against the cover-up of dominant culture.

The double use of "mutual" in verse 3 with its acknowledgment of suffering and sadness, plus the list of concerns (our fears, hopes, aims, comforts, and cares) in verse 2 and, in verse 3, our mutual woes and mutual burdens altogether attest to an intense practice of communal solidarity in which the lives of many persons are deeply interwoven. Such a practice and affection are an important contradiction of the ideology of privatism that so permeates our society, all the way from privatizing our public institutions (health care, schools, and prisons) to privatized piety as though faith did not require community. The ideology of privatism pits each person against all in an endless and ruthless competition. The Christian congregation knows better. It knows that God does not love us only one at a time but has bound ("tied") us into a common destiny of well-being for which the tag word is "shalom." The church knows that there is no "private shalom," no "separate peace."

We sing this hymn because it ends in hope. Verses 4–5 honestly voice the reality of pain and death, but the singing continues to affirm that beyond death there is "hope to meet again" in a context where freedom, perfect love, and friendship prevail. These verses do not claim too much. They do not, like much popular eschatology, offer a blueprint of an afterlife. They only accept the promise of the gospel that death does not terminate the good rule of God. That good rule of freedom, love, and friendship, moreover, displaces the vexation of sorrow, toil, pain, and sin that mark our present life in the world.

This vigorous act of hope contradicts the deep despair of a dominant culture that believes there is no life beyond this life, that there is no God who persists beyond death, and that God's kingdom will not come among us in power and goodness. In its dominant mode, the world ends in despair that there are no meaningful gifts to be given and that we live in a zero-sum universe. That despair is evident in the phony promises that "products" will keep us young, drugs will keep us healthy, and arms will keep us safe, when in fact youth, health, and safety cannot be guaranteed by any such frightened strategies.

Thus we sing because such a hymn is a welcome chance to affirm the truth of faith in a culture that has long since given up such truthfulness:

- We sing to affirm *a gracious sovereignty* that moves in, with, and under our life against a self-contained, self-preoccupied world.
- We sing to affirm that *truth telling* is the clue to well-being against a culture of denial that pretends it's happy when it is not.
- We sing to affirm *glad community solidarity* against an ideology of privatism that refuses the common good.
- We sing as an act of *hope* against a culture of despair.

We sing to celebrate, construct, and receive a world other than the one given us by dominant culture. It is no wonder that Fawcett chose to continue his life and ministry amid such a singing environment.

I am bound to notice that this hymn by itself can be recognized as myopic. What it does, it does very well. But it does not do—and does not intend to do—everything. Thus the imaginings of this hymn are contained within the congregation and the affection its members have for one another. There is here no outreach, no mission, no contact to the larger world of society, no urgent summons to the contested issues of justice. Such inward-looking celebration, however, has it place in Christian worship even as many of the epistles are concerned with the right ordering of the community. It is important to affirm the good "ties" of members to one another and the good life such ties generate, as long as this hymn is accompanied by other hymns that the believing community sings beyond itself. As the life of this beloved congregation is "like to that above" where God's rule is unchallenged, so the congregation, by its very existence, can be an invitation to broader culture to reorder its life, policies, and practices toward such mutuality of well-being. The larger implications of such an embodied model are clear and immense!

GOD OF GRACE AND GOD OF GLORY

Harry Emerson Fosdick, 1930

1 God of grace and God of glory,
on thy people pour thy power;
crown thine ancient church's story;
bring its bud to glorious flower.
Grant us wisdom, grant us courage,
for the facing of this hour,
for the facing of this hour.

2 Lo! the hosts of evil round us
scorn thy Christ, assail his ways!
From the fears that long have bound us
free our hearts to faith and praise.
Grant us wisdom, grant us courage,
for the living of these days,
for the living of these days.

3 Cure thy children's warring madness;
bend our pride to thy control;
shame our wanton, selfish gladness,
rich in things and poor in soul.
Grant us wisdom, grant us courage,
lest we miss thy kingdom's goal,
lest we miss thy kingdom's goal.

4 Save us from weak resignation
to the evils we deplore.
Let the gift of thy salvation
be our glory evermore.
Grant us wisdom, grant us courage,
serving thee whom we adore,
serving thee whom we adore.

Glory to God (2013), no. 307

Chapter 6

God of Grace and God of Glory

Harry Emerson Fosdick, writer of this well-known hymn, was a celebrity preacher and a controversial figure because of his theological "modernism." In 1930 he began a remarkable ministry at the newly built Riverside Church in New York City, built for him by Rockefeller money. Just prior to beginning that wondrous ministry, Fosdick wrote this widely cherished hymn. His work at Riverside Church was just across the street from Union Theological Seminary, where he also taught. Union Seminary, among other things, hosted the celebrity theologian Reinhold Niebuhr, who became increasingly critical of the theological "liberalism" that Fosdick so much championed.

Niebuhr is credited (in a not undisputed way) with being the source of the "Serenity Prayer":

> God, grant me the serenity
> to accept the things I cannot change,
> courage to change the things I can,
> and wisdom to know the difference.[1]

I cite this from Niebuhr because it calls us to "serenity," "courage," and "wisdom." It interests me that Fosdick's great hymn is also a petition for wisdom and courage: "Grant us wisdom, grant us courage." I'm not suggesting that Fosdick was informed by this famous prayer, and we can readily see that while he accented two points voiced in the prayer, there is no mention of the third, "serenity." Perhaps it did not fit the meter of the hymn. But Fosdick was not especially interested in "serenity" because his passion was for daring change. We must look elsewhere, in other hymns, to find mention of serenity.

Fosdick's hymn was written in 1930 in the midst of the Depression. The moment was an instant between the two world wars when the international community struggled with systemic disarmament. Thus it was, for one with the celebrity status of Fosdick, a moment when great challenges were to be faced and great issues had to be faced in faith. The repeated refrain "Grant us wisdom, grant us courage," while cast as a petition to God, was as well an assertion that this is no time for "business as usual." This moment, so Fosdick insists, is no time for reliance on old certitudes or old formulations. It was a time for courage to think new thoughts and risk new actions. It is also a time for wisdom that paid attention to the facts on the ground, that took seriously the gospel call to obedience, and that was informed by alert critical thinking. Fosdick was determined that Christian faith should be intellectually responsible and engaged with the best learning of the day.

The context in which wisdom and courage were required, signaled in the refrain, is "this hour" and "these days," thus immediacy in which decisions will and must be made in relation to the "goal" of God's kingdom. Fosdick was an adherent of the social gospel, in which human decision making, rightly responsible, would abet the kingdom of God in this hour and in these days. The final line of the last verse keeps the focus on God; the hymn is thoroughly theocentric, though the scorn of Christ is mentioned in verse 2. The final refrain is to serve God "whom we adore." This move toward doxology affirms that the practice of wisdom and courage, now required, is in obedience to God. Fosdick's orthodox opponents in Presbyterianism had attacked him for his modernism, which they judged was too soft on gospel truth. Thus even today Fosdick is at the center of the still ongoing dispute in the church, only now Fosdick's liberalism is termed "progressivism." The final refrain of the hymn shows that Fosdick well understood the God-centered, doxology-evoking truth of our faith.

The opening phrasing of the hymn, which functions as its title, voices the two accents of the God of the gospel. The accent on "grace" is of course the great theme of Paul's theology that came to vibrant expression in Luther's Reformation; it is an affirmation that the God of the gospel is a self-giving God who in utter generosity accepts us unconditionally as we are. That accent was given popular expression by Fosdick's near neighbor Paul Tillich, a colleague at Union Seminary, in his famous sermon "You Are Accepted." But Fosdick knew (as did Tillich) that a singular accent on God's grace would by itself lead to an easy offer of "cheap grace."

For that reason, the hymn promptly voices a counteraccent on God's glory, an assertion that God is "wholly other," a truth that precludes God from being an intimate friend or a good buddy. The accent on God's glory witnesses to the transcendence of God that assures that God is beyond our explanatory categories, one who must be "adored," worshiped, and not presumed upon.

The combination of "grace" and "glory" expresses the most elemental claim for God, that God is *for us*, but that God is also *for God's own self* and will not be mocked. In recent times, given the force of a psychology of acceptance, the accent among us has been on God's grace. The counterpoint of glory, however, is a stark reminder that in truth we are dealing with "God," a reality in the life of the world who eludes all our efforts at domestication. The holiness of God is a mighty resistance against our seductions of prideful self-sufficiency and our contemporary temptation to reduce the life of the world to the crassest forms of brutality and ugliness.

The continuation of verse 1 is a petition for "power" from God for the church in order to live into the demanding claims of the church's "ancient story." The accent on "story" shows that Fosdick was a "narrative theologian" long before that become popular. He understood that all of our resolves for faithfulness are grounded in the ancient story of Scripture that provides ballast for our present-day faith. Thus we can imagine that Fosdick would gladly sing both "I love to tell the story" and "We've a story to tell to the nations." The former is an affirmation that the story of the gospel is a welcome disclosure of well-being in God's grace, of which we require frequent reminder. The latter is a reminder of the missionary dimension: that the news is not to be kept just for us and for our kind and that the gospel narrative dispatches the church into venues that require courage and wisdom.

Before he finishes this first verse Fosdick will call attention to the ongoing dynamism of the gospel narrative that reflects his passion for the contemporaneity of the gospel that was at the heart of his modernism. Fosdick is determined that the gospel faith of the church should not be contained in old formulations of certitude that his orthodox opponents so vigorously defended. He understood that the Scripture has a dynamism toward the future that evokes fresh formulation and that summons to new mandates. This dynamism is voiced in verse 1 in two figures. First, the imperative petition "crown" signifies an expectation that the beautiful, sweet finish of the "ancient story" is yet to come in the future by fresh revelation and interpretation. Second, with the image of a flower, the old story is still only a "bud." The imperative "bring" expects that the bud of Scripture will blossom to "glorious flower" in time to come. In both images the best of Scripture (the ancient story) lies in the future. Negatively, such phrasing is a rejection of strict constructionism and fundamentalism that imagines Scripture is frozen "back there." Positively, the hope expressed in these two imperatives echoes the old Puritan conviction that "God has yet more light to break forth from his word." Or in an updated version, my church, the United Church of Christ, asserts, "God is still speaking." Thus the phrasing of the hymn confirms Fosdick's "progressive" credentials.

Verse 2 reflects an ominous social context in which dominant values aggressively contradicted the way of Christ. The imperative "free" bids for God's grace-filled emancipation from fear of the dominant social realities. The words suggest that genuine gospel faith is "on the run" in retreat from that social reality. The petition assumes that a fearless, unintimidated church will practice unrestrained confident praise and will get on with faithful living that defies the "hosts of evil."

Verse 3 offers an acute critique of a society that is hell-bent on self-indulgence and self-sufficiency. It alludes to the "warring madness" in which nation-states imagine military solutions to every problem. The verse, moreover, sees that the unrestrained materialism of society is a cause of "warring madness." Perhaps the most remarkable phrase in the hymn comes in verse 3, "rich in things, poor in soul." The word "soul" is an odd one for a progressive, but we know what Fosdick means. The mad self-indulgence of consumerism diminishes the human dimension of social reality, in which everything and everyone is commoditized so that authentic relationships grounded in "soul" become scarce and difficult. The double contrast of "rich"/ "poor" and "things"/ "soul" echoes the verdict of Jesus that we must choose between "God and wealth" (Matt. 6:24: Luke 16:13). The prayer that the God of grace and glory "shame" to well-being perhaps alludes to the rich man in the parable of Luke 12 who was "not rich toward God" (v. 21). The petition that God should "shame our wanton, selfish gladness" suggests that unrestrained materialism is a cause for shame. That line, however, does not recognize that when we are trapped in such indulgence, we are not likely to be shamed out of it. Thus Jeremiah can recognize that his indulgent contemporaries were beyond such shame:

> . . . they were not at all ashamed,
> they did not know how to blush.
> Jer. 8:12

Abraham Heschel can observe,

> Embarrassment is a response to the discovery that in living we either replenish or frustrate a wondrous expectation. . . . It is a protection against the outburst of the inner evils, against arrogance, *hybris,* self-deification. The end of embarrassment would be the end of humanity.[2]

Fosdick's verse 3, which is cast as a petition with three powerful imperatives ("cure," "bend," and "shame"), is in fact a confession of sin. It is remarkable that the contrast of "things"/ "soul" is already made definitional in 1930, when consumerism as we have it today had not yet heated up.

In verse 4 we again begin with an imperative: "Save." It is important, however, that the prayer is not that we be saved from the "evils we deplore." It is rather a prayer to be rescued from "weak resignation" in the face of those evils.

Progressive that he is, Fosdick did not believe that God would, in any direct way, rescue from evil. He regarded that as a human task. It is a human assignment to confront and overcome evil (see Rom. 12:21). But if God does not directly deal with evil, our expectation in the hymn is that God can move (inspire?) us to wisdom and courage to act against evil. God is the essential legitimator of such courageous action, without whom we are unlikely to resist evil in bold ways. Positively this final verse culminates in "the gift of salvation" that is the ground from which all else follows. The verse affirms that if we receive and relish the gift of salvation, we need not settle in passive, indifferent resignation before evil. Although the hymn does not identify the evils we deplore, it hints at materialism that leads to war and materialism that eventually leads to human diminishment. Thus the hymn is an invitation to reorder priorities and reclaim faithful energy for the immense tasks at hand. The phrasing of the hymn compellingly links *the rule of God* to *the real world* in its vexation with the most elemental *assurances of faith.* This indispensable linkage contrasts with so much contemporary evangelicalism that has lost contact with the evil of the real world in a world-denying way, and with much contemporary theological progressivism that has lost contact with the gospel roots of ethical imagination in a God-disregarding way.

What strikes me most about this hymn is that it is grounded in a series of imperative petitions: "pour," "crown," "bring," "free," "cure," "bend," "shame," and "save." The hymn is the prayer of a congregation that is alert to the dangerous place in which God has placed us, alive to the responsible role assigned to us, and convinced of the indispensability of God's rule (grace and glory) that equips us for the assignment. Such petition, moreover, is reinforced by the eight uses of "grant," two in each verse. The expectation of this repeated petition is that if God does grant us wisdom and courage, we will not fail to face this hour, to live these days, and to reach the goal of God's kingdom. It is a daring conviction. This is resolved evangelical talk from a convinced progressive; it affirms ultimate dependence on God even while it anticipates immense human responsibility. That human responsibility, however, is deeply situated in gospel reality. Everything depends on God, the one whom we adore. We may deeply affirm with the hymn that, given the divine grant of wisdom and courage, human capacity is immense:

"For mortals it is impossible, but for God all things are possible." (Matt. 19:26)

What becomes possible is that we will be free to praise; we will have courage to meet the evil we deplore. We will have wisdom to face this hour faithfully. We will live these days wisely and courageously. We will reach the goal of the kingdom of God in joy. But best of all, we will serve the one whom we adore. We will do that, even in the midst of warring madness; we will become "rich in soul." We may embrace an alternative life that is our true God-given life, given in glory, dispatched to us in grace.

HE WHO WOULD VALIANT BE

John Bunyan, 1684

1 He who would valiant be
'gainst all disaster,
let him in constancy
follow the Master.
There's no discouragement
shall make him once relent
his first avowed intent
to be a pilgrim.

2 Who so beset him round
with dismal stories
do but themselves confound,
his strength the more is.
No foes shall stay his might,
though he with giants fight;
he will make good his right
to be a pilgrim.

3 Since, Lord, thou dost defend
us with thy Spirit,
we know we at the end
shall life inherit.
Then fancies flee away;
I'll fear not what men say,
I'll labor night and day
to be a pilgrim.

The Hymnal 1982, according to the use of the Episcopal Church, no. 564

Chapter 7

He Who Would Valiant Be

John Bunyan was an English Puritan and a convinced preacher. When royal authority tried to silence his preaching, he refused; as a result he was imprisoned for twelve years. In 1684, four years before his death, he published *The Pilgrim's Progress*. The book is his spiritual biography and has subsequently become a classic of spiritual literature. In the book Bunyan traces the "pilgrimage" of a resolved Christian who, on his way in gospel obedience, encounters many seductions and impediments to his journey in faith. The hymn we consider was included in the second part of his book, it being the only hymn Bunyan wrote.[1]

The theme of the book and of the hymn is that of being a pilgrim. This is reflective of the pilgrimage "in faith" narrated in Hebrews 11 where "by faith" these celebrated characters of the biblical tradition faced many "toils and snares," overcame many dangers, and resisted many temptations. "Faith" in this rendering is a determined resolve to remain faithful to the promise of the gospel, no matter what the cost.

A remarkable feature of these pilgrims in faith is that they did not arrive at their destination of "a better place":

> All of these died in faith without having received the promises, but from a distance they saw and greeted them. They confessed that they were strangers and foreigners on the earth, for people who speak in this way make it clear that they are seeking a homeland. . . . They desire a better country, that is, a heavenly one. Therefore God is not ashamed to be called their God; indeed, he has prepared a city for them. . . . Yet all these, though they were commended for their faith, did not receive what was promised. (Heb. 11:13–16, 39)

They lived by promises and could anticipate their arrival at a new promised land that was never achieved by them. There was such a destination, a city prepared, and they did not doubt it. But arrival there would depend on coming generations of pilgrims who would continue and arrive at "something better": "Since God had provided something better so that they would not, apart from us, be made perfect" (Heb. 11:40).

These many pilgrims who did not arrive are celebrated for the tenacity of their resolve and their endurance. The present generation of pilgrims (at any time) is a part of the sequence of generations of pilgrims. The lead pilgrim in this horizon is Jesus, "pioneer and perfecter of our faith" (Heb. 12:2). There are many generations to come whose task is to "make perfect" the pilgrimage of those who trusted but did not arrive.

Bunyan was and understood himself to be a part of this continuing sequence of pilgrims who withstood immense external pressure from those who wanted to silence him. His testimony, however, is that the great withstanding he had to do concerned spiritual seductions and temptations that would cause him to compromise or abandon faith. This locus between generations of pilgrims is apparent when we consider that Father Jacob attests the sojourn of his ancestors (Gen. 47:9) and that the epistle of 1 Peter identifies believers as "aliens and exiles" who are summoned to refuse accommodation to "the desires of the flesh" that assault "the soul" (1 Pet. 2:11). Bunyan would have been among those aliens and exiles who knew, in his earnest faith, that he did not belong in this present society but was on his way elsewhere.

When we sing this hymn, we identify with and join Bunyan in the trek of faith. His notion of "pilgrim" has among us been compromised in many ways: (1) We have become too easily at home in a society of scarcity, fear, greed, and violence, and regard such a context as our natural habitat; (2) we have a romantic notion of pilgrims from Plymouth Rock that easily morphed into a nationalist movement that eventually abused and overwhelmed a native population; and (3) we have romanticized pilgrimage as spirituality as an easy bourgeoisie practice. Against all such easy accommodations Bunyan's hymn is a mighty affirmation of the demands of faith.

In the three verses of the hymn that we have in our hymnals specific references to God are sparse. In verse 1 we acknowledge resolve to follow "the Master." In verse 3 there is direct address to the "Lord" and an affirmation of "the spirit." But as we shall see, these uses are a bowdlerization of Bunyan's more imaginative rhetoric. But that is all. Reliance on the truth of the gospel, the reality of God's governance, and the grace of Christ are assumed. The hymn is not at all theologically curious or speculative. It focuses rather on the practicalities facing the pilgrim. Thus all three verses end with resolve to be an uncompromising pilgrim on the way in the gospel in defiance of external challenges and internal impediments.

The opening term "valiant" in verse 1 is an old-fashioned term for brave loyalty to duty. Thus Bunyan affirms that pilgrims are under mandate even in the face of disaster. The disaster he identifies in the larger narrative concerns all the passions that will talk him out of faith, out of his resolve to be a pilgrim. The counter to all these passions that makes valor possible is "constancy," an unceasing, single-minded intent to be a follower, that is, a disciple. This valor requires immense intentionality that is never for an instant relaxed into complacent accommodation. The result, in verse 1, is that no impediment will interrupt pilgrimage resolve. The cadence of "discourage*ment*," "re*lent*," "in*tent*" in lines 5–7 reinforces constancy. Reference to "first avowed intent" may be an allusion to the reprimand addressed to the church in Ephesus:

> "But I have this against you, that you have abandoned the love you had at first." (Rev. 2:4)

We know about initial zeal that then cools. So it was when Christian community became Christian institution. Bunyan will allow for no such cooling. The first intent with all its initial passion persists. The pilgrim is as resolved every day as on the first day, no relenting, no relaxation, no complacency, no ease in Zion!

Verse 2 is an act of resistance against companions who tell him "dismal stories," perhaps stories of excessive risk or narratives of easier accommodation. Such stories are dismal because they contradict and detract from the true story of the gospel that Bunyan did not doubt. Such distractions, however, only expose the tellers of such tales. They do not harm the pilgrim who, in the face of such distraction, is only strengthened in great resolve.

Verse 2 presents the constancy of the pilgrim in deep combat. There are "foes," those who refuse and resent such pilgrimage. But Bunyan, in his imaginative wording, makes the foes much more real and graphic. The foes are as awesome as giants. The "giants," before reductionist editing in the hymn version, are in parallel to "lions" in Bunyan's original poem: "No lion can him fright."[2] This phrase may allude to Hebrews 11:33, which is in turn a reference to Daniel 6:10–24. The reference to giants may connect to the spies in the Joshua narrative who, in their anxiety, imagined the inhabitants of the land to be as fearsome as giants (Num. 13:33). Giants and lions are enough to intimidate. But in both of these OT cases, the threats in fact have no force.

The giants, in the face of Joshua's steadfastness, turn out to be a fantasy. The lions for Daniel turned out to be no danger. The "foes" are not ominous when faced with constancy. In Bunyan's rhetoric, it is a "right" as well as a duty to be a pilgrim. It may be that the rhyme required "right" to go with "fight," but the usage makes it a nice corrective to any notion of a burdensome duty. In any case the pilgrim is undaunted by apparent threats.

In verse 3 our familiar rendering is a limp purgation away from Bunyan's more graphic imagination. In his original wording,

> Hobgoblin nor foul fiend
> Can daunt his spirit;
> He knows, he at the end
> Shall life inherit.[3]

Bunyan gives us a much more fearful context than our bowdlerized version. Bunyan is assaulted by two fears. On the one hand, he faces hobgoblins, fantasy forces that may occupy his imagination. But he sees that they are not real and have no force. On the other hand, "foul fiends," demonic forces that try to dissuade him from radical faith, try to talk him out of constancy. Bunyan no doubt had a notion of spiritual warfare against such foes. But never mind! These imagined threats are in fact no serious challenge to his constancy; his spirit is undaunted because he remains fixed on his destination, which is "life." In our hymn version the rhyme of "spirit" and "inherit" is preserved, but now the graphic threats have been eliminated, and the "spirit" is no longer that of the pilgrim but now is that of the "Lord."

As in so much gospel talk, that notion of a promised life is left unspecified. In the Synoptic Gospels, it is "the kingdom of God" (or alternatively "kingdom of heaven"). In the Fourth Gospel, it is "eternal life," as well as "life abundant." In Hebrews 11 it is a "city," "a better country," "a heavenly city." In much popular piety these anticipations have morphed into "life after death." But authentic spirituality, as with Bunyan, leaves the destination unspecified, a goal that cannot be readily reduced to prose designation. It is for that reason that Christian anticipation must appeal to a rich variety of images and metaphors, each of which by itself can be reduced to one-dimensional reality, but each of which must be corrected and enriched by other images and metaphors.

In verse 3 the last lines make sense when we appeal to Bunyan's original wording. In our purged version, "fancies" has no antecedent. In the original, the "fancies" are "hobgoblins and foul fiends" that have no actual reality.[4] The last lines of verse 3 look back to all the threats heretofore named that have attacked him for his constancy. The pilgrim, however, will be fearless, unswayed by false talk among his companions. He will get on with the labor of pilgrimage. And it is, as Bunyan knew, real work, an onerous duty that requires 24/7 engagement. The pilgrim finishes this hymn of resolve unharmed, still fully constant, with undiminished zeal, even in the face of assault and distraction.

I first encountered Bunyan's classic in college in a course on "Christian Classics" taught by my beloved teacher and subsequent colleague Eugene Wehrli. Of course, as a college student I had no clue about religious classics or the hymn Bunyan offered in his classic. I was of late drawn back to the hymn by reading a biography of Clement Attlee, the great underrated Prime Minister of Great Britain, written by John Bew.[5] In the wake of World War II and the immense impact of Churchill, Attlee labored all his life, "night and day," for his societal vision. Bew writes that Bunyan's hymn was Attlee's favorite, and even though he was an avowed atheist, the hymn was sung at Attlee's funeral.

In his life and career, Attlee labored night and day in constancy. The subtitle of Bew's biography is "The Man Who Made Modern Britain." And indeed Attlee did! In the wake of the war, he introduced legislation that created a sustainable safety net and social infrastructure that continues to mark Britain, even in the wake of Margaret Thatcher's relentless assault on that safety net and infrastructure. That safety net was created for the sake of the vulnerable, most notably in the national health-care system that Bishop Stephen Sykes has termed the core of Britain's "civil religion." Attlee was a self-effacing man without great ego needs who in his constancy, resolve, and courage decisively altered the social map of Britain. What I learned from Attlee concerning the hymn is that "pilgrimage" is not about piety, spirituality, or comfortable tours of ancient religious sites. It is rather *an act of sustained obedience to a vision of an alternative world that is intended by God.* Attlee understood as well that the practice of "pilgrim" is not a solo flight of spirituality; it is a life that is clearly situated in a network of generative social relationships. Attlee was unfailingly loyal to his companions on his trek of obedience. Even though their pilgrimages took very different forms, there is a compelling continuity from Bunyan to Attlee in the awareness that the gospel (even for an atheist) invites us to a *God-willed future* that is different from the present. To be sure, Attlee had a theological grounding in his background; the primary motivation for his astonishing work, however, was his awareness of deep need among his fellow citizens.

This hymn is no invitation to complacent singing or self-satisfied faith. My sense about most of us in fading Christendom is that we are, liberal and conservative, inured to the political economy of the status quo. The sharp edges of faith have been tamed and silenced to accommodation. Yet this hymn summons us to night-and-day constancy, a summons that we regularly may fend off and resist. The seductions, temptations, and dangers—the hobgoblins and foul fiends, the giants and lions—pull our imagination into fear and resignation.

The news of Bunyan's hymn is that the context of late capitalism, enforced by the politics of exceptionalism, is not our true home, attractive as it is. Our true home, to which we are on our way as pilgrims, is "elsewhere" in the providence of God. It is our duty and our "right" to be on the way that we may "life inherit." The hymn is a huge wake-up call to the pilgrim community that mostly does not any longer intend to be on our way to a "better country."

HOLY, HOLY, HOLY
Reginald Heber, 1827

1 Holy, holy, holy! Lord God Almighty!
   Early in the morning our song shall rise to thee.
   Holy, holy, holy! merciful and mighty!
   God in three persons, blessed Trinity!

2 Holy, holy, holy! all the saints adore thee,
   casting down their golden crowns around the glassy sea;
   cherubim and seraphim falling down before thee,
   who wert, and art, and evermore shalt be.

3 Holy, holy, holy! though the darkness hide thee,
   though the eye of sinfulness thy glory may not see,
   only thou art holy; there is none beside thee,
   perfect in power, in love and purity.

4 Holy, holy, holy! Lord God Almighty!
   All thy works shall praise thy name, in earth and sky and sea.
   Holy, holy, holy! merciful and mighty!
   God in three persons, blessed Trinity!

Glory to God (2013), no. 1

Chapter 8

Holy, Holy, Holy

This stately, regal hymn voices a dimension of gospel faith that is almost lost in the sweet romanticism of much recent and contemporary church music. In a frightened, lonely culture of alienation like ours, the accent of much current church music, especially voiced in so-called "praise hymns," concerns intimate one-on-one contact with God. The lyrics and the music together offer a warm intimacy of companionship that reassures.

In the midst of such popular church music this hymn stands as a mighty insistence that the reality of God cannot be reduced to comfortable, reassuring companionship. The hymn insists, to the contrary, that the God the church worships is an awesome sovereign to whom willing yielding is appropriate.

In current church usage the hymn is regularly linked to the celebration of "Trinity Sunday" in the church year, as the hymn quite intentionally asserts that distinct formulation of God in the full majesty of mystery. The ground for that linkage is that the three-fold "holy" is taken as an allusion to the "three persons" of the Trinity. That is a legitimate ecclesial extrapolation, even though in the biblical texts, as we will see, there is no appeal to "Trinitarian" categories. Rather the three-fold "Holy" in the biblical texts is a rhetorical extravagance and a linguistic superlative to voice the awesome wonder of the sovereign God. This ecclesial linkage, moreover, is reinforced by the majestic music of John Bacchus Dykes that he titled "Nicaea," an intentional allusion to the ecumenical Council of Nicaea in 325 CE that fully embraced the Trinitarian formula. This ecclesial rendering is compelling in church liturgy even though it represents a significant departure from the biblical texts on which it is based.

The first text that has evoked and funded the hymn is Revelation 4:6–11. This text offers a vision of "living creatures" (v. 6) and elders all gathered in doxology around the heavenly throne singing,

> "Holy, holy, holy.
> the Lord God the Almighty,
>   who was and is and is to come." . . .

> "You are worthy, our Lord and God,
>   to receive glory and honor and power,
> for you created all things,
>   and by your will they existed and were created."
>   vv. 8, 11

This vision in the book of Revelation is an anticipation of a world to come that is alternative to the present brutalizing world of Roman imperialism. The hymn of the "living creatures," like all of the book of Revelation, does not doubt that this awesome God will eventually prevail over the empire of force. It does not doubt, moreover, that the faithful who trust the gospel will end in doxological joy at God's prevailing after they have endured the suffering imposed by the present empire. Thus the doxology is an anticipatory celebration of God's sure and certain victory over historical evil. The God who is celebrated is the nearly unutterable creator God who created all things, who "calls into existence the things that do not exist" (Rom. 4:17), and who is before all created time, after all created time, and governor of all created time. From the outset the church, after the manner of Israel, has known that such an unutterable claim for God can only be expressed in poetic, doxological cadence. It is most unfortunate that the doxological, poetic formulation of the Trinity, "God in three persons," has been flatly reduced from poetic liturgical formulation to a propositional claim that pretends that the claim can be parsed in conventional human rationality. To the contrary, the purpose of doxology is to defy such explanatory reasoning, which is why at its best the church *sings* rather than *reasons* or *disputes*.

Behind Revelation 4, to which our hymn appeals, is a thick allusion to Isaiah 6:1–8. The three-fold "holy" in the text of Revelation is undoubtedly derived from Isaiah 6. That text narrates a tumultuous experience of the prophet Isaiah in Jerusalem, wherein the prophet has a vision of the awesome sovereign God and in response accepts the burdensome assignment of a prophetic vocation.

The vision Isaiah narrates is of YHWH as king, high and lofty in the heavenly throne room where the "living creatures" of Revelation, winged creatures (seraphim and cherubim), swarm around the throne of God in unending doxology. They cover their faces with two wings because they dare not see the Holy One. Their song is the three-fold "Holy" echoed in Revelation and in our hymn:

> "Holy, Holy, Holy is the LORD of hosts;
> the whole earth is full of his glory."
> Isa. 6:3

The temple cannot contain the divine glory that spills over throughout all creation. (On the inability of the temple to contain the holy God, see 1 Kgs. 8:27.)

The prophet's response to this vision of God is an awareness of his own sinful unworthiness, his ritual uncleanness before holiness. Isaiah is startled beyond explanation that in his disqualification he nonetheless can receive this vision of the holy God. More than a vision, this holy God, via the ministry of the winged creatures, removes his guilt and blots out his sin. It is astonishing that the Holy One will invest in pardon! Isaiah's response to this wonder is readiness to be dispatched on behalf of this three-times-holy God.

It is worth notice that the lines that follow in Isaiah 6 are most often not mentioned or quoted among us, because they are hard words in which the holy God provides that Israel, in its recalcitrance, will not be able to "comprehend," understand, or "turn and be healed" (vv. 9–10). The people of God, "before Jehovah's awful throne,"[1] are to be subjected to profound judgment; that is the burden of the prophetic vocation of Isaiah. While we regularly choose to disregard this note (as does Revelation), it is important to notice that the New Testament repeatedly cites this text as a judgment on the "older people of God" (Israel) from which we can readily in our context extend to the "newer people of God" (the church) (Matt. 13:14–15; Mark 4:12; Luke 8:10; John 12:37–43; Acts 28:26–27; Rom. 11:7). In Isaiah 6 the vision of God's holiness is awesome, but it is also ominous, thus precluding any easy intimacy that we would much prefer.

Verse 1 moves beyond Isaiah and Revelation and situates our own singing in the doctrinal formulation of Nicaea: "God in three persons, blessed Trinity." The opening "Lord God Almighty" is a faithful echo of Isaiah's attestation that he had "seen the King, the LORD of hosts" (Isa. 6:5). The "hosts" that surround the king are the "living creatures," the angels and minigods, including the seraphim and cherubim. Since the throne room is peopled in the vision by a great doxological company, it is not a big leap to imagine this three-fold emergence of the divine presence. This is no one-dimensional monarch but a great company of agents.

The first verse includes two other notes. First, the presiding king is recognized as "merciful and mighty." These two themes together stretch the rich complexity of God's capacity: might that bespeaks, sovereign authority that will not be mocked, on the one hand, and mercy that opens divine majesty to gracious mutuality, on the other hand. Ronald Clements has said that such a pairing of themes that characterize God becomes a pattern of articulation in Israel: divine might and mercy; might that brings judgment, mercy that enacts restoration. The prophetic literature acquired an overarching thematic unity that centered on the death and rebirth of Israel, interpreted theologically as acts of divine judgment and salvation.[2]

While the two themes map out Israel's history of *exile and restoration* and while they reappear in the Jesus narrative as *crucifixion and resurrection*, they come to constitute recurring realities in the life of God, even though we have a great propensity to prefer one of them to the other. The two themes of might and mercy live in deep tension with each other, and so keep us mindful that we are dealing with a God of deep primal relatedness and not a one-dimensional god who could not bear such a tension.

It is precisely this tension between might and mercy that keeps the future open. It is no wonder then that already in this first verse we affirm that we will sing praise to this God at the break of sunlight, just as morning has broken. The wonder of this three-times-holy God of might and mercy does not invite explanation. Rather, it evokes doxology that must begin promptly as we awaken. Thus the hymn performs, in our mouths, the very act that it describes. We sing about praise at daybreak as we ourselves sing praise at daybreak.

Verse 2 attests the God who persists in might and mercy in all times, before time and after time, thus enveloping our modest historical moments of hope and fear. The wonder of such an engaged ultimacy (engaged in great acts of sustenance, impingement, and restoration) makes praise the only appropriate response, a glad acknowledgment of this reality that defies our critical capacity for explanation. The doxological drama unfolds in heaven (the venue of the gods) as well as on earth, where we reiterate the scene from the throne room of heaven. The doxological scene has among its glad participants "all the saints" who willingly forgo their own crowns of victory, virtue, and achievement (Rev. 4:10). There is no reluctance among the saints to yield their largest claims, for the vision of God overwhelms. Alongside the saints—those who have suffered greatly at the hands of the empire for their confession and who are now validated—is the thronging company of the throne room who attend to God, as we have seen in Isaiah's vision (seraphim and cherubim). In our singing we participate in the glorious drama along with God's more immediate attendants. The scene is one of unmitigated joy in celebration of the King-God who has defeated the powers of evil and who offers a new regime of glad well-being.

Verse 3 further exposits this celebrated Lord of might and mercy by a formula of incomparability: "there is none beside thee." The formula allows that there are other gods round about, but none of them can compare to this practitioner of might and mercy. There is no one like this God, no rival, no alternative, no better offer. This formula, perforce, is oft reiterated in the biblical text because everything stands or falls on this claim:

> "So that you may know that there is no one like the LORD our God, the frogs shall leave you and your houses and your officials and your people." (Exod. 8:10–11; see 9:14)

> "There is no Holy One like the LORD,
>   no one besides you."
>   1 Sam. 2:2

> There is none like you, O LORD;
>   you are great, and your name is great in might.
>   Jer. 10:6

> There is none like you among the gods, O Lord,
>   nor are there any works like yours.
>   Ps. 86:8; see 1 Kgs. 8:23; 1 Chr. 17:20

The incomparability of YHWH, the hymn attests, is in the combination of "power," "love," and "purity." Of these three terms at the end of the verse, the first two, "power" and "love," reiterate "merciful and mighty." The third term is a fresh note in the hymn that reflects the unqualified innocence and purity of the saints in Revelation whose lives have been purged by suffering. Or it reflects the action of the seraphim in the Isaiah vision who dealt decisively with the prophet's disqualifying "uncleanness" and made him clean and rendered him pure, fit to be in God's presence. It could be, improbably, that there is somewhere a god of power or even a god of love, or perhaps a god of purity. There is, however, none like YHWH, who combines in his character these three features in a dramatic and effective way that makes our life with God possible and joyous.

The other note in verse 3 that claims our attention would seem to have no rootage in the text from Revelation, for there is nothing there of either the elders or the living creatures being sinful. The verse recognizes the profound and unbridgeable distance between God and the worshipers, a distance that may have two different justifications. First, God may be hidden from us because our sin has disabled our eyes and skewed our vision so that, in the words of Richard, Bishop of Chichester, and the musical *Godspell*, we cannot "see thee more clearly." Sin keeps God hidden from us. In Isaiah, however, the text allows otherwise. The prophet in astonishment acknowledges that even though he and his people were "unclean" (ritually unqualified), "[his] eyes have seen" (Isa. 6:5). In that moment God is willing to overcome his ritual disqualification so that Isaiah may indeed see God. But a second possibility is that the "darkness" that hides God in verse 3 of our hymn is a liturgical arrangement that precludes inordinate access to God, precludes in order to maintain divine awe or perhaps to protect worshipers from the danger of direct access. The sequence of words suggests that it is God's incomparability that is the ground of hiddenness. I suggest that the hymn leaves the issue open, even as Scripture is ambiguous and unsettled on the question. It is the propensity of much interpretation to imagine that it is only our obstinacy that blocks our vision of God. That is, it is our failure, as though we were able to determine whether God would be seen or not, and the third verse allows for that understanding. But it could be that the root reality is not in our failure but in God's singularity, which does not intend to be fully on exhibit. Thus God asserts to Moses that "seeing God" is too risky:

> "You cannot see my face; for no one shall see me and live." (Exod. 33:20)

Even in that encounter, however, the fact of God's hiddenness does not preclude God's mercy:

> "I will be gracious to whom I will be gracious, and will show mercy on whom I will show mercy." (Exod. 33:19)

The juxtaposition of verses 19 and 20 suggests that divine hiddenness serves to maintain God's freedom to act as God will, even in mercy. Thus we are back to the hymn's double claim of might and mercy, power and love, hiddenness and accessibility. This ambiguous divine reality is only recognized in wonder that evokes eager praise.

Verse 4 reiterates much of what we have already sung. Again it is "merciful and mighty.'" Again it is "God in three persons, blessed Trinity," in an appeal to the three-fold "holy." We do find here, however, one new accent in the second line, that "all thy works [creatures?] shall praise thy name." These works/creatures are inhabitants of "earth and sky and sea," that is, the totality of all that is. The triad reflects the ancient three-story universe, but the list bespeaks comprehensiveness, no creature left behind. There is no creature who will not praise.

In this liturgical act, God the creator will gladly acknowledge a responsive, dependent relationship of all creatures to the creator. The appropriate stance of all creatures, from lowly radish and slippery eel to the ones "in the image of God," is one of doxology:

> Earth and all stars! Loud clashing planets!
> Sing to the Lord a new song!
> Hail, wind, and rain! Loud blowing snowstorm!
> Sing to the Lord a new song!
> God has done marvelous things.
> We too sing praises with a new song!
>
> Trumpet and pipes! Loud clashing cymbals! . . .
> Harp, lute, and lyre! Loud humming cellos! . . .

Engines and steel! Loud sounding hammers! . . .
Limestone and beams! Loud building workers! . . .

Knowledge and truth! Loud sounding wisdom! . . .
Daughter and son! Loud praying members! . . .[3]

That all creatures will join in praise is already celebrated in such psalms as Psalm 148:

Praise the LORD!
Praise the LORD from the heavens;
    praise him in the heights!
Praise him all his angels;
    praise him, all his host!

Praise him, sun and moon;
    praise him, all you shining stars!
Praise him, you highest heavens,
    and you waters above the heavens!
. . . .
Praise the LORD from the earth,
    you sea monsters and all deeps,
fire and hail, snow and frost,
    stormy wind fulfilling his command!

Mountains and all hills,
    fruit trees and all cedars!
Wild animals and all cattle,
    creeping things and flying birds!

Kings of the earth and all peoples,
    princes and all rulers of the earth!
Young men and women alike,
    old and young together!

Let them praise the name of the LORD.
            Ps. 148:1–4, 7–13

This vision of a doxological creation is echoed by St. Francis, who lived close to creaturely reality:

All creatures of our God and King,
Lift up your voice and with us sing![4]

The awareness that all such creatures stand alongside us in glad doxology might rescue us from the flat view of modernity that creaturely reality is only a material phenomenon for us to use, enjoy, and exploit. To the contrary, every element is a doxological creature who sings with us.[5]

As in Psalm 148, our hymn concerns God's name (identity and reputation):

> Let them praise the name of the LORD,
> for his name alone is exalted.
>
>   v. 13

In the book of Amos, God's name is "Lord of hosts," which means the sovereign and commander of the whole company of angels, the stars, and all living creatures (see Amos 4:13; 5:8–9; 9:5–6). That such creatures join in praise reflects a conviction that there are no inanimate or subcovenantal creatures; it is all relationality and mutuality among willing partners who gladly celebrate a defining dependence on and grateful responsiveness to the creator God. Thus our hymn boldly links the mystery of the Trinity to all, even the lowliest creaturely species. With appeal to Dante's *Divine Comedy*, Hardy and Ford conclude,

> This sees praise and adoration of God, and in appropriate ways of people, as the essence of every person's vocation. . . . What was the positive contribution of the doctrine of the Trinity? Praise is, among other things, a form of thinking, and aims to "think God" as adequately as possible.[6]

This claim takes one's breath away, because it contradicts all of our ordinary thinking. In the process, moreover, we have been given a vast vista of the world responding to God in acknowledgment of its true status before God. Such a way of thinking (and singing) refuses our reductionist imagination, which seeks to control rather than to yield gladly. It also exposes the tackiness of so much church music that is privatized and domesticated so as to resist the great drama in which we are situated among God's glad and grateful creatures.

I SING THE MIGHTY POWER OF GOD

Isaac Watts, 1715

1 I sing the mighty power of God that made the mountains rise,
   that spread the flowing seas abroad and built the lofty skies.
   I sing the wisdom that ordained the sun to rule the day.
   The moon shines full at God's command, and all the stars obey.

2 I sing the goodness of the Lord who filled the earth with food.
   God formed the creatures through the Word, and then pronounced
      them good.
   Lord, how thy wonders are displayed, where'er I turn my eye,
   if I survey the ground I tread, or gaze upon the sky!

3 There's not a plant or flower below but makes thy glories known.
   And clouds arise, and tempests blow, by order from thy throne,
   while all that borrows life from thee is ever in thy care,
   and everywhere that we can be, thou, God, art present there.

Glory to God (2013), no. 32

Chapter 9

I Sing the Mighty Power of God

Isaac Watts, in his prolific hymn writing, remains closely attentive to the decisive claims of the gospel; his hymns are theologically self-conscious. In this hymn we have the voice of a single singer, "I." We can imagine, however, that the "I" who sings "I" is situated in a robust community of "we," each of whose members sings as "I" but also sings with the other members of the community. The mood of the hymn is confessional. That is, it stakes and affirms the most elemental claims of gospel faith; all of these claims, of course, concern the reality and the truth of God.

FIRST RHETORICAL UNIT

The hymn rhetorically divides into two parts. In the first part—verse 1 and the first half of verse 2—the singer celebrates three characteristic markings of God: God's power, God's wisdom, and God's goodness.

"I sing *the mighty power of God*": Since the beginning of revelatory history, God is linked to generative power, the capacity to enact the divine will. Here the evidence of God's generative power is a recital of the overwhelming wonder of creation that is all around and unmistakable. It is that generative divine power that caused mountains to rise on the landscape, seas to gather the waters, and skies that hover above. In this triad, Watts appeals to the old image of the "three-storied universe" that is narrated in the creation story of Genesis:

> And God said, "Let there be a dome in the midst of the waters, and let it separate the waters from the waters." So God made the dome and separated the waters that were under the dome from the waters that were above the dome. And it was so. God called the dome Sky. . . .
> And God said, "Let the waters under the sky be gathered together into one place, and let the dry land appear." And it was so. God called the dry land Earth, and the waters that were gathered together he called Seas. And God saw that it was good. (Gen. 1:6–10)

The same triad is celebrated in our greatest creation hymn:

> You stretch out the heavens like a tent,
>   you set the beams of your chambers on the waters,
> you make the clouds your chariot,
>   you ride on the wings of the wind,
> you make the winds your messengers,
>   fire and flame your ministers.
>
> You set the earth on its foundations,
>   so that it shall never be shaken.
> You cover it with the deep as with a garment;
>   the waters stood above the mountains.
> At your rebuke they flee;
>   at the sound of your thunder they take to flight.
> They rose up to the mountains, ran down to the valleys
>   to the place that you appointed for them.
> You set a boundary that they may not pass,
>   so that they might not again cover the earth.
>   Ps. 104:2–9

This doxology of course offers a prescientific picture of created reality. It does not, however, intend to be descriptive. It intends to be doxological; the wonder of it all requires a poetic pushing back beyond observed creation to the agency of the creator God "who calls into existence the things that do not exist" (Rom. 4:17). Thus the creator God engages in no struggle but in a decisive and uncontested way shapes the world according to God's own purpose of faithfulness. Thus in Genesis 1 what follows is God's faithfulness. What follows in Psalm 104 is water that makes life possible (vv. 10–18).

"I sing *the wisdom that ordained . . . at God's command*": God's wisdom ordered the universe as a fully functioning network that features the proper ordering of sun, moon, and stars, all situated and serving at God's unchallenged behest. In the lore of Israel, the principal function of sun and moon is to divide the span of time into livable ordered units:

> And God said, "Let there be lights in the dome of the sky to separate the day from the night; and let them be for signs and for seasons and for days and years, and let them be lights in the dome of the sky to give light upon the earth." And it was so. God made the two great lights—the greater light to rule the day and the lesser light to rule the night—and the stars. God set them in the dome of the sky to give light upon the earth, to rule over the day and over the night, and to separate the light from the darkness. And God saw that it was good. (Gen. 1:14–18)

In the psalm as well, sun and moon govern light and darkness:

> You have made the moon to mark the seasons;
>   the sun knows its time for setting.
> You make darkness, and it is night,
>   when all animals of the forest come creeping out.
> The young lions roar for their prey,
>   seeking their food from God.
> When the sun rises, they withdraw
>   and lie down in their dens.
> People go out to their work
>   and to their labor until the evening.
>   Ps. 104:19–23

The ordering permits the several creatures to live their lives without getting in the way of their neighbors. Thus human persons work all day and retire to rest at night. Conversely, predatory animals rest all day and seek food all night. The pattern is a schedule that makes for good outcomes for all creatures.

The accent of the hymn's second affirmation is on God's wisdom. In the biblical attestation of this ordering for life, the sweep from Proverbs 8:22–31 to John 1 affirms that it is God-ordered wisdom that has been operative from the beginning of time.[1] It is God's wisdom that is the "master worker" in making the world sustainable. Wisdom declares,

> When he established the heavens, I was there,
>   when he drew a circle on the face of the deep,
> when he made firm the skies above,
>   when he established the fountains of the deep,
> when he assigned to the sea its limit,
>   so that the waters might not transgress his command,
> when he marked out the foundations of the earth,
>   then I was beside him, like a master worker.[2]
>   Prov. 8:27–31

Israel will not imagine created reality without observing in it a wise ordering of life that is of God:

Wisdom's witness to creation testifies to the security and rich complexity of a world that sustains her growth and inspires her delight. Just as children develop fully within secure and enriching surroundings, growing into adults who can go forth in confidence to establish their own place in the community, so Wisdom matures and ventures forth to build her house and to host the community ([Prov.] 9:1).[3]

It is this ordered regularity, willed and guaranteed by the wisdom of God, that makes scientific investigation viable:

Wisdom's all-encompassing play, the Hebrew text suggests, interconnects all creation, dynamically so. At the quantum level, interconnectedness transcends even space itself. Beginning with Einstein, and later confirmed experimentally, researchers have confirmed "an instantaneous bond between what happens at widely separated locations.". . . Welcome to the quantum "entanglement."[4]

Brown observes that no mention of human creatureliness is offered in this lyrical text in Proverbs. The ordering by God's wisdom is vast and provides a structure in which human community may flourish.

"I sing *the goodness of the Lord*": This half verse appeals directly to the creation narrative of Genesis that reiterates that creation is "good" and ultimately "very good" (Gen. 1:31). In this third clause of the hymn creatures are mentioned, but there is no specific acknowledgment of human creatures. The one specificity is "food": God has made the world to be generative of food that sustains all creatures. While we take such generous assurance of food for granted, the poetry of Israel recognized the wonder of such assured food:

These all look to you
    to give them their food in due season;
when you give to them, they gather it up;
    when you open your hand, they are filled with good things.
                                                                    Ps. 104:27–28

The eyes of all look to you,
    and you give them their food in due season.
You open your hand,
    satisfying the desire of every living thing.
                                        Ps. 145:15–16

It is this food in abundance (impeded only by skewed monetized production, distribution, and consumption) that assures that God's world teems with well-being. The pharaonic obsession with monopoly evokes scarcity (Gen. 47:13–25), just as the narrative of manna in the wilderness outside of the reach of Pharaoh's predatory system indicates that God the creator can jump-start the supply of abundant food yet again:

Those who gathered much had nothing over, and those who gathered little had no shortage; they gathered as much as each of them needed. (Exod. 16:18)

In the afterlife of this narrative, there is no doubt that Jesus is portrayed as the inexplicable agent of God's wondrous abundance in the wilderness (see Mark 6:30–44; 8:1–10). It is this inexplicable abundance in defiance of pharaonic scarcity, moreover, that is celebrated in the Eucharist of the church. And thus we sing,

> I sing the mighty power of God. . . .
> I sing the wisdom that ordained. . . .
> I sing the goodness of the Lord. . . .

Doxology offers this sweeping triad of power, wisdom, and goodness, a configuration that the interpretive community of faith continues to parse, even in the face of the intractable riddle of theodicy. In this doxology the church (as with Israel) is untroubled by such a riddle and does not linger over it. In such doxologies as this one by Watts, the church echoes the ancient doxology of Israel that aims to defy and defeat all idols:

> It is he who made the earth by his power,
>   who established the world by his wisdom,
>   and by his understanding stretched out the heavens.
>   Jer. 10:12; see 51:15

In its doxology, the church explains nothing. Such doxology is propelled well beyond explanation by the wonder of creation. While the ordered evidence of creation evokes and empowers scientific investigation, it also evokes wonder and this lyrical singing.

SECOND RHETORICAL UNIT

Halfway through the hymn, in the middle of verse 2, Watts abruptly shifts rhetorical gears. This shift is marked by the direct address "Lord." Up until this point God (the Lord) has been treated in the third person. Now it is all "thee," congruent with Martin Buber's "Thou," who evokes and generates the "I" of creatureliness and consequently the "I" of doxology.

What follows the direct address to the "thou" of God is a fresh recital of the wonder of creation that is not unlike the initial inventory of the first part of the hymn. The difference is that now it is all "*thy* wonders"; creation is referred back to the creator. The term "wonder" recurs in Israel's doxologies to attest inexplicable transformative acts that in the terms of Enlightenment rationality are slotted as "miracles." Thus Buber can characterize as "miracle" any happening that evokes "abiding astonishment" (see Ps. 145:4–7).[5] In this hymn it is the manifold wonder of creation that leaves the singer awed and astonished.

The particular use of the term "survey" is of interest because Watts employs the same word in his better-known hymn "When I Survey the Wondrous Cross." By juxtaposing these two uses of the word by Watts, we can see that both *creation* and *cross* are God's wonders; both creation and cross, moreover, are to be surveyed so that we allow for complete astonishment at these two divine actions that escape our explanation. We cannot "explain" creation even though scientists rightly keep working at it (see Prov. 25:2–3).[6] We cannot "explain" the cross even though theologians continue to propose variant "theories of atonement."

The acknowledgment that the wonders of creation all belong to God invites a parallel to the unofficial U.S. anthem "O Beautiful for Spacious Skies." That song also "surveys" the "wonders" of the U.S. landscape with an inventory of waves of grain, purple mountains, and fruited plains. The difference is that Watts's hymn affirms that it is all of God, whereas the U.S. inventory of our landscape comes close to suggesting that the beauty of our land is intrinsic to "America's" achievement (conquest?), without any acknowledgment of the creator except that the creator should belatedly bless what is already there in its beauty. The creator may be marginally implied in that song, but it is far from explicit.

In verse 3 of our hymn, the "survey" continues concerning "plant," "flower," "clouds," and "tempests." These all belong to God and have no autonomous life of their own. Such growing things as plant and flower attest God's glory and operate according to the ordering of the creator:

> As long as the earth endures,
>   seedtime and harvest, cold and heat,
> summer and winter, day and night,
>   shall not cease.
>   Gen. 8:22

The final lines of the hymn make yet one more notable maneuver in three parts. First, it is recognized that all wondrous creatureliness "borrows life from thee." Plants and flowers have life only because God loans them life; they live on "borrowed time." They have no intrinsic capacity for life, which is every time an inexplicable miracle. And of course if it is so for plants and flowers, how much more so for human creatures, who also have no intrinsic capacity for life but borrow it daily from the creator God. (On the "how much more" of human creatures, see Matt. 6:26.) Second, all of God's creatures live in God's continuing care. The act of creation is not a one-time start-up; so much for the deist clock maker! Creation is rather an ongoing, divine act of sustenance and maintenance. I suppose that is the reason that we may wonder at the fact that new creaturely species continue to emerge through the dynamic processes of creation. Not on the horizon of this hymn but surely on the horizon of creation is the negative counterpoint that willful, destructive (human) creaturely agents can do severe damage to God's sustenance. Thus E. O. Wilson can report on the great threat to the wonder of creation wrought through careless policy and action of human agents who neglect their responsibility to protect the other creatures.[7] The concrete consequence of such carelessness is the constant loss of countless species from the fabric of creation.

Third, the final line of the hymn attests that the creator God is present in, with, and under creaturely life: God is there! In an inchoate way, Watts has adumbrated what is now called "panentheism"[8]—God is in all. This is not to be confused with "pantheism." The hymn thus invites affirmation of two important theological awarenesses. On the one hand, we get a strong dose of "natural theology," that is, reasoning from creation to the creator. Thus John Barton can judge with reference to the prophets,

> Now if I am correct in thinking that Amos and Isaiah present a view of ethics which can fairly be described as "natural law," then this restriction of natural law to the background or the periphery of thought in ancient Israel is mistaken.[9]

Karl Barth's well-known resistance to natural theology is to be taken in his particular context of National Socialism, a context now being reiterated before our very eyes by neo-Nazis who yet again champion "blood and soil." We do better to adhere to the irenic good judgment of William Brown, who sees, without polemic, the generative interface of biblical witness and scientific investigation. All of this is nicely voiced in Watts's closing lines.

On the other hand, the phrase "ever in thy care" evokes an affirmation of divine providence wherein God is actively operative, even if hidden, in the life of all God's creatures. This hymn refuses any thought of a world without God. As Barth writes,

> This God is never absent, passive, non-responsible or impotent, but always present, active, responsible, and omnipotent. He is never dead, but always living; never sleeping but always awake, never uninterested, but always concerned, never merely waiting in any respect, but even where He seems to wait, even where He permits, always holding the initiative.[10]

This affirmation of God's care for the created world amounts to a profound repudiation of modernist notions that creation is simply a valuable commodity to be exploited and used up at will.[11] Resulting from this, of course, is the recognition that God's care for the created world is a barrier against commoditization, monetization, and abuse of creatureliness. When that divine limit is violated, creation suffers. Watts's hymn does not venture into the negatives that are implied in his affirmation of natural theology and divine providence, but they are powerfully tacit in his affirmation. In the end the created world belongs to God and is under God's care. God's care, moreover, consists in *the exercise of generative power, the administration of ordering wisdom,* and *the willing of goodness.*

There is ample ground for our singing "the mighty power of God," "the wisdom that ordained," and "the goodness of the Lord." Such singing is a vigorous, celebrative affirmation. It is also a rigorous warning against every imagination that wants to take the world on its own, without reference to the good rule of God.

JESUS CALLS US O'ER THE TUMULT

Cecil Frances Alexander, 1852

1 Jesus calls us; o'er the tumult
  of our life's wild, restless sea,
  day by day his clear voice soundeth
  saying, "Christian, follow me."

2 As, of old, Saint Andrew heard it
  by the Galilean lake,
  turned from home and toil and kindred,
  leaving all for his dear sake.

3 Jesus calls us from the worship
  of the vain world's golden store;
  from each idol that would keep us,
  saying, "Christian, love me more."

4 In our joys and in our sorrows,
  days of toil and hours of ease,
  still he calls, in cares and pleasures,
  "Christian, love me more than these."

5 Jesus calls us! By thy mercies,
  Savior, may we hear thy call,
  give our hearts to thine obedience,
  serve and love thee best of all.

The Hymnal 1982: according to the use of the Episcopal Church, no. 550

Chapter 10

Jesus Calls Us o'er the Tumult

This familiar hymn is rooted in the scriptural narrative of Jesus' call to Peter and his brother Andrew to be his first disciples. He calls, and they answer "immediately" (Matt. 4:20). The hymn segues from that ancient call to Peter and Andrew to a contemporary call to discipleship. When it was written in 1852, it was intended especially for children, but it has become greatly loved by people of all ages.

The hymn is distinguished by the fact that three times Jesus is "quoted." That is, every time the congregation sings a line, we are singing back quotes that are credited to Jesus. But, in fact, of the three "quotes" placed in the mouth of Jesus, only the first is found exactly so in Scripture. In verse 1 of the hymn, the imperative of Jesus is "Christian, follow me." The "follow me" is the imperative summons issued to Peter and Andrew to depart their conventional lives as fishermen and to sign on for Jesus' radically alternative life (Matt. 4:19; Mark 1:17; in Luke 5:27 the same mandate is issued to Levi). Of course Jesus never called anyone "Christian," so this is clearly a modern adjustment. But such an adjudication indicates that in the context of the hymn, the call to discipleship is not addressed to those who had never known him but to those who are already signed on as Christians (baptized!) but who have not yet "followed" with great attentiveness.

In verse 3 of the hymn the second "quote" from Jesus is not an actual quote, but it offers a second imperative: "Christian, love me more." The word "love" is never used in the Synoptic Gospels as a bid to love Jesus. Instead it alludes to the Fourth Gospel, where love of Jesus is urged (John 21:15–17). In this hymn quote the "more" is unspecified. It might mean only that you have loved me in the past, but now love me more than in the past; or it might mean more than the "idols" just mentioned in the previous hymn line. The summons purports to be an intensification from the "follow me" of verse 1. Except in our cultural setting, loving Jesus is not nearly as radical as following Jesus because love has been infused with excessive sentimentality. Again the address is to "Christian," a sign that suggests that the call is to those already in the church.

In the third "quote" of verse 4, the address to "Christian" is again reiterated, thus recurring in all three "quotes." Now the imperative of verse 3 is reiterated in verse 4 with the "more" specified by "more than these." In context the "these" would seem to be an allusion to the "cares and pleasures" just mentioned. Love Jesus more than cares. Love Jesus more than pleasures. The imperative seems to be an allusion to Jesus' question to Peter in John 21:15: "'Do you love me more than these?'"

Three matters interest us in this usage. First, the "these" in John 21:15 refers to the other disciples in the preceding paragraph. It is a curious usage that invites comparison between the faithfulness of Peter and the other disciples. Peter's response affirms love for Jesus, but he does not champion himself at the expense of the other disciples. Indeed John 21:22 explicitly precludes such comparison: "'What is that to you? Follow me!'" In the context of the hymn the "these" does not refer to other disciples (Christians) but to "cares and pleasures" of the preceding phrase. Thus the hymn shifts the meaning significantly. Second, the question to Peter in the Scripture passage, "'Do you love me?'" morphs into the more practical responsibilities of "'Tend my sheep'" (v. 16) and "'Feed my sheep'" (v. 17), so that there can be no sentimentality in loving Jesus. Third, in the passage in John, the conclusion of the interaction is "Follow me" (v. 19), thus a return to the first quote of the hymn. John 21:19, moreover, alludes to the costly death Peter will suffer because of his love of Jesus. This sober note is in some tension with the jazzy way we usually sing this hymn. Thus all three "quotes" of Jesus are addressed to those already in the household of faith; it summons them to a more intentional and serious discipleship of obedience, with all the costs that relate to the call.

One other matter about the call is indicated in the second verse. The Scripture reference in Matthew 4 concerns both Peter and Andrew, and the allusion to John 21 concerns only Peter, while verse 2 of the hymn concerns exclusively Andrew. (Perhaps that specific reference to Andrew is the reason that the verse is often omitted in contemporary hymnals.) In verse 2 Andrew is celebrated for his immediate responsiveness to Jesus, evidenced in his readiness to forgo everything in his previous life. The specificity of Andrew leads to a recognition that the hymn words, written in 1852, were intended especially for the celebration of St. Andrew's Day in Britain. Curiously, Andrew is the patron saint of Scotland, and the hymn's writer, Cecil Frances Alexander, was Irish; but the hymn is an offer to all British children. Thus the three "quotes" attributed to Jesus are all addressed to Andrew, who is, along with Peter, taken as the first "Christian." Indeed Andrew, along with his brother, had already signed on with Jesus and now is being summoned to radical obedience.

In the hymn we may notice three dimensions of context for the call to "Christian." In the first verse the voice of Jesus Christ that summons to radical and immediate obedience is heard "over the tumult." The "tumult" is the loud crashing waters of a storm at sea; the imagery is made specific in verse 2 by "the Galilean lake" and likely alludes to the storm of Mark 4:35–41 (see Matt. 8:23–27; Luke 8:22–25) that frightens the disciples, over which Jesus magisterially presides. Or the phrasing may alternatively allude to the narrative of Matthew 14:23–33 (see Mark 6:45–52; John 6:15–21) wherein Jesus walks atop the storm and reassures his fearful disciples, "'Take heart, it is I; do not be afraid.'" Both episodes reflect "the tumult of our life's wild, restless sea." The voice of Jesus was loud and clear enough to override the threatening sea, loud enough to reassure the disciples, clear enough to silence the storm.

But of course in biblical imagery the "sea" that preoccupied Jesus and the disciples was an allusion to the "mighty waters" of primordial chaos out of which creation came (see Gen. 1:1–2) and which continues to threaten ordered creation. Thus the narrative of Jesus to which the hymn alludes intends to signal a much greater threat than "the Sea of Galilee": the threat of chaos that will undo creation. The affirmation is that Jesus is the master of "life's wild, restless sea" because he performs the functions of the creator.

When we sing this hymn then, we affirm that Jesus' call to discipleship is a call amid chaos that threatens to undo our lives. Alongside the potential man-made chaos of global warming, the imagery pertains to the unmanageable crises in one's personal life (sickness, broken relationships, financial risks) and to the great public threats of terror, injustice, oppression, and inequality. The hymn affirms that the Lord Jesus will faithfully preside over all such chaotic realities. What astonishes us is that the hymn, beyond this opening line, does not focus on assurance but on a call to radical obedience. Indeed, chaos is just the right time to be responsive in obedience to Jesus!

We may, beyond "life's wild, restless sea," identify two other realities from which Jesus in this hymn calls us away. First, in verse 3 there is reference to "each idol that would keep us." This line does not specify idols, but we know that idols are objects of loyalty, trust, and obedience that compete with God and that will, if they can, talk us out of trust in God. It is not necessary to provide a list of idols, as every list would need to reflect specific circumstances.

If, however, we ask about loyalties that disrupt our trust in the gospel and that compete with the gospel for our attention and energy, we may identify such ideological forces as nationalism, racism, sexism, and classism. But verse 3 gives us one specificity: "the vain world's golden store." While "golden store" could be anything we hold precious, anything at all, a first inclination is to judge that the phrase means money or wealth. There is no doubt that in biblical horizon money is a primary object of loyalty that talks us out of the gospel and has been so since the episode of the golden calf of Aaron (Exod. 32). Jesus, moreover, asserted that we cannot serve God and money, suggesting that money and our various forms of commoditization are real rivals to the claims of the gospel (see Matt. 6:24; Luke 16:13; 1 Tim. 6:9–10; Jas. 5:1–6). Thus Jesus could observe, "'How hard it will be for those who have wealth to enter the kingdom of God'" (Mark 10:23).

In addition to idols and treasures verse 4 suggests that an alternative to Jesus is in our "cares and pleasures" that preclude gospel trust. "Cares" means worries or demanding responsibilities that weigh us down. Indeed, Jesus warns about creaturely cares that propel us against faith and make us unbearably anxious:

> "Therefore I tell you, do not worry about your life, what you will eat, or about your body, what you will wear. For life is more than food, and the body more than clothing. . . . And can any of you by worrying add a single hour to your span of life?" (Luke 12:22–25)

Alongside "cares" verse 4 recognizes that "pleasures" can also become forces of resistance against the gospel. Pleasures become alternatives to the gospel because they require time, energy, and self-indulgence that may preclude love of God and love of neighbor, or even require addictive behavior that turns our lives in on themselves.

The third call of Jesus is to "love me more than these." We have seen how "these" in John 21 contrasts to other disciples. But here "these" becomes "cares and pleasures." We are to love Jesus more than our cares, more than what we worry about. We are to love Jesus more than our pleasures, more than the great enjoyments of our lives. Thus when Peter and Andrew left everything and followed, we may imagine that they left behind their defining cares and their great pleasures.

The final verse of the hymn is a response to this three-fold imperative of Jesus. The verse reiterates the same awareness: "Jesus calls us!" It is in the purview of Jesus' work to continue to invite people into discipleship. He never quits calling! Continually, incessantly, clearly! This verse moves to a resolve to hear and answer that call. But the lines reflect the awareness that our ability to answer the call of Jesus itself depends on God's mercy. Thus the call of Jesus is an act of mercy, albeit demanding mercy. And the response likewise depends on God's goodness toward us.

The third line of the last verse begins with a peculiar imperative: "give," which is a petition addressed to our savior Jesus. That is, you give our hearts over to obedience. We would give our hearts, that is, our ultimate loyalty, but we cannot do it by simple willpower. Our giving and yielding to Jesus' call depend on his work so that faith itself is a gift from God. In light of that anticipated giving by God, the final line promises glad obedience. "Love" is reiterated but now defined by the more specific verb "serve," thus a reminiscence of the way in which the "love" of Peter in John 21 morphs to "tend" and "feed." Such love is not romantic or sentimental but entails self-giving engagement with neighbors. But such "service" is not do-goodism. It is an active way to love Jesus, thus "'to one of the least of these," so "to me" (Matt. 25:40), and to recognize that in all things Jesus is our primary love, this love that is "best of all," better by far than our treasures and idols, better by far than our cares and pleasures.

So why do we sing this hymn? It was originally written as an invitation for children to celebrate St. Andrew's Day. Andrew has been made a saint, and on his saint day children are invited to sign on with him to the ready discipleship that he embraced without reservation. He turned away from "home and toil and kindred," from a safe setting and good work (fishing), "all for [Jesus'] dear sake." The hymn is a bid for childlike naiveté that can respond to Jesus and his mission without restraint or caution. But of course the hymn could not be contained as an address to children. It came to be a summons to adult men and women of faith as well—those already baptized—that new resolve concerning obedience to Jesus could be embraced.

So why would we sing this hymn? Likely we sing it for its upbeat melody without much notice of its lyrics. If, however, we linger long enough to notice the lyrics, the hymn has peculiar pertinence to our moment in history.

- **We sing because Jesus three times issues a summons to discipleship.** That fresh summons is issued to those already signed on who have compromised the call or grown indifferent to it. Such a fresh summons pertains to us because in our culture we have largely compromised Jesus' call to discipleship until it has lost all of its radical pertinence for life in the world. Such a fresh summons offers a second chance for fidelity, or a third chance, or a ninth chance; many chances are offered and required because we are regularly talked out of the sharp edge of discipleship.
- **We sing this hymn because it honestly acknowledges the "wild, restless sea" on which we live**, a wild sea that threatens the foundations of our common life. We know about global warming that jeopardizes our environment, about international disorder that makes the world an unsafe place, about an economy that can no longer sustain a viable middle class, and about a culture of meanness and violence in which rage and bullying are the order of the day. Such "tumult" of disorder

makes it difficult to hear a summons to discipleship, but this hymn makes that compelling voice of Jesus heard.

- We sing this hymn because we know about idols that offer false security and phony certitude, and we know about treasures that we have accumulated in fearful greed. We know that we will never have enough of those treasures to make us safe.
- We sing this hymn because we know about "cares" that sap our energy and that paralyze us in fatigue and anxiety; we are brought up short with the reminder that all such care will not and cannot add a nanosecond to our lives nor an ounce of well-being or joy.
- We sing this hymn because we know about "pleasures" that sap our energy and occupy our attention, as though the purpose of our lives was to satisfy our various appetites, a purpose that is ignoble once we remember who we are.
- We sing this hymn because we are recalled to our first love of Jesus; we know that Jesus is "best of all," better than any alternative source of well-being. That initial love of Jesus has among us greatly eroded.

Although this hymn may have been initially offered to children on St. Andrew's Day, it will not stay focused on children, for it calls us all with its summons. Nor will the hymn stay focused on St. Andrew's Day, because every time we sing it, we notice that the call to Andrew and Peter is also addressed to us. We remember how they left their boat and their father—or as the hymn has it, "home and toil and kindred"—and followed. They did so "immediately" (Matt. 4:20)! We sing to overcome our hesitation and our reluctance; we are led by these lyrics to the edge of readiness alongside them.

LOVE DIVINE, ALL LOVES EXCELLING

Charles Wesley, 1747

1 Love divine, all loves excelling,
   Joy of heaven, to earth come down,
   fix in us thy humble dwelling;
   all thy faithful mercies crown.
   Jesus, thou art all compassion;
   pure, unbounded love thou art;
   visit us with thy salvation;
   enter every trembling heart.

2 Breathe, O breathe thy loving Spirit
   into every troubled breast;
   let us all in thee inherit;
   let us find the promised rest.
   Take away the love of sinning;
   Alpha and Omega be;
   end of faith, as its beginning,
   set our hearts at liberty.

3 Come, Almighty, to deliver;
   let us all thy life receive;
   suddenly return, and never,
   nevermore thy temples leave.
   Thee we would be always blessing,
   serve thee as thy hosts above,
   pray, and praise thee without ceasing,
   glory in thy perfect love.

4 Finish then thy new creation;
   pure and spotless let us be;
   let us see thy great salvation
   perfectly restored in thee:
   changed from glory into glory,
   till in heaven we take our place,
   till we cast our crowns before thee,
   lost in wonder, love, and praise.

Glory to God (2013), no. 366

Chapter 11

Love Divine, All Loves Excelling

Charles Wesley, the great Methodist (Anglican) hymn writer, provided us with many fine hymns. But he wrote none better than this one that he authored in 1747. It is a well-nigh perfect hymn that sounds all the great notes of evangelical faith, being eminently singable according to two fine tunes, both of which are much used in the church.

The first verse reflects the warm evangelical piety of Wesley and his brother John Wesley, founder of the Methodist church, with a close focus on Jesus. The opening assertion is that God is totally, unconditionally love. God's love surpasses in depth and durability all other loves, including love of one spouse for the other spouse, love of parent for child, love of patriot for country, and even love of money by the greedy. Trinitarian that he was, Wesley begins with reference to the Father's love in heaven (or alternatively, love of the Son who "was in the form of God" [Phil. 2:6]) but then moves promptly to the embodied love of God in Jesus on earth (who "emptied himself, taking the form of a slave" [Phil. 2:7]). His presence and ministry on earth bespeak all the joyous love grounded in the wonder of God's heaven. This embodied love found a "humble dwelling" place on earth in human flesh, in the Bethlehem

113

manger, and among the underprivileged peasants in Galilee. The Wesleys were greatly attentive to the "humble" in their own eighteenth-century context, so that the move from humble Galilee to humble London, with its many poor in humble dwellings, was a ready move for them; in our singing we make a parallel move to our own context of the humble where Jesus dwells, thus giving body to what liberation theology calls "God's preferential option for the poor." Surely Jesus invested the love of God among the marginal and uncredentialed, just as the Wesleys kept their eye on the mandate of Jesus toward the vulnerable.

The hymn's first verse addresses Jesus directly. It affirms in doxology that Jesus, in his compassion, is an embodiment of unconditional (unbounded) love, the joy of heaven now occupying the earth. The verse finishes with an imperative petition, "Visit." Or we might say, "Come by here" (Cumbayah)! Because where Jesus comes, there is well-being (salvation). Wesley's pietism sees the gift of grace in Jesus initially addressed to specific individual persons; that of course is attested in the Gospel narratives wherein Jesus deals with specific persons in need—lepers, a hungry crowd, even the dead Lazarus. They are the ones with "trembling hearts," whose hearts may have trembled in profound need or perhaps in profound expectation. Or perhaps the phrase alludes to the dread curse of Deuteronomy 28:26 ("Your corpses shall be food for every bird of the air and animal of the earth"), thus to be surprised by love when wrath is rightly anticipated.

Verse 1 is thus a mighty affirmation and hope that the love of Jesus should be extended from heaven not only to earth but, in the intimacy of pietism, to *you and me* with our trembling hearts. We love to sing this hymn because it lets us recognize our very selves, with our needs and our hopes, as the intimate targets of the love carried by Jesus.

The second verse of the hymn begins with an imperative "Breathe, O breathe" and appears to continue to be addressed to Jesus. We know, as we confess, that God's "loving spirit" is the divine agent in evoking the life of the world (Gen. 1:2; 2:7). We know with the psalmist, moreover, that the absence of God's breath (spirit) brings dismay (trouble) to creation:

> When you hide your face, they are dismayed;
>   when you take away their breath, they die
>   and return to their dust.
> When you send forth your spirit, they are created;
>   and you renew the face of the ground.
>   Ps. 104:29–30

When the matter is referred specifically to Jesus as in our hymn verse, we are led to the resurrection appearance of Jesus:

> Jesus came and stood among them and said, "Peace be with you." After he said this, he showed them his hands and his side. Then the disciples

rejoiced when they saw the Lord. Jesus said to them again, "Peace be with you. As the Father has sent me so I send you." When he had said this, *he breathed on them* and said to them, "Receive the Holy Spirit." (John 20:19–22, emphasis added)

It is by the breath of Jesus that the disciples receive the "Holy Breath." The hymn asks for the life-giving breath of Jesus because without it our hearts (breasts) remain troubled (dismayed).

But then the imagery of the verse shifts abruptly to the rhetoric of inheritance and rest. The reference is to Israel's entry into the land of promise as an inheritance. When Israel was securely settled in the land, it had "rest on every side," that is, safety and security from all enemies (Josh. 21:43–45). In Christian imagery the reception of the land is morphed into the "rest of God," whether life beyond death (eternal rest) or simply the well-being of companionship with God. Thus the verse asks for admission into the blessed companionship with God. But Hebrews 3–4, with reference to Psalm 95:11, knows that disobedience to God will cause exclusion from God's rest. Thus our verse promptly asks Jesus to take away the love of sinning, so sinning does not preclude rest. This is not simply a bid for forgiveness but a larger hope that the desire to be out of sync with God will lose its power and attractiveness. When we no longer "love . . . sinning," we may be admitted to God's "promised rest." Thus far in the verse we have two metaphors (breath, rest), each of which is voiced as a petition.

To complete the verse we get two more petitions, thus four in all (five counting "take away"). The third petition is "Alpha and Omega be." It is a strange request that urges Jesus to function and perform in a sweeping way to be everything for us from *A* to *Z*. The petition refers to the ultimate promise of Revelation 21:6: "'It is done! I am the Alpha and the Omega, the beginning and the end.'" In Revelation's anticipatory vision God now declares in a loud voice from the throne a new governance that totally redefines the shape of reality. There is nothing before the rule of Christ; there is nothing after the rule of Christ. There is nothing other than the rule of Christ, who says, "'I am making all things new'" (Rev. 21:5). This is the one who ends all weeping, misery, and death—the one who provides living water to an arid creation. The declaration tumbles with images as the speaker seeks to find words that match the wonder of the new governance of Christ. Quite remarkably Wesley's artistry has permitted him to voice all of this in the petitionary phrases. Thus three positive petitions—"Breathe," "let us . . . inherit," "be"—and one negative ("take away") offer a rich inventory of biblical images, all of which together attest a new beginning of life that is grounded in God's love, which overrides our inclination to self-destruction.

The verse concludes with a fifth imperative, "set our hearts," which when coupled with the final term "liberty" means "free, emancipate." The emancipated heart at the end looks back to its equivalent troubled breast at the beginning. The heart that was troubled is now the heart that is emancipated. Wesley does not say for what the heart is freed, but the preceding petition, "take away," suggests that our hearts are freed from recalcitrance against the rule of Christ, which is the rule of love. Thus the convergence of all the second verse's imperatives constitutes a mantra of transformation. Verse 2 thus acknowledges that this transformation of the heart is the gift of Christ, something that we cannot do for ourselves by our willpower.

In verse 3 the sequence of imperatives continues with two more petitions reinforced by a series of jussive verbs ("let us") that function as petitions. The first imperative, "Come," is addressed to the "Almighty," perhaps still Jesus, who is the new ruler, or perhaps the Father-Creator; the petition need not be precise. The purpose of the coming of the Almighty is deliverance from the world of death; this is the final prayer of the church: "Amen. Come, Lord Jesus!" (Rev. 22:20). It is urgent that the rule of Christ should intrude upon the creation, because without that divine intrusion of love, the power of death is unrestrained. The first imperative of verse 3 is followed by the jussive "Let us all thy life receive." God's coming into the world of death is the inescapable, irresistible gift of life.

The second imperative is "return." The term has an apocalyptic dimension, thus congruent with the great expectation of Revelation 21–22. This coming of God will be sudden! While the Wesleys work passionately at social amelioration, they did not think that God's rule would come gradually through their efforts. God's rule would be imposed abruptly. The language of this anticipation is an allusion to Ezekiel 43–44 wherein the God of glory who had departed the unbearable abomination of the old Jerusalem temple now returns to the new temple (in the imagination of the prophet) that has been purged of all that is profane. The return of the God of glory is a wondrous triumphal entry:

> As the glory of the LORD entered the temple by the gate facing east, the spirit lifted me up, and brought me into the inner court; and the glory of the LORD filled the temple. (Ezek. 43:4–5; see Exod. 40:34–38)

Once the glory of God has returned to the temple, the gates are shut (see Ezek. 44:1–2). The divine glory would not depart again.

The vision voiced in verse 3 of the hymn assures that the returned rule of God (the "second coming" of the "rule of Christ") means that the gospel of God will now occupy the earth, and we will gladly abide in obedience to that new rule. In the promissory vision of Revelation 21–22, God will dwell in the new holy city:

> "See, the home of God is among mortals.
> He will dwell with them;
> they will be his peoples,
> and God himself will be with them."
> Rev. 21:3

The vision of Revelation cited in our hymn verse utilizes the vision of Ezekiel but now imagines the dwelling of God amid creation, without all the sacerdotal apparatus that was so important for Ezekiel. Now the connection of God and world and their interaction is direct and immediate: "God himself will be with them." Thus the initial petition of our verse, "Come," is enacted, and the second petition, "return," is implemented. God has come to occupy God's creation.

Verse 3 is an artistic wonder. Through the hymn's sequence of imperatives, we sing *petitions*, but then the lyric reverses field, and we voice a *response* affirming that the petitions have been answered. Now we "speak" a response back to God in answer to God's generous self-giving to us. We make vows and pledges about what we will do; it turns out that the "we" is not only the immediate congregation that sings this hymn but also the whole company of faithful peoples and eventually the whole of creation that joins in a mighty chorus of glad affirmation. "We"—all of us—will continually "bless the Lord" (see Ps. 103:1–2, 20–22). We will enhance and magnify the wonder of God.

"We"—all of us—will serve the Holy One; we will do so as "the hosts above," that is, the whole company of angels and lesser gods who fill the throne room of the heavenly king. The imagery of heaven (the place of the gods) offers a place other than our place where God's rule is honored fully and without reservation. That is why we pray that God's rule will be on earth as it already is in the throne room of heaven. Thus we sign on for the kind of ready obedience practiced by the angelic company.

"We"—all of us—will praise. The throne room of God is filled with endless doxology, an act of gladly ceding over to God all that we are, have, and can be, with nothing held back for self. This response to God in gladness is an appropriate match to "Love divine, all loves excelling." Our love back to God is full and without restraint.

"We"—all of us—will pray without ceasing. Such prayer, we imagine, is not an endless torrent of words but rather an unmitigated mindfulness of living always in the presence of God.

And finally, "we"—all of us—will "glory" in perfect love, in "love divine, all loves excelling," in love that surpasses all our explanatory capacity. This act of exuberant "glory" in the presence of God is an echo of the ancient answer of the Westminster Catechism: The chief concern of human persons is to glorify God and enjoy God forever. Those in sync with God find joy in God's company.

In this third verse, we—all of us—recognize that glorifying God is our proper vocation. Such an affirmation is a recognition that giving most of our human energy to having, owning, and controlling is a misguided habit. It is no doubt the case that most of our preoccupations and busyness are varied attempts to fend off our mortality and, if we can, defeat the threat of death. In a world of perfect divine love, however, death is not a threat. Therefore our habits of getting and having are unnecessary and inappropriate. Thus our hearts are "set at liberty." We are free to deploy our energies differently. Now, in that new governance of the gospel, our energies can be readily and gladly mobilized to bless, serve, pray, praise, and glory, all without ceasing. By this lyrical narrative, we are moved to an alternative existence.

The final verse of the hymn concerns final things. It begins with one more powerful imperative followed by two jussive verbs. The opening word is a petition: "Finish." The word is like a command that the creator God should complete the newness that is not yet accomplished. The language of new creation appeals to the grand vision of Isaiah 65:17–25: ". . . new heavens, . . . new earth, . . . Jerusalem as a joy" (vv. 17–18). The specificity of that prophetic poem concerns both new economy and new intimacy with God so that there will no longer be hurt and destruction because of the rule of God. It is clear that Israel's hope for newness is not otherworldly; it is the expectation that God's rule will transform the earth and its political-economic practices.

That Israelite vision of newness is then reiterated with reference to Christ in Revelation 21–22. While that vision is easily read in a mode of otherworldliness, the this-worldly accent in Israel's poetry is a check on such a temptation in the church. The hymn's verb "Finish" in verse 4 is reminiscent of the report that God "finished" creation (Gen. 2:1), the finish of the tabernacle as God's new dwelling place (Exod. 39:32; 40:33), and Jesus' declaration on the cross, "'It is finished'" (John 19:30). God can and will make the new creation complete. In basketball we criticize players who cannot "finish." God is one who can and does finish!

The Wesleys worked and lived in a context of transforming and transformed "holiness," that is, with an accent on ritual-ethical requirements of a life appropriate to the presence of God. In this final verse, we may imagine that the "finish" is not unlike the final delicate act of completing a new building—the close finishing work that requires attention to detail and aesthetic beauty. Here the finish of the new creation reverts to sacerdotal rhetoric of being qualified for entering into the presence of God, "pure and spotless," without fault or blemish. The jussive "let us be" in verse 4 is a bid that the finishing work of the creator is to make us fit and competent to live life fully in the presence of the Holy One. The second jussive, "let us see," asks that we may be witnesses to the perfected new creation.

As we are rendered "pure and spotless" by the goodness of God in Christ, and as we witness the perfected new creation, we will, so the hymn anticipates, be changed. We expect to be transformed as we are invited into the awesome presence of God's holiness. That is, we will be made new by the presence and vision of God. The hymn stages this unspeakable transformation as before and after, marked by the double "till": until we arrive in heaven, the perfect place of the gods to which we are given access, and until we gladly submit our crowns, our best accomplishments and marks of status that we so much prize.

That is where we are headed when we are fully caught up in divine love. The ultimate goal and outcome of human life is that our "selves" of *fear, anxiety, and responsibility* are caught up in a complete yielding to *wonder, love, and praise:*

- Wonder at the unimaginable splendor of God's person
- Love that arrives back at love divine that was our beginning
- Praise, glad ceding of life over to God in ways that enhance God's awesomeness

In this transformation we are transported from the old order of fear, anxiety, and responsibility to wonder, love, and praise. The first triad bespeaks our recalcitrant need for control. The second triad is possible when we are freed from the need for control, overcome by love divine.

It is easy enough to read this final verse of "last things" in another-worldly way, that the destination of life is eternal life in heaven. And Wesley surely had a compelling vision of that ultimate goal. It is also possible, however, that this "transport" to "a better place" is a ritual activity here and now, not delayed until death. Indeed, the hymn itself is a vehicle for such transport, which is Wesley's gift to us. The singing assemblage itself can be and sometimes is a transport into another world of wonder, love, and praise that invites us and permits us to redefine our lives so that fear, anxiety, and responsibility are made at best penultimate. When we are fully enveloped by "love divine, all loves excelling," we may relinquish, for the sake of a different life, the destructiveness of seeking to live beyond the reach of Alpha and Omega. This divine love overreaches such self-deceiving futility.

O FOR A CLOSER WALK WITH GOD

William Cowper, 1769

1 O for a closer walk with God,
a calm and heavenly frame,
a light to shine upon the road
that leads me to the Lamb!

2 Where is the blessedness I knew
when first I saw the Lord?
Where is the soul-refreshing view
of Jesus and his word?

3 What peaceful hours I once enjoyed!
How sweet their mem'ry still!
But they have left an aching void
the world can never fill.

4 Return, O holy Dove, return,
sweet messenger of rest;
I hate the sins that made thee mourn,
and drove thee from my breast.

5 The dearest idol I have known,
whate'er that idol be,
help me to tear it from thy throne,
and worship only thee.

6 So shall my walk be close with God,
calm and serene my frame;
so purer light shall mark the road
that leads me to the Lamb.

Hymns to the Living God (2017), no. 252

Chapter 12

O for a Closer Walk with God

This well-loved hymn was written all at once on December 9, 1769, by William Cowper in response to the illness of a friend that left him feeling bereft. The song is a yearning for a more intimate companionship with God that the writer, at the moment of writing, senses that he has lost.

The hymn is framed by verses 1 and 6, which both use the same phrasing to voice a wistful wish—a prayer—for the nearness of God. Cowper tells us that the phrase "walk with God" is an allusion to Genesis 5:24, wherein Enoch "walked with God." The phrase suggests intimate companionship, the kind reflected in the clichéd hymn "In the Garden":

> I come to the garden alone . . .
> And He walks with me
> And He talks with me
> And He tells me I am His own . . .[1]

Or in a jazzier lyric:

> Just a closer walk with Thee,
> Grant it, Jesus, is my plea,
> Daily walking close to Thee,
> Let it be, dear Lord, let it be.[2]

That walk includes intimate conversation that yields comfort, assurance, and joy, exactly that for which Cowper hoped.

The image of "walk," however, includes a second dimension, namely, the walk of obedience in the path of torah or in the way of discipleship. Thus the early Christians were followers of "the Way" (Acts 24:14). Enoch, moreover, is regarded in the tradition as an icon of utter fidelity to God, for "God took him" into the divine presence. From that terse "departure," moreover, Enoch subsequently became a central figure in apocalyptic imagination for those who embraced the alternative of God's kingdom. Thus the opening phrase of verses 1 and 6 bespeaks both *companionship* and *obedient discipleship*, a combination that, so the hymn anticipates, will illumine "the road" (path, way) that will lead to God's presence. The imagery of "Lamb" (in addition to a sight rhyme with "frame") alludes to "the Lamb who was slain" (*crucifixion* of Jesus)and the "Lamb who is victorious" (*resurrection* of Jesus) (Rev. 5:12–13). Thus Cowper anticipates that his hoped-for *companionship and discipleship* will be situated precisely in the crucifixion and resurrection of Jesus. Thus the God with whom he wants a "closer walk" is the God known and performed in the life of Jesus.

Verses 2 and 3 are a pained acknowledgment of the bereft state of the speaker, who has lost, at least for now, the good companionship of God that was previously known. The second verse consists in two rhetorical questions that admit of no answer. The questions are in fact a memory of a better day, not unlike Job's recall of better days:

> "O, that I were as in the months of old,
>   as in the days when God watched over me;
> when his lamp shown over my head,
>   and by his light I walked through darkness;
> when I was in my prime,
>   when the friendship of God was upon my tent;
> when the Almighty was still with me,
>   when my children were around me;
> when my steps were washed with milk,
>   and the rock poured out for me streams of oil!
> When I went out to the gate of the city,
>   when I took my seat in the square,
> the young men saw me and withdrew,
>   and the aged rose up and stood;
> the nobles refrained from talking,

and laid their hands on their mouths;
the voices of princes were hushed,
and their tongues stuck to the roof of their mouths."
Job 29:2–10

Job's memory of what he had lost is much more worldly than is that of our hymn, but it is the same anguish and wish for what has been lost. In the hymn the loss is the well-being (blessedness) of a vision of the Lord, a view of Jesus that was "soul-refreshing." The questions are given no direct answer, but the clearly implied answer is "Gone. Gone without retrieval, gone to be left without blessedness and without soul-refreshment." The loss is parallel to that of Job:

"And now my soul is poured out within me;
days of affliction have taken hold of me.
The night racks my bones,
and the pain that gnaws me takes no rest.
With violence he seizes my garment;
he grasps me by the collar of my tunic.
He has cast me into the mire,
and I have become like dust and ashes.
I cry to you and you do not answer me;
I stand, and you merely look at me.
You have turned cruel to me;
with the might of your hand you persecute me."
Job 30:16–21

Job is more vigorous and vivid, but in both cases it is love lost for a while.

The statement attests that the speaker was in a deep faith crisis. That crisis may have been triggered for Cowper by the illness of his friend, but the loss is deeper and more far-reaching than that. The poignancy of loss—surely like the "dark night of the soul" known by the great mystics of faith—is reinforced in verse 3 by the specific recall of how wondrous it was with God before that companionship was disrupted. The memory of that companionship is "sweet." That sweetness, however, is contrasted with the present circumstance, one of "aching void." God is gone! The speaker has no access to God. The void is unrelieved, and the "world" cannot fill that void. Cowper knows that there is no substitute for the presence of God in his life. The end of verse 3 brings us to the nadir of spiritual abandonment.

The six verses of the hymn, I suggest, pivot on the big petition of verse 4: "Return." We have had a wistful wish before this but no direct imperative. The verb "return" issues an urgent summons that indicates that God has indeed departed his life, and now there is only hope that that divine departure and absence can be reversed. The verb is an echo of the great imperative petition of Psalm 90 that acknowledges God's absence from the speaker and that hopes for a return of divine presence and favor:

> Turn, O LORD! How long?
>   Have compassion on your servants!
> Satisfy us in the morning with your steadfast love,
>   so that we may rejoice and be glad all our days.
> Make us glad as many days as you have afflicted us,
>   and as many years as we have seen evil.
> Let your work be manifest to your servants,
>   and your glorious power to their children.
> Let the favor of the Lord our God be upon us,
>   and prosper for us the work of our hands—
>   O prosper the work of our hands!
>   Ps. 90:13–17

The initial "turn" (that in the Hebrew could be rendered as "return") is followed by a torrent of imperative petitions addressed to God:

- "Have compassion . . ." after compassion has been absent.
- "Satisfy . . ." with covenant fidelity that is the only satisfaction that will suffice.
- "Make us glad . . ." matching the years already suffered.

The imperatives are followed in verses 16–17 by two jussive verbs:

- "Let your work . . ." (of rescue)
- "Let the favor . . ." (grace)

The last line of the psalm is a final imperative: "Prosper"!

Verse 4 of the hymn is as bold as the psalm in its address to God. In the first line of verse 4, moreover, the petitionary verb is repeated: "Return . . . return." The two verbs sandwich an address to God's Holy Spirit under the image of a dove. It is the spirit of God that can counter the "aching void." The spirit is God's "messenger" who brings news of "rest" that is a counter to the profound restlessness of verse 3. Thus for all the "aching void," the hymn does not doubt that God's own presence will be a complete antidote to the deep troubles of life.

The last two lines of verse 4 and verse 5, however, are honest in acknowledging that God's departure and absence are not random or arbitrary. The divine departure and absence are caused by "sins" that have made God sad and that drive God away. Thus the speaker understands and affirms that the divine absence that produces aching void is caused by human sin, or more precisely, caused by the sin of the hymn singer.

This confession is based in the awareness that the holy God cannot and will not remain in a place (or with a people) who practice sin, for sin is inimical to God. The most vivid and dramatic scene in Scripture wherein God departs a sinful venue is in Ezekiel 8–10, which is a rumination on the "exile of God" from Jerusalem that is linked to the "exile of Israel" from its land. Ezekiel reports on the "abominations" in the Jerusalem temple that shocked and offended God. The crisis, in prophetic purview, is unavoidable given the violation of God's temple:

> So I went in and looked; there, portrayed on the wall all around, were all kinds of creeping things, and loathsome animals, and all the idols of the house of Israel. (Ezek. 8:10)

Then in chapter 10 the cherubim, winged heavenly creatures, become flying vehicles that transport the "glory of God" away from the temple into Babylonian exile:

> Then the glory of the LORD went out from the threshold of the house and stopped above the cherubim. The cherubim lifted up their wings and rose up from the earth in my sight as they went out with the wheels beside them. They stopped at the entrance of the east gate of the house of the LORD; and the glory of the God of Israel was above them.
>   These were the living creatures that I saw underneath the God of Israel by the river Chebar. (Ezek. 10:18–20)

As God departed the Jerusalem temple because of sin, so in our hymn's verse 4 it is sin that drove God "from my breast" . . . no more intimate companionship.

In verse 5 the hymn acknowledges that it is idolatry that caused God to depart, as it is in Ezekiel. The hymn singer, moreover, is helpless before the power of the idols. It is only the God who is affronted by the idols who can rescue from the idols. For that reason verse 5 gives us one more urgent petition to God: "Help me"! The human task is to "tear" the idols from their throne. But that tearing banishment of idols cannot be done without God's help. Thus the return of God asked in verse 4 will happen only when the idols are removed, and that will happen only with God's help. The speaker can anticipate that when the idols are removed, the speaker will worship only God, worship here both remembered from good times past and anticipated for time to come when God returns. The Ezekiel tradition anticipates that when the temple is purged of offensive idols and images, the divine glory will indeed return:

> The vision I saw was like the vision that I had seen when he came to destroy the city, and like the vision that I had seen by the river Chebar; and I fell upon my face. As the glory of the LORD entered the temple by the gate facing east, the spirit lifted me up, and brought me into the inner court; and the glory of the LORD filled the temple. (Ezek. 43:3–5)

Thus verses 4–5 of the hymn feature a deep engagement with the God who is gone. That, however, is matched by a deep resolve of repentance undertaken by the speaker. These verses have already moved well beyond the illness of a friend and map out the core drama of evangelical faith.

Verse 6 returns to the words of verse 1. Only now the frame of reference has shifted. In verse 1 we had only a wistful wish for divine companionship and obedience. Now in verse 6 we get an assurance and an affirmation that there will be that close walk that leads to the Lamb. That assurance is based on the readiness of the Lamb to "return" (to the temple in Jerusalem or to the breast of the believer). That affirmation, moreover, is based on the readiness to purge the idols from one's life. This is no easy reconciliation but rather a costly reorientation. The "idols" are not identified. Room is left for every singer to identify them, only with the recognition that they are immensely powerful in falsely defining our lives.

When we trace the dramatic movement of these six verses, we see a beginning in *wistfulness,* then a *bold imperative petition* to God, followed by a deep act of *repentance,* and a *confident hope* of restoration. This is the drama of gospel faith that may be triggered, as for Cowper, by an incidental crisis; but in fact the drama reaches more powerfully into the truth of our life.

So why do we sing this hymn? First, we may notice that the lyric is intuitively Trinitarian. The framing in verses 1 and 6 concerns "God." The term itself is left uninflected, but we may assume that the singer would most easily assume, in conventional terms, that this God is "Our Father," though the hymn itself remains gender free. But God, in both verses 1 and 6, is named by the end of each verse as the "Lamb," that is, Jesus. In verse 2 Jesus is named explicitly, thus specifying the reference to "Lamb." His "word" in verse 2 is at the same time his embodied life "become flesh" and the good news voiced in Scripture. At the central imperative the "dove" of the Spirit is addressed. I do not imagine that Cowper set out to be Trinitarian. He is, however, so deeply situated in the tradition that his articulation in this mode is natural and, I suspect, inevitable.

Second, in the same way I do not suggest that Cowper's words intentionally allude to the wistful memory of Job 29 that recognizes and rehearses goodness lost, or to Job 30 concerning present unbearable circumstances, or to the report of divine departure in Ezekiel 8–10 or the return of divine glory in Ezekiel 43, even though the allusion to Enoch (Gen. 5:24) is explicit. It is rather the case, I am sure, that those well situated in the tradition (like Cowper) inescapably retrace the major moves of the drama because we have no better way to tell the truth of our life than in the words of the tradition that is entrusted to us.

We sing this hymn because of its deep honesty about human tribulation that is expressed with thick reference to the tradition. The many alterations made subsequently to the hymn text call attention to the deep, thick force of the original. We do best to sing it in that version. I have become aware that present hymnals have "gerrymandered" the text so that the dramatic structure of the original hymn has been distorted or lost. Thus *Glory to God* omits verses 2 and 3 and the articulation of the "aching void" and moves directly from verse 1 and its wistful yearning to verse 4 with its strong petition. The Episcopal hymnal does better by adding verse 2 but still omits verse 3 with its aching void. The *New Century Hymnal* does the same by including verse 2 but omitting verse 3; its bowdlerizing further violates the poetry by changing "walk" to "bond," thereby losing the allusion to Enoch (Gen. 5:24) and forgoing as well the notion that life with God is an active "walk" of companionship and obedience. This is a little curious in that the United Church of Christ, with its characteristic accent on justice obedience, here has lost the "walk" of obedience to the more elusive "bond." One wishes, in each of these cases, that more attention had been given to the dramatic movement of the whole, for it is exactly the "aching void" of verse 3 that evokes the strong imperative of verse 4.

Fourth, this hymn provides a compelling script for the performance of the core drama of the gospel that includes a wistful memory of *an idyllic interaction with God,* an *honest acknowledgment of alienation from God,* and a *convinced expectation of restoration of life* with God. These three elements of the drama together constitute the movement of evangelical faith and are in fact the basis of the infamous "three-point sermon" around which Luther organized his catechism. All three accent points constitute a summons to a deep honesty about the truth of our life. This hymn is an immense resource for us. It is, however, a splash of very cold water on so much contemporary ("traditional" and "contemporary") worship that is "user friendly" to the point of indulgence and surface staying and does not go deeply or honestly into the truth of our life concerning alienation and reconciliation with God. Only this acknowledgment becomes the ground for vigorous petition to God and for lively hope of restored "calm and serene" companionship with the Lamb.

O MASTER, LET ME WALK WITH THEE

Washington Gladden, 1879

1 O Master, let me walk with thee
in lowly paths of service free;
tell me thy secret; help me bear
the strain of toil, the fret of care.

2 Help me the slow of heart to move
by some clear, winning word of love;
teach me the wayward feet to stay,
and guide them in the homeward way.

3 Teach me thy patience; still with thee
in closer, dearer company,
in work that keeps faith sweet and strong,
in trust that triumphs over wrong,

4 In hope that sends a shining ray
far down the future's broadening way,
in peace that only thou canst give,
with thee, O Master, let me live.

The Hymnal 1982: according to the use of the Episcopal Church, no. 659

Chapter 13

O Master, Let Me Walk with Thee

This hymn was originally composed as devotional poetry by Washington Gladden in 1879. Gladden was an outspoken advocate on social-justice issues in his time, but here his words voice a quiet tone of resolved discipleship. The poem is framed by two jussive verbs that amount to softly spoken petitions:

- "Let me walk with thee" (v. 1).
- ". . . let me live" (v. 4).

The jussives might be heard as requests for permission but in fact consist in a petition for authorization and empowerment to live as a faithful, effective disciple.

The prayer is addressed to "Master" Jesus: "O Master, let me. . . ." The vocative has been bowdlerized in *The New Century Hymnal* to "O Savior, let me. . . ." The shift from "Master" (that *The New Century Hymnal* takes to be patriarchal and hierarchical) to "Savior" unfortunately softens the resolve to discipleship in the new rendering.

The initial petition is to "walk with Jesus," the walk of obedient discipleship.

The entire summons of Jesus to "follow me" is an invitation to walk in the path of Jesus after the risky manner of Jesus (Mark 2:14; 8:34; 10:21). Perhaps the most poignant text for this imagery is the walk to Emmaus, when two disciples are accompanied by the risen Jesus, whom they did not recognize (Luke 24). They report that they met him "on the road" (v. 35) and that he "walked ahead" (v. 28), as one would expect the Lord to precede the followers. This episode "on the road" bespeaks intimacy that is mediated through "the breaking of the bread" (v. 35) an allusion to his presence in the Eucharist. A glad, obedient "walk with God," moreover, is tersely asserted concerning Enoch:

> Enoch walked with God; then he was no more, because God took him.
> (Gen. 5:24)

This simple statement suggests that Enoch was a model of trust and obedience and that his obedient walk with God is the basis for which God "took him," presumably into abiding, obedient fellowship. It is of course on that basis that later Judaism generated an immense literature about the afterlife of Enoch in God's inscrutable future.

In the hymn's first verse, the accent is on service, that is, discipleship. The lines recognize that discipleship after Jesus entails *toil* with its strain and *care* with its fret. The lines do not imagine that discipleship is easy, happy, or comfortable. The toil that is involved, in Gladden's trajectory, is to be engaged down and dirty with hard, intransigent justice issues, the kind in which Gladden himself endlessly engaged. It involved, moreover, care that attends to individual persons at the point of their need; such care, moreover, evoked endless worry and concern (fret).

Thus if we correlate toil with public issues and care with personal needs, we see that the final phrase of verse 1 concerns both public and personal costs of discipleship, all of which is acknowledged here. The double imperative of verse 1, "tell me," "help me," acknowledges that the toil and care are a heavy burden that we cannot undertake on our own without ready burn-out. The first imperative, "tell me," wants in on Jesus' secret, that is, the mystery of a sustained life of toil and care with a good heart and a resilient spirit. The line recognizes that it was Jesus' deep linkage to God his Father (however that relationship is understood) that made his life's work possible. The second imperative asks for help for the sustenance and a discipleship of ongoing toil and care.

Verse 2 pivots on two imperatives, both of which are a reaching out to others in ministry and mission, seemingly of an evangelistic kind. The opening verb "Help" reiterates the imperative of verse 1; only now the energy is directed outward, whereas the same petition in verse 1 was inward. Now the prayer is that the singer should have aid in moving the "slow of heart," the reluctant, to a life with Jesus. The petition reflects a commitment to recruit others to Jesus, but to do so by the attractive power of love. The second imperative, "teach me," reflects the function of the "Master," who will nurture the followers; the speaker wants to learn the skills and capacity to bring others home, that is, to life with God. The verse lacks specificity about the substance of this missional effort, but much is implied by the phrases that end the two clauses: "word of love" and "homeward way." Gladden would not have been a hard-sell evangelist, but he does recognize that without the walk toward home with Jesus, we remain alienated from our true selves.

In verse 3 the opening petition is "Teach." The speaker asks to be taught patience, perhaps looking back to the "strain" and "fret" of verse 1, for moving the "slow of heart" is indeed exasperating and tries one's patience. Anyone who stays at pastoral work, ordained or lay, in the face of such exasperation, can readily lose patience. The speaker then asks God to relieve the exasperation by blessing with the "fruit of the Spirit," patience (see Gal. 5:22). The opening imperative is limited to only four words and is not further developed. The phrase "still with thee" governs the remainder of the verse through three uses of "in":

First, "in closer dearer company": We are back to the initial jussive, "Let me walk with you," only now there is a craving for a deep intimacy with Jesus. The thought is not developed, but we may infer a tilt in a mystical direction; the singer wants palpable, experienced company with the living Jesus that will sustain toil and care.

Second, "in work that keeps faith sweet and strong": The juxtaposition of "work" and "faith" calls to mind the old irrepressible tension between Paul's accent on faith ("For by grace you have been saved through faith, and this is not your own doing; it is the gift of God—not the result of works." [Eph. 2:8–9]) and the counterpoint of James's accent on work ("Faith by itself, if it has no works, is dead" [Jas. 2:17]). Gladden had the pastoral insight, surely also reached by the apostle Paul, that "faith" (that is, utter reliance on God's grace), while an end in itself, is funded by practical action and implementation. Jesus endlessly propels his followers to missional engagement, sometimes in interpersonal engagement, sometimes in quite public ways, and it is such missional engagement that over and over confirms to us the truth of our faith. Or more simply put, "Use it or lose it." The modifiers for such work, "sweet and strong," are an exact, happy choice by Gladden. Faith is "sweet" when it is filled with imagination and innocence. But when faith is not articulated in joyous toil and care, it may become sour, cynical, authoritarian, and uncaring. See the awareness of Paul in 1 Corinthians 13:1–3. It is the day-to-day evidence of God's grace in actual human life that keeps us strong, that leaves us convinced of the truth of the gospel. It is glad, obedient work that generates specific human evidence of the truth of grace and the appropriateness of faith. Without that palpable funding, faith loses its incarnational anchor. Conversely, when we treat our commitment to Jesus as an end in itself without missional engagement, it becomes tepid, rote, and eventually quite unimportant in our lives.

Third, "in trust that triumphs over wrong": This phrase nicely moves from "faith" in the second phrase to "trust" in order to accent the living relationship of reliance on Jesus that is entailed in the walk of discipleship. It is wondrous to rely on this "secret" of Jesus in risky ways that will finally prevail. While Gladden is not explicit about it, we can see in the phrase a vague affirmation of the theology of the cross, for it is Jesus' full confidence in the Father God that he triumphed over the power of death, which in his context meant defeat of the power of the Roman Empire. It was his vulnerable way on Friday that defeated the empire of force.

In all three "in" phrases the singer wants to stand in the "patience" of Jesus:

- Patience to be lived in the close dear company with Jesus
- Patience that allows works which sweeten and strengthen faith
- Patience that prevails even over the power of death

In the fourth verse the word sequence of verse 3 is inverted. Whereas in verse 3 the lines begin with an imperative and a phrase that introduces three "in" phrases, in verse 4 two "in" phrases ("In hope . . ."; "in peace . . .") are followed at the end by a jussive: "with thee . . . let me live." At the end, and only at the end, the vocative "O Master" is reiterated from verse 1, so that the two vocatives provide an envelope for the entire hymn. In *The New Century Hymnal*, the bowdlerized first vocative, "O Savior" is also reiterated in the final verse.

Thus the singer wants not only to *be* with Jesus and to *walk* with Jesus but to *live* with Jesus. This commitment to Jesus is a whole-life undertaking that, we may anticipate, requires and deserves full energy with nothing held back. The two "in" phrases of verse 4 trace out the marks of that life together:

"In hope that sends a shining ray": This life together is filled with hope "down the future's broadening way." Life with Jesus does indeed entail a theology of hope, a conviction that God's promised future will prevail over the resistant powers of this age that aim to sustain the status quo to perpetuity. The new future that Jesus performs can only be voiced in parables, but it hosts a new world in which the last will be first, and the humbled, exalted. Life with Jesus is drawn to a future that is a deep contradiction to present-world arrangements.

"In peace that only thou canst give": This life together is one of peace that comes only from God. This peace is a real-world anticipation of a time and circumstance when debts are forgiven and swords are indeed beaten into plowshares. In the meantime, however, before the arrival of that altered world, peace as the mark of Jesus is given by God in a way that surpasses all human understanding (Phil. 4:7). The anticipation of such peace that defies circumstance is welcome in a world that is fiercely organized against the peace of God. Those who walk the walk are already engaged in that future of peaceableness.

Accomplished poet that he was, Gladden offered a prayer that permitted one to wrap one's self in Jesus, but only by way of obedient discipleship. The prayer is bracketed by two vocatives addressed to Jesus, the Master. It is governed by a series of urgent petitions (including three jussives) that seek gifts from God that permit an alternative life in the world. It is quite noteworthy that none of these appeals voice the kind of conventional "grocery list" of needs we regularly voice in petitions for ourselves and for those closest to us. There is nothing here of requests for self or even for one's loved ones. It is all a quest to be better equipped for missional obedience.

And finally, the petitions are fleshed out by a series of "in" phrases that characterize the life that comes in close companionship with Jesus. The accent is kept insistently focused on the mission that is ready and able to move beyond self, recognizing that Jesus' self-giving is his way for the sake of the world. The aim is not self-comfort or satisfaction but the intention, in the wake of Jesus' own intention, to enact God's rule in the earth. It is legitimate to address Jesus as "Savior," as in *The New Century Hymnal*, but here, before that bowdlerization, it is asserted that glad obedience to Jesus and readiness to follow his path is the point of faith. The hymn does not sugarcoat the cost of obedience so evident in Jesus' own life and so urgent in our world today.

The theme of this hymn, discipleship, calls to mind Bonhoeffer's poignant phrase "the cost of discipleship." By his phrase "cheap grace," Bonhoeffer meant that we finally cannot have it both ways but must choose.[1] In the time of Jesus, it was the either/or of God or wealth (Matt. 6:24: Luke 16:13). In Bonhoeffer's context it was God or National Socialism. In our time perhaps it is God or the rat race of military consumerism. The theme also calls to mind the normative Statement of Faith in my church, the United Church of Christ:

> You call us into your church
> to accept *the cost and joy of discipleship,*
> to be your servants in the service of others,
> to proclaim the gospel to all the world
> and resist the powers of evil.[2]

Along with cost there is joy. This hymn affirms the deep joy and well-being of the close walk. It also knows that joy and cost are deeply intertwined and cannot be separated from each other.

ONCE TO EVERY MAN AND NATION

James Lowell, 1845

1 Once to every man and nation
   Comes the moment to decide,
   In the strife of truth with falsehood,
   For the good or evil side;
   Some great cause, God's new Messiah,
   Offering each the bloom or blight,
   And the choice goes by forever
   'Twixt that darkness and that light.

2 Then to side with truth is noble,
   When we share her wretched crust,
   Ere her cause bring fame and profit,
   And 'tis prosperous to be just;
   Then it is the brave man chooses
   While the coward stands aside,
   Till the multitude make virtue
   Of the faith they had denied.

3 By the light of burning martyrs,
   Christ, your bleeding feet we track,
   Toiling up new Calvaries ever
   With the cross that turns not back;
   New occasions teach new duties,
   Time makes ancient good uncouth;
   They must upward still and onward,
   Who would keep abreast of truth.

4 Though the cause of evil prosper,
   Yet 'tis truth alone is strong;
   Though her portion be the scaffold,
   And upon the throne be wrong,
   Yet that scaffold sways the future,
   And, behind the dim unknown,
   Stands our God within the shadow
   Keeping watch above his own.

The Worshipbook: Services and Hymns (1970), no. 540

Chapter 14

Once to Every Man and Nation

It is most unfortunate, in my judgment, that this poem-hymn has dropped out of the church's working repertoire. I have found it in none of the new wave of denominational hymnals. The words of the hymn were written by James Russell Lowell in 1845. They were written on protest against the U.S. war against Mexico under the presidency of James Knox Polk, a protégé of Andrew Jackson. In order to understand the urgency of Lowell's words, the context of the Mexican-American War is important. The war was waged by the United States in order to serve expansionist notions of U.S. territory. The phrase "Manifest Destiny" was coined in 1845 to serve the expansionist vision of the United States. The phrase affirms that it is the God-given destiny of the United States to expand, and because the "destiny" is God given, it was to be enacted in aggressive ways that were regarded as legitimate. Thus the phrase helped to fund the nationalist imagination required for the war with Mexico and has funded and legitimated U.S. military aggression in the service of "exceptionalism" on many occasions since then. The major impetus for that expansionism, however, was to add slave states to the Union so that the balance of power between slave states and free states would be maintained. Thus opposition to the war included opposition to the expansion of slave states.

The early view of Abraham Lincoln is typical of such opposition to the expansion of slave states. Lincoln conceded, at the outset, that slavery was protected by the Constitution in the original slave states. But he resisted expansion of slave territory because it gave unfair advantage to the plantation economy with its free labor in competition with the labor of small farmers like his father who could not compete against the advantage of the plantation economy. Thus opposition to the war was in part moral but also in part economic.

The moral passion of Lowell's words intends to dramatize the radical either/or of a decision about the war and thus a decision about the expansion of slave territory with all of its moral and economic implications. The prophetic rhetoric of Lowell's words, like all such prophetic rhetoric, is to insist that the "choice" about the war is an immense, urgent either/or of huge theological and moral import. It is characteristically the work of prophetic rhetoric to attest the urgency of such either/or decisions, for without such rhetoric, the choice might be made almost without notice, as though nothing momentous were at stake. Thus the urgency of the hymn is to practice the prophetic work of witnessing to urgent moral choices that would otherwise be routine.

The continuing force of the hymn rests in our imaginative capacity to transpose the moral urgency of 1845 to contemporary moral choices that are as urgent in our time as the war was in Lowell's time. Thus the singing of the hymn is always contemporary in its moral urgency, even while we acknowledge that Lowell's gender-exclusive male language is reflective of his time and place. Thus, for example, as I write these lines the U.S. government, under the guidance of President Donald Trump's draconian deportation policy, is this week to deport Maribel Trujillo-Diaz, a Hispanic mother in Cincinnati who has committed no crime beyond her status as an undocumented immigrant. Without this hymn or something like it, the decision to deport seems to be simply an implementation of policy. In the context of this hymn, however, the decision to deport is not only an urgent human crisis for Ms. Trujillo-Diaz and her family; it is also an urgent moral crisis for our government and for those of us who are governed by such policy. Thus when we sing this hymn, we not only acknowledge the huge crisis of the Mexican-American War (and its durable thirst for expansion under the rubric of Manifest Destiny), but we also sing concerning our own moral crisis in which the quality and future of our common humanity is at stake. In such singing we are always readily ranging back and forth between old remembered issues and present unavoidable issues.

The hymn begins with a summons to recognize the moral urgency of a decision now faced by society, in this case a decision about the Mexican-American War. The words affirm that it is a real "choice"; policy makers (and voters who endorse policy makers) have options. The United States was not fated to go to war. Expansion in this aggressive way was not inevitable. The words entertain alternative options.

The choice can be made only "once," and then it must be lived with forever. That choice, moreover, is deep and total. Thus the first verse gives us four word pairs, all of which witness to the deep either/or that is to be faced:

- "Truth and falsehood"
- "Good or evil"
- "Bloom or blight"
- "Darkness and . . . light"

The words imply that going to war is a choice for "falsehood," "evil," "blight," and "darkness." The choice is not routine, commonplace, or inevitable. Decision makers are moral agents, and going to war is a moral decision with huge and long-lasting implications. It is worth notice that only in the final word pair are the terms reversed so that the negative element, "darkness," comes first. But perhaps that is dictated only by the requirement of rhyme to make "light" match "blight." Substantively, we might easily transport the hymn to our own moment of decision making: whether to deport Trujillo-Diaz or not. It is also a decision for truth or falsehood, good or evil, bloom or blight, and darkness or light. In the case of Trujillo-Diaz, the decision to deport was made only once. And then, in the aggressive relentlessness of current immigration policy, it was made yet again, only once, each time decisively and brutally. Each time, it was brutally "only once."

The second verse of the hymn extends the argument to celebrate "truth." The words make clear that truth is not a body of certitudes but a praxis that "performs truth" by making a concrete decision in the right direction. It may be, the words suggest, that truth will someday bring fame, profit, and prosperity. But before that, long before that, truth gets only wretched crust, only crumbs from the table of the advocates of evil. Thus the decision for truth must be made "ere," that is, before any visible gain can come from it. The enactment of truth, we affirm as we sing, can be not only inconvenient but costly.

The last four lines of the second verse offer yet another either/or, but now the contrast is different. Now it is the brave who choose to do the truth. The antithesis to "brave," however, is not "evil" but simply cowardice. Lowell saw that the war could be decided not by heroic decision making but by abdication of responsibility and refusal to face up to the implications of the decision. The brave see what is at stake and are ready for "wretched crust." The opening "till" of line 7 matches "ere" in line 3. "Till" anticipates that eventually the crowd will celebrate the virtue of the right decision, the decision to forgo war; but the crowd will only arrive at that awareness late. So it was in the Vietnam War. In retrospect the protesters against the war were right, but only the brave knew it at the time. In retrospect Martin Luther King Jr. was right about civil rights, and now he is much celebrated. But only the brave stood with him then. We dare imagine, moreover, that eventually protection of undocumented workers like Trujillo-Diaz will be seen by "the multitudes" as right policy that will bring fame, profit, and prosperity. But only then, belatedly, not now! And decisions must be made now, "once."

We sing as far as the third verse before we arrive at any voicing of the presence of Christ amid the urgency of the once-for-all choice. Lowell dares to imagine that those who refuse popular aggressive expansionism belong in the company of the Christian martyrs. The martyrs, then and always, walk a hard path of suffering and end with bloody feet for walking that hard path. The imagery may call to mind the roster of the faithful in Hebrews 11 who walked "by faith." And of course it is like that in opposition to any war, as it was in 1845. It is like that in the championing of the protection of undocumented immigrants. Given a certain U.S. chauvinism, such regard for undocumented immigrants is unwelcome, if not "unpatriotic." The third and fourth lines of the third verse go even further. Now the resisters to a popular jingoistic decision are not only like the martyrs. They are likened to Christ himself, who walked the impossible walk to Calvary, carrying for himself the instrument of the Roman Empire for his execution. And since the court decision for deportation of Maribel Trujillo-Diaz has been made through the course of the Christian Holy Week, it is not inappropriate to see advocacy for her as a new journey to Calvary in which a decision is urged that defies the predatory practices and policies of the imperial state.

The most famous line in Lowell's hymn is the sixth line of the third verse, which acknowledges that there has been an "ancient good," that is, an accepted moral practice, in this instance, the legitimacy of slave states and of the institution of slavery. Slavery had been accepted as "normal," so abolitionists were seen to be dangerous oddballs in their dissent from the so-called norm. But, the line insists, times change; circumstances alter. "Ancient good" becomes "uncouth," ill-mannered, gross, and unacceptable. It took a very long time, but finally slavery and all powerful, coercive forms of racism have indeed become uncouth and unacceptable.

So it will be with undocumented immigrants. The "ancient good" is that the United States belongs only to "us," to white Europeans, thus the wholesale injustice toward Native Americans and African Americans who were brought here as slaves. But times change; circumstances make demands. It is uncouth in the extreme to imagine that the United States is to be all white or, for that matter, all Christian. It is uncouth to want to deport wholesale in a way that breaks up families and disrupts peaceable communities. Without this hymn (or some statement like it) we may unthinkingly accept that the ancient good remains normal and correct for all time, undisturbed by changing social reality.

No one can deny, however, that there are "new occasions [that] teach new duties" (v. 3). The "new occasion" for Lowell was the conduct of the

Mexican-American War in the midst of the vigorous public debate about slavery. Everyone knew that slavery was by now unsustainable. Everyone knew that this "ancient good" (the good of cheap labor) had to end, even if the way forward was not clear. Everyone sensed, even those who denied it, that there were "new duties" that had to be performed, duties that recognized that slavery was unsustainable, that a slave was not simply three-fifths of a person, that slaves had to be emancipated, and that there must not be new slave territory.

Thus our "once" is the awareness that it is a new occasion for eleven million undocumented immigrants. It is time to reembrace that welcoming posture of the United States that is the very fabric of a U.S. economy that depends on welcome of new participants and contributors. All of the white European immigrants who came here knew about and know about that welcome. The new duty is to practice that welcome without the requirement of white racist quotas. Looking back to verse 2 there is no doubt that eventually such welcome of undocumented immigrants will morph into profit and prosperity, as it is easy enough for us to recognize that the U.S. economy depends on such welcome. It is the brave who already know all of this.

The last line of verse 3 affirms that "truth" is dynamic and on the move; we have to run to keep up with it. This is a courageous, astonishing affirmation that truth is not a settled package of unchanging convictions. Such an affirmation rejects the so-called "originalism" of Justice Scalia that pretends that the Constitution had an "original" meaning that can simply be reiterated. It rules out as well religious fundamentalism that imagines an old package of unchanging certitudes. It recognizes that truth—the kind embodied in Jesus who is "'the way, and the truth, and the life'" (John 14:6)—is radically out in front of us, and we must make new decisions to stay current with God's new insistences. There is no doubt that ancient U.S. policy concerning undocumented immigrants was tailored toward the maintenance of a homogeneous white society in which the only nonwhites were those in degraded social positions. It is comforting to some simply to reiterate that "ancient good" without recognizing that it has become "uncouth." But the world does not stand still, and God's will is on the move with new expectations from the faithful.

In verse 4 Lowell offers yet one more either/or, this time "evil"/"truth." He has taken the terms from verse 1 and has given us a new mix and match. In 1845 "evil" was resistant to the new truth of God that slavery was wrong and must not be expanded. In our time the new truth is that such deportation is evil and cannot be countenanced. There was not and is not any doubt that such evil (war or massive deportation) will be popular—it appeals to our instincts that traffic in fear. But truth is strong and will not yield to those fears. Truth is strong enough not to yield, even as the martyrs and Christ himself did not yield to the deathliness of popular policy that wanted him crucified. Wrong prevails! Wrong is dominant! Right is rejected, executed on the guillotine. Lowell could see what was happening through popular support for the war. And we can see what is happening. Xenophobia has its day! But we know better. The guillotine will perform its lethal work against truth, and the multitudes will applaud. One can imagine today the rhetoric of sycophants for policies concerning "successful" deportation. But we know better. Or we will come to know better. We will come to see, the hymn has no doubt, that truth cannot be eliminated by violent action, no matter how popular.

The reason that evil cannot finally win—whether in the continuation and expansion of slavery or with the practice of deportation—is that God is present in the process. The last lines of the hymn are the first explicit mention of God. Lowell has withheld God until the final lines, and now plays the theological "trump" card. God is "within the shadow," not visible, not intrusive in a way that would embarrass progressives, not in direct ways that would comfort evangelicals, but constant in the process. Thus Lowell articulates confidence in the *pro-vidence* of God; God can see and provide what is needed, and will not finally be defeated or deterred in that governance.

The shadowing governance of God assures that we do not live in a relativistic world where our nativist propensity can best the durable truth of God. It is the reality of God that gives substance in verse 1 to truth over falsehood, good over evil, and light over darkness. In verse 2 the reality of God gives success to the brave over the cowardly; in verse 3 that same reality gives truth leverage over ancient good now become uncouth; and in verse 4 it keeps faith strong in its sway over the future. God will not be outflanked by evil, by falsehood, by darkness, or by cowardice. It is the reality of God that gives urgency to this "once" of life or death. Without this God, everything evil is possible. Slavery can last forever; deportation can proceed endlessly. We insist otherwise, however, because of God.

This God is "keeping watch":

> He will not let your foot be moved;
>   he who keeps you will not slumber.
> He who keeps Israel
>   will neither slumber nor sleep.
>
> The LORD is your keeper;
>   the LORD is your shade at your right hand.
> The sun shall not strike you by day,
>   nor the moon by night.
>
> The LORD will keep you from all evil;
>   he will keep your life.
> The LORD will keep
>   your going out and your coming in
>   from this time on and forevermore.
>   Ps. 121:3–8

God attends to "[God's] own." And who are God's own? The hymn does not say. Clearly God's own are the brave who have chosen differently and did not give in to popular opinion. They are those who act in the awareness that we are pressed to new duties. They are those who recognize that when truth is on the scaffold, it is not thereby rendered obsolete.

Beyond that, we may imagine that God's own are not only those who perform new duties but also those who are the subject of such new duties, that is, the slaves for whom God wills futures and the undocumented immigrants for whom God wills well-being. God's own are those who are cast out "once" by "ancient good" but who become the face of "new truth."

The hymn does not go very far with articulating this God in the shadows. In the Christian congregation, however, that God in the shadow has come to transformative vitality in Jesus. Jesus did indeed embody new truth. Jesus embraced new duty. Jesus ended on the Roman "scaffold." But his scaffold, his crucifixion, his execution, constitutes power to a new future.

It is grossly unfortunate that this hymn has been dropped from the repertoire. Maybe the congregation in a therapeutic culture cannot tolerate such moral urgency and outrage, or it cannot host such a summons.

PRAISE, MY SOUL, THE KING OF HEAVEN

Henry Frances Lyte, 1834

1 Praise, my soul, the King of heaven;
   to his feet your tribute bring;
   ransomed, healed, restored, forgiven,
   evermore his praises sing:
   Alleluia, alleluia!
   Praise the everlasting King.

2 Praise him for his grace and favor
   to his people in distress;
   praise him still the same as ever,
   slow to chide, and swift to bless:
   Alleluia, alleluia!
   Glorious in his faithfulness.

3 Fatherlike he tends and spares us;
   well our feeble frame he knows;
   in his hand he gently bears us,
   rescues us from all our foes.
   Alleluia, alleluia!
   Widely yet his mercy flows.

4 Angels, help us to adore him;
   you behold him face to face.
   Sun and moon, bow down before him,
   dwellers all in time and space:
   Alleluia, alleluia!
   Praise with us the God of grace.

Glory to God (2013), no. 620

Chapter 15

Praise, My Soul, the King of Heaven

This wondrous hymn parlays the beautiful Psalm 103 into singable, rhyming meter. The initial work of Henry Lyte that used monarchical language ("king," etc.) to render YHWH as Lord has since been "gender corrected" to "God," a term taken to be a more neutral address.[1] However God is voiced in this psalm, it is clear that everything depends on the good, trustworthy sovereignty of God, whether rendered in the Hebrew YHWH, the monarchical "king," or the gender-neutral "God." Because the hymn tracks the psalm so closely, it seems wise to me to consider the psalm itself; after we have done that, it will be easy and obvious to see what is happening in the hymn.

Psalm 103 is readily parsed as a series of rhetorical clusters, each of which attests to God's goodness. In the opening summons, the "self" addresses the "self" with four imperatives:

> Bless the Lord, O my soul,
>   and all that is within me,
>   bless his holy name.

> Bless the Lord, O my soul,
>   and do not forget all his benefits.
>   vv. 1–2

It is curious that in the process of "cleaning up" the language of the hymn, recent "correctors" do not quibble with the opening word "soul," a word that tilts toward excessive inward spirituality. The better reading, however, is "self," the whole self summoned by the self to enhance God by praise. The word "self" is preferred to "soul" because "soul" spiritualizes the subject away from the material bodily reality of the self. The term in the psalm refuses such spiritualizing and includes the whole self, including material, bodily reality.[2] This opening summons of self to self is matched at the end of the psalm by a five-fold imperative (vv. 20–22). Whereas the opening addresses only the self, at the end all of God's creaturely subjects are addressed and summoned to enhance God: "O you his angels" (v. 20), "all his hosts, his ministers that do his will" (v. 21), "all his works" (v. 22), and finally, yet again, "O my soul" (v. 22), the self. Thus verses 1–2 and verses 20–22 frame the psalm by mobilizing all those who enhance God.

Within this bracket of imperatives, we may identify four rhetorical riffs. First, verses 3–6 feature a recital of YHWH's "benefits," God's good recurring actions. This series of strong verbs of transformation provides a summary of God's actions that characteristically permit otherwise failed lives to flourish: *forgive, heal, redeem, crown, satisfy,* and *vindicate.*

Second, in verses 7–8 we are given a historical recall of the Mosaic tradition. Moses is named; then in verse 8 we get a characteristic inventory of YHWH's defining attributes: *mercy, grace,* and *steadfast love,* a great triad of covenantal faithfulness reinforced by the assurance that God is "slow to anger." This highly stylized formulation, often repeated in Israelite tradition, is rooted in the divine declaration of Exodus 34:5–6 whereby YHWH restores Israel's covenant after it had been violated.[3] This triad of terms (plus one) attests YHWH's tenacious fidelity and reliability, which was evidenced in the narrative of Exodus 32–34 by YHWH's capacity to move beyond the affront of the golden calf to revitalize the covenant of Sinai.

In what follows, the psalm takes up the two defining issues of "the human predicament," sin and finitude. In verses 9–14 the third rhetorical riff of the psalm asserts YHWH's generous graciousness in the face of human (Israelite) immorality. The psalm acknowledges sin, iniquity, and transgression. These realities, however, are no match for *the compassion of God,* who is like a generous father (or parent). Again the term "steadfast love" is sounded, already used twice in verses 4 and 8. These verses allude to the paradigmatic covenantal violation of Genesis 2–3; verse 14 recalls that the initial human couple in Genesis was formed (the old translation had "framed") out of dust (Genesis 2:7). For that reason God has only limited expectations of such frail, fragile creatures and does not retain anger toward them in their infidelity. The fatherly (parental) imagery rings true, for characteristically all "good enough" (à la D. W. Winnicott) parents make allowances for their children in default.

In verses 15–18, the psalm in a fourth rhetorical riff affirms the finitude of human persons; everybody dies! We do not last long on earth; we flourish briefly like grass or like flowers, and we dry up and wither away. Thus inescapable mortality is acknowledged; it is, however, promptly countered by the adversative "but" in verse 17. YHWH's steadfast love decisively counters human mortality. *God endures in fidelity*; that fidelity is persistent and is not interrupted by our deaths. Thus God's "steadfast love" is asserted a fourth time in the psalm. The point of this assertion is to recognize that the defining human reality is not human virtue or human durability. The defining reality is the truth of God's fidelity through every circumstance of failure and fragility.

Thus we have four rhetorical riffs sandwiched between the opening and concluding imperatives:

- The verbs that recite God's characteristic actions (vv. 3–6)
- The catalogue of the markings of God in the tradition of Moses (vv. 7–8)
- The compassion of God that counters sin (vv. 9–14)
- The durability of God that counters death (vv. 15–18)

Taken altogether we can see why the imperative summons of verses 1–2 and 20–22 have such force. Given these claims for God, who would not want to sign on for celebrative adherence to this sustaining, transformative God? It is easy to see why the self, along with all of God's great creatures, joins the celebrative song in these four rhetorical clusters.

In the hymn by Lyte, the summons to "praise" (a substitute for "bless"), frames verse 1 as it does the psalm in the beginning and concluding imperative summons. These two imperatives bracket the verbs taken from verses 3–6 of the psalm: "ransomed, healed, restored, forgiven." The outcome of such a recital is a vigorous responsive "Alleluia," the last syllable of which, the final "a," is shorthand for "Yah," that is, YHWH. Thus, praise YHWH! For all of the grand accent points of the psalm, finally we are drawn back to the enigmatic, untranslatable proper name of Israel's God (see Exod. 3:14).

In verse 2 of the hymn we read of God's being "slow to chide, and swift to bless," a reference to verses 9–11 of the psalm. In these verses God is like a father (parent) who does not keep score or retain grudges but is marked by covenantal "faithfulness." The Christian tradition (in the interest of social control, I believe) has been overly occupied with sin and guilt. Here such matters are quickly disposed of by a ready and willing compassionate parent.

Verse 3 continues reflection on the problem of alienation that is dealt with in "fatherlike" ways, or "like a loving parent." The hymn, like the psalm, issues a mighty alternative to any thought of an angry, punishing sovereign.

We might particularly notice how that wondrous affirmation gives the lie to ignorant Christian caricatures of the Old Testament in which it is all too often mistakenly taken as an attestation to an angry, judging God. Such caricatures are regularly offered by those who have not troubled to notice the actual witness of the text of the Old Testament.

It is curious that this hymn does not at all take up the claim of verses 15–18 in the psalm concerning God's durable fidelity in the face of human mortality. Rather in verse 4 the hymn moves directly to the sweeping summons of verses 20–22 in the psalm and finishes, as in the psalm, with a grand vision of all of God's creatures engaged in praise. Thus when a congregation sings this hymn, it does so alongside angels who have direct access to the sovereign God in the throne room of heaven. These angels are not cute cherubic figures as in much artistic lore but the agents of and attendants to the God of heaven who oversee the proper function and administration of God's governance. These angels, along with a choir full of majestic creatures—including sun and moon—worship. And finally "dwellers all in time and space," all creatures of every species in creation, all creatures over time and since the beginning of time, are at their proper vocation of praise. Thus the singing of the congregation is not a trite, rote, or incidental act. It is rather participation in the ongoing anthem of the entire world.

The reason for this hymn, sung by us and by all our creaturely companions, is to "bless" God, to enhance, celebrate, and elevate God over all alternatives. When we ask about alternatives to this glorious God known in the traditions of Israel, we may imagine cosmic or historical forces who bid us worship them and who do not forgive, do not heal, do not redeem, do not crown, and do not satisfy (see Luke 4:1–13). The alternatives to this creator God are not marked by mercy, grace, or steadfast love. They do not readily forgive but keep their anger forever. They do not remember our feeble formation in Genesis and so do not have low expectations for us. They do not endure in fidelity in the face of our mortality.

I take the trouble to line out these negative alternatives to YHWH because our daily lives are much occupied by alternatives to this faithful God, alternatives such as exclusionary ideologies of race, gender, or nation; by reductionist technology; or by consumer propaganda—all of which make promises they cannot keep. When we come together to join in this ongoing cosmos-embracing hymn, we defy these seductions that beset us. We contradict the claims of such idols. We affirm that we live by the sustenance of a durable fidelity that is not on offer from any of these gods who compete with the creator God. We sing this hymn because we know it is best that this God should be celebrated and that the fake gods should be minimized, downgraded, and dismissed. Praise in this hymn is no innocent enterprise. It is engagement in a life-or-death dispute about the future well-being of the world and hope for future life that is not defined or circumscribed by either our guilt or our mortality.

Chapter 16

Sparrows as Models of Faith

Jesus famously summoned us to notice the birds (Luke 12:24). He likely meant that reference to birds generically, but the NRSV translates it as "ravens," the same ones who wondrously fed Elijah (1 Kgs. 17:4–6). Jesus might have also included swallows and sparrows in his summons. All of them, he observed, find ample food without any effort on their part to be predatory or acquisitive. They are cited, along with lilies, as examples of God's creatures who rely on the faithful sustenance of the creator. They embody a model of trust that Jesus commends to his disciples, who are to be neither predatory nor acquisitive; they are to be quite unlike the farmer in the parable that precedes the instruction about birds, that is, quite free of anxiety (Luke 12:13–21). The raven, sparrow, and swallow have figured out, long ago I presume, that you cannot serve God and pursue commodities (food!) via predation and acquisitiveness (Luke 16:13). Neither, avers Jesus, can anyone who enlists in the Jesus movement.

A bit further afield, we may mention two other attestations of sparrows as model citizens in the kingdom of God. In Psalm 84, the sparrows and swallows (in poetic parallelism) are cited as welcome residents in the temple of YHWH where they find a safe home:

147

> Even the sparrow finds a home,
>   and the swallow a nest for herself,
>   where she may lay her young,
> at your altars, O LORD of hosts,
>   my King and my God.
>   Ps. 84:3

These birds are welcome to roost right on God's altar! They are observed, in the psalm, as nest builders, that is, as homemakers who practice family values and care well for their young. The next verse of the psalm imagines that sparrows and swallows join in the doxology of all creatures, "ever singing your praise" (Ps. 84:4).

Special attention should be given to Jesus' teaching in Luke 12:6–7 (also see Matt. 10:29–30):

> "Are not five sparrows sold for two pennies? Yet not one of them is forgotten in God's sight."

Sparrows in the course of the day are sold cheaply indeed. Two pennies! But cheap as they are, so cheap as to be easily discarded, every one of them is remembered by God! None is left behind. None is forgotten or neglected, because the creator pays attention to every creature. The object lesson of sparrows, however, is designed to assert that the disciples are precious in God's sight, are valued, and not forgotten or neglected by Jesus. They are so precious to God that God knows the number of hairs on their heads (Matt. 10:30; Luke 12:7). They are so precious as to be worth many times the value of a sparrow.

The intent of Jesus' teaching is to urge his disciples to make a bold, risky confession of the gospel before the authorities. Although such a confession might lead to punishment or even torture and execution, says Jesus, these risks can be run because God never forgets or neglects. The outcome of the teaching is for high-risk discipleship and confession. The concrete grounding for the teaching is an observation about sparrows, those well-beloved creatures of God who are never forgotten, neglected, or discarded.

The defining Reformation teaching, the Heidelberg Catechism, has as the first question "What is your only comfort, in life and in death?"[1] Its first answer goes like this:

> That I belong . . . to my faithful savior Jesus Christ who . . . protects me so well that without the will of my Father in heaven not a hair can fall from my head; indeed, that everything must fit his purpose for my salvation.

Our faithful savior, Jesus Christ, is so profoundly our comfort in life and in death because even the hairs on our heads are noticed and numbered by our heavenly Father. The catechism cites our verses in Luke and Matthew as a reason "that everything must fit his purpose for my salvation." The catechism's answer has behind it stunning confidence in the well-ordered sustenance of a good creation by the creator. The creation is so well managed by the creator that even sparrows count with the creator . . . how much more those created in God's image!

In the chapters that follow we will consider three very different hymns, each of which appeals to the image offered in Scripture of a well-loved sparrow as a model of faith and trust that lives by God's goodness and that gives back to the creator in gladness. The implied teaching in each of these hymns is "How much more . . . us!"

GOD'S EYE IS ON THE SPARROW

Civilla D. Martin, 1905

1 Why should I feel discouraged,
   why should the shadows come,
   Why should my heart be lonely,
   and long for heaven and home,
   When God is ever my portion?
   My constant friend will be:
   God's eye is on the sparrow,
   and I know God watches me;
   God's eye is on the sparrow,
   and I know God watches me.

   Refrain:
   I sing because I'm happy,
   I sing because I'm free,
   God's eye is on the sparrow,
   and I know God watches me.

2 "Let not your heart be troubled,"
   Christ's tender word I hear,
   And resting on God's goodness,
   I lose my doubts and fears;
   Though by the path God leads me
   but one step I may see;
   God's eye is on the sparrow,
   and I know God watches me;
   God's eye is on the sparrow,
   and I know God watches me. (*Refrain*)

3 Whenever I am tempted,
   whenever clouds arise,
   When song give place to sighing,
   when hope within me dies,
   I then draw close to my Savior,
   from care I am set free:
   God's eye is on the sparrow,
   and I know God watches me;
   God's eye is on the sparrow,
   and I know God watches me. (*Refrain*)

The New Century Hymnal (1995), no. 475

Chapter 17

Sparrow Song One: God's Eye Is on the Sparrow

This well-loved hymn was written as a poem by Civilla Durfee Martin in Elmira, New York, to comfort a friend with chronic illness. It was first combined with its well-known tune in 1908. The poem, like the Scripture to which it appeals, moves from awareness of God's care for an insignificant sparrow to an affirmation of trust that God cares even more for me (for us; for them), even in desperately hopeless circumstances. Martin's friend was able to trust the assurance about "each little sparrow" to affirm, "He loves and cares for me."

Verse 1 begins with three questions that might readily arise for anyone who faces chronic illness, or any number of other losses or wounds:

- Why . . . discouraged?
- Why . . . shadows?
- Why . . . lonely and longing?

The questions acknowledge these crowding, inescapable realities. Clearly, however, it is recognized in the questions themselves that they are finally inappropriate because "God is my portion." The reality of God is a decisive counter to such sensibility. The notion of God as "portion" echoes "God is the strength of my heart and my portion forever" (Ps. 73:26). God as portion in the ancient tradition is an alternative to "land as portion." God is the inheritance of those who have lost their place. Having that sure portion, moreover, is a counter to discouragement, shadow, and loneliness. A more direct answer to the three questions, however, is promptly given: God is a constant friend, one who is always there to comfort and reassure. The hymn voices a direct, simple piety that knows the Lord Jesus to be a real, attentive, and reliable presence in one's life. This terse affirmation is filled out with the refrain stemming from Jesus' teaching that we have already considered: "sparrow . . . me (us)!" Jesus is particularly watching over us in the way a parent watches over a child or the way the creator watches over birds and the hairs on our heads.

The hymn does not doubt the complete, attentive fidelity of God, even though that assurance offered in the gospel teaching has now been distanced from any call to bold confession, though it might be understood that the capacity to say "my constant friend" in the face of chronic suffering is itself a bold confession.

The three-fold affirmation, "*I know* God watches me" leads to a transformative outcome: "*I'm happy . . . I'm free.*" In this direct, simple piety an assurance of the attentive, reliable care of God is a counterreality that, in the world of this hymn, defeats the disabling power of discouragement and loneliness. Of course for those who inhabit this world, the companion of God in Christ is a lived reality; it is not a thought experiment or an act of imagination but the taproot of reality that empowers a more excellent way in the world.

The second verse begins with a quote from John 14:1, the verse most frequently cited at Christian funerals. The use of this phrase of assurance in the hymn shows how Scripture, when read in faith, is readily adaptable from one context to another. In this verse yet again, it is the utterance of trusted words from Jesus that reorder the world away from "doubts and fears." The second motif of verse 2 is something of a surprise; the singer understands self as a follower of Jesus, walking in the path of discipleship. And as all serious disciples readily learn, we cannot see the destination of the path of discipleship. We know only the next step; we walk by faith and not by sight (2 Cor. 5:7). Such a walk is congruent with the reality of those who face chronic pain or any durable, burdensome difficulty. One cannot see the end; one cannot know the outcome. One must get through the day. A troubled heart will perforce be filled with "doubts and fears," and likely (back to verse 1), discouragement, shadows, loneliness, and longing. But when one's life is situated in the reliable assurance of Jesus, that heart trouble is overcome. Even in such circumstances, those who walk with Jesus can be, the song affirms, "happy" and "free." The lines do not offer emancipation from pain or loss but from doubt and fear, thus with sufficient resources for the day. I suppose it is this assurance and the promise of Jesus that are the grounding for the remarkable assurances of Paul:

Rejoice always, pray without ceasing, give thanks in all circumstances; for this is the will of God in Christ Jesus for you. (1 Thess. 5:16–18)

I have learned to be content with whatever I have. I know what it is to have little, and I know what it is to have plenty. In any and all circumstances I have learned the secret of being well-fed and of going hungry, of having plenty and of being in need. I can do all things through him who strengthens me. (Phil. 4:11–13)

Paul commends joy, thanks, and constancy in every circumstance! The gospel invitation overrides circumstances; at its best it is not an act of denial but an act whereby lived reality is resituated in the context of a deeper, more reliable reality.

The third verse begins with four phrases triggered by "when" phrases followed by an offer of immense honesty about real circumstances:

- "Whenever I am tempted"
- "Whenever clouds arise" (an allusion back to "shadow" in verse 1)
- "When song give place to sighing"
- "When hope . . . dies"

The singer acknowledges that the wondrous affirmation of the three-fold chorus (clouds, sighs, the loss of hope) does not always prevail. Sometimes (often?) the reality of circumstance prevails, and we find ourselves recaptured by the grim realities of our life.

That reality, however, is promptly contradicted in the next clause: nearness to Jesus emancipates from worry. As elsewhere the singer does not explain but simply confesses . . . a bold confession of a counterreality. As with all gospel confessions, the confession makes no sense to those who live outside this frame of reference. That is why it is a confession and not an objective statement. As an outsider could not understand or even suspect, the confession is very "thick"; its truth is mediated to the confessor via text, proclamation, sacrament, and a company of human companions who offer the sweet comfort of Jesus. Given all these modes of mediation, however, the simple truth of the confession is that Jesus is a comfort. This conclusion does indeed "surpass all understanding." It defies explanation. Thus Paul in his great reassurance to the Philippians can assert,

> Do not worry about anything, but in everything by prayer and supplication with thanksgiving let your requests be made known to God. And the peace of God, which surpasses all understanding, will guard your hearts and minds in Christ Jesus. (Phil. 4:6–7)

Peace with God is a reassuring companionship that is the outcome of making one's requests known to God. The way to companionship with God is found in honest, demanding dialogue in which the petitionary speaker addresses God with requests and seeks redress of needs. The wonder of voiced petitionary utterance when one knows one's self to be acknowledged and seriously engaged is that it is an emancipatory act. The silence is broken. The need is legitimated. And the Lord addressed is drawn into one's situation in a way that alters reality in exactly the way in which the entry of a trusted person into a crisis changes everything. The outcome is that our "hearts and minds" are guarded, that is, kept safe from disabling doubt and erosive fear. The entire process, however, from the courage to petition to the outcome of peace all begins in Paul's affirmation that "the Lord is near" (Phil. 4:5). In Paul's horizon the phrase concerns apocalyptic expectation that the reentry of the risen Christ into the world will end the power of evil. Our singer, however, draws such vivid apocalyptic rhetoric into the immediate reality of suffering. In the hymn, "closer to my Savior" is no longer about a decisive, divine reentry into human history but about the intimate companionship of a constant friend in the midst of lived reality that is unbearable alone. Thus the apocalyptic phrasing has been reconfigured to serve in a new lived circumstance. In both cases, however, that of Paul and that of us belated singers, the outcome of "nearness" is happiness and freedom.

Everything depends on the eye of God, the remarkable capacity of God the creator to pay attention. Melissa Florer-Bixler, in her exposition on sparrows, reports that devoted bird-watchers endlessly and vigilantly pay attention to every little movement of the bird.[1] So it is with the "good enough" mother on a playground who keeps her eye diligently on the child or a "good enough" father with a kid in a swimming pool. So it is with this "good enough" God, who keeps a close eye on God's covenanted creatures. Thus in Deuteronomy 32:10 Jacob (Israel), even in the wilderness, is kept safe by the watchful God:

> He sustained him in a desert land,
>   in a howling wilderness waste;
> he shielded him, cared for him,
>   guarded him as *the apple of his eye.*
>   Deut. 32:10, emphasis added

In Psalm 17 the imagery is transferred from the covenant people to an individual person who dares to address an urgent imperative petition to God:

> Guard me as the apple of the eye;
>   hide me in the shadow of your wings.
>   Ps. 17:8

The petition is uttered in a dangerous, desperate situation of threat and eventuates in a vigorous attempt to mobilize God against ominous enemies:

> Rise up, O LORD, confront them, overthrow them!
>   By your sword deliver my life from the wicked,

from mortals—by your hand, O LORD—
from mortals whose portion in life is in this world.
Ps. 17:13–14

We can readily imagine that the chronically ill, without the brutality of this text, may transfer the imagery from God to Jesus, from ancient circumstance to the immediacy of the present situation.

We are able to see that this hymn is deeply grounded in Scripture. It is, moreover, deeply attuned to practical reality. The song can readily bracket out all kinds of critical complexities concerning present trouble as every bold confession must do. In the end it comes to a simple conclusion: God cares for every modest creature. How much more does God care for me, us, the suffering, and the left behind!? It is no wonder we sing, "What a friend we have in Jesus." He is indeed our best friend. Like every good, trusted friend, it is an emancipatory relief to have a best friend drawn into our circumstance, rendering us watchful care. One can imagine that the sparrow mentioned in Matthew 6 and Luke 12 senses the same reassuring reality. That is why sparrows are not productive or acquisitive. God will take care of them—of you! Who needs to know more than that?

GOD OF THE SPARROW

Jaroslav J. Vajda, 1983

1 God of the sparrow
God of the whale
God of the swirling stars
How does the creature say Awe
How does the creature say Praise

2 God of the earthquake
God of the storm
God of the trumpet blast
How does the creature cry Woe
How does the creature cry Save

3 God of the rainbow
God of the cross
God of the empty grave
How does the creature say Grace
How does the creature say Thanks

4 God of the hungry
God of the sick
God of the prodigal
How does the creature say Care
How does the creature say Life

5 God of the neighbor
God of the foe
God of the pruning hook
How does the creature say Love
How does the creature say Peace

6 God of the ages
God near at hand
God of the loving heart
How do your children say Joy
How do your children say Home

Glory to God (2013), no. 22

Chapter 18

Sparrow Song Two: God of the Sparrow

This wondrously singable hymn was written in 1983 by Jaroslav Jan Vajda, a Lutheran pastor, for a church anniversary at Concordia Lutheran Church in Kirkwood, Missouri. I know that church because I visited it as a part of my "field work" (as we called it then) in seminary and interviewed the pastor of that time. The hymn is all the more remarkable because it is so open-ended; it poses questions that it does not seek to answer. This is remarkable for a Missouri Synod Lutheran pastor writing for a Missouri Synod Lutheran congregation because Missouri Synod Lutherans are not greatly noted for their propensity for open-ended questions or for leaving important theological questions unresolved and unanswered.

We may be glad for the lyrical freedom sketched by Pastor Vajda, surely a response to his subject matter about the vigor, freedom, and open-endedness of creation. The music and words together readily summon us out of an explanatory mode into celebrative wonder. Since this hymn concerns creation, it voices a summons away from old quarrels about creation and evolution; it refuses the reductionist explanatory ideology of the so-called "new atheists," and it resists the didactic ideology on exhibit in the Creation Museum in Northern

Kentucky that seeks to reduce lyrical poetry about creation to manageable straight-jacket prose. In the face of all of those reductions, this hymn recognizes creation as an invitation to wonder:

> Though separated by over two and a half millennia, the authors of ancient Scripture and numerous scientists of today find themselves caught up in a world of abiding astonishment. Like the ancients, many scientists admit to being struck by an overwhelming sense of wonder—even "sacredness"—about nature and the cosmos. What a far cry from Francis Bacon's objectification of the natural realm as humanity's slave.[1]

The hymn is God-centered. In each of six verses God is mentioned three times, eighteen in all. This is the God who is the creator. Nothing more is said directly about God, but much is tacit in the words that follow. God is the Lord of all creatures, "great and small." And all creatures, by their created nature, are designed to respond back to the creator. Thus creation is a dialogic enterprise initiated by the creator but continued by the ready responsiveness of every creature.[2]

Each of the six verses names three creatures, except for a variation in the final verse. The list of creatures constitutes a representative inventory of all of God's creatures, all evoked by the creator, all designed for response to the creator. I do not think too much should be made of the specific juxtaposition of any triad of creatures in any verse, as I suspect they could be rearranged in any configuration of triads. We can nonetheless tease out more from the several triads:

Verse 1: "sparrow," "whale," "stars": I was led to this hymn as the second of three "sparrow hymns" by the opening reference to "sparrow." The sparrow, however, occupies no special place here, no more than any other creature. We know from the preceding sparrow hymn, however, that sparrows are models of trust who are not productive or acquisitive. This tiny, vulnerable bird is grouped here with two other enormous creatures to signify all creatures great and small, a whale, perhaps the largest mammal, and stars that open to seeming limitlessness attestation to the Lord of all galaxies.

Verse 2: "earthquake," "storm," and "trumpet blast": This triad bears honest recognition to the unsettled, unsettling quality of creation, for we all know about earthquakes, storms, floods, and tsunamis that wreak incredible destruction that we call "acts of God." The "trumpet blast" perhaps has apocalyptic overtones that signal the end of the presently ordered world (see Rev. 1:10; 4:1; 8:2, 6, 13; 9:14). Each member of this triad bespeaks enormous upheaval. These upheavals, however, do not outflank the rule of the creator who presides over all such disruptive occurrences. Elsewhere we know that God the creator can still the storm (Mark 4:35–41) or rescue from the storm (Ps. 107:23–32). But there is nothing of that here. Rather we might imagine the creator engaged in pyrotechnics as manifestations of power.

Verse 3: "rainbow," "cross," "empty grave": In a curious juxtaposition this triad bespeaks divine restoration. The rainbow answers the storm of verse 2. The cross and empty grave, via divine efficacy, attest God's defeat of the chaotic power of death and disorder. Thus verses 2 and 3 seem to have a close linkage.

Verse 4: "hungry," "sick," "prodigal": Now the hymn draws closer to concrete, lived reality. It identifies the vulnerable who lack resources and who depend on the generosity of the creator and of other creatures. The hungry, of course, are of special concern to the creator God. In grand doxology the creator gives food:

> The eyes of all look to you,
> and you give them their food in due season.
> You open your hand,
> satisfying the desire of every living thing.
> Ps. 145:15–16

Mary anticipates revolutionary divine action on behalf of the hungry:

> He has filled the hungry with good things,
> and sent the rich empty away.
> Luke 1:53

And Jesus names the hungry among "the least" who are strangely identified with Jesus himself (Matt. 25:37–40). The sick are the recipients of God's healing capacity since YHWH turned out to be "the doctor" of the emancipated slaves from Egypt (Exod. 15:26). The mention of the "prodigal" is a bit curious here, because it is undoubtedly an allusion to the parable of the Prodigal Son (Luke 15:11–24) and so has a specificity lacking in the other two cases. Nevertheless, as the story goes, the prodigal ended up as needy and resourceless as the hungry and the sick. All the vulnerable are among the creatures of God who live in response to the creator.

Verse 5: "neighbor," "foe," "pruning hook": The neighbor and enemy are a natural juxtaposition. From the outset of Mt. Sinai, "neighbors" are fellow members of the covenant community; the people of God are summoned to "love of neighbor" as the whole sense of the Torah (Lev. 19:18; Gal. 5:14; 6:2). But of course that more-or-less-conventional ethic is challenged by the insistence of Jesus, who sees gospel conduct as a reach beyond neighbors to the embrace of enemies:

> "You have heard it that it was said, 'You shall love your neighbor and hate your enemy.' But I say to you, Love your enemies and pray for those who persecute you. . . . And if you greet only your brothers and sisters, what more are you doing than others? Do not even the Gentiles do the same?" (Matt. 5:43–47)

As difficult as neighbor love is in a fearful political economy, in the horizon of Jesus it is no big thing, for even "Gentiles" do that. The serious gospel ethic is love of enemy. That demanding embrace brings us to the third member of the triad, the pruning hook. The term is a direct reference to the prophetic expectation of disarmament that will reforge the weapons of war into the peaceable tools of agriculture (Isa. 2:4: Mic. 4:3).

Verse 6: "ages," "near at hand," "loving hearts": This final triad begins with the large sweep of time, as large as stars, whales, and earthquakes. It then moves very close, as close as neighbors and enemies. In the third member of the triad it draws even closer, to "loving hearts," to those who fully embrace the ethic of the pruning hook. The phrase is perhaps an allusion to "Jesus, thou joy of loving hearts," wherein the hymnist—long assumed to have been the old monk, Bernard—understood that those with loving hearts had joy in Jesus:

> Jesus, thou joy of loving hearts,
> thou fount of life, thou light of all,
> from the best bliss that earth imparts
> we turn, unfilled, to heed thy call.[3]

The triad bespeaks the human community, the humanity of all times and specifically of our time. In verse 6 the next phrase offers a variant from the other five verses; the "children," the human community, accept God as our father/mother who gives bread and not stones, who cares for those of all ages and now us with parental attentiveness.

The sum of these representative creatures is more than the specificity of the enumeration. All together we have a breathtaking affirmation that God does indeed have the entire world in God's good hands. The sweep of the whole surely must evoke wonder of an immense magnitude.

The hymn then, in each verse, turns to the vocation of response on the part of the creatures. These words do not doubt that the creatures respond to God, for it is in their nature as God's creatures to do so. They are made for responsiveness! The only question is how. The creatures "say" (in one case "cry"). They do not do so in our human tongue, but they do so. And what they say is given us in two terms in each verse, twelve in all. All creatures engage in this worship and communion with the creator, albeit in modes other than our own. I am not sure that there is an intentional logic to the arrangement of the twelve factors of dialogic response, but we may consider them at least in the word pairs in the six verses.

In verse 1 the creatures (sparrow, whale, star) speak "Awe" and "Praise." This first word pair is focused on the wonder and unimaginable worthiness of the creator. I suppose in all these cases there is a practice of "natural theology" in which we are pressed by what we see in creation back to the Lord of creation who calls it all into being. Thus we imagine, in our own dialect, every creature responding in self-abandoning praise back to the one who has made its life possible and "very good."

In verse 2 the creatures (earthquake, storm, trumpet blast) "cry." This the only case of "cry" as divergent from "say." The use of "cry" is appropriate because the subject is the "woe" of creatures who face deep trouble. The particular creatures who know woe are the agents of chaotic upheaval, earthquake and storm. Along with the cry of woe (congruent with the shrill cry of Israel in need, as in Exod. 2:23–24; see Luke 18:1–8), this is a cry of "save," an imperative petition to God in one's helplessness. These creatures, at the end of their own resources, know that they must turn to the creator, the one with a capacity for rescue.

In verse 3 the creatures (rainbow, cross, empty grave—markers of well-being and restoration) say "Grace" and "Thanks." These creatures know that the "save" of verse 2 has been answered. Flood is answered by rainbow. Empire is answered by cross. Death is answered by empty grave. In the face of flood, empire, and death, there is good and compelling reason for thanks, because each of these rescues embodies grace upon grace, exhibiting the creator's readiness to be the savior.

In verse 4 the creatures (the hungry, sick, and prodigal) say "Care" and "Life." In each case life has been in jeopardy: the hungry by starvation in food deserts, the sick by the force of death or poor health care, the prodigal in degrading homelessness. In each case, the creator God has cared enough to intervene. The God of food ministered to the hungry. The God of health restored the sick. The God of homecoming welcomed the prodigal. It is because "God will take care of you" that life is restored and can be celebrated.

In verse 5 the creatures (neighbor, foe, pruning hook) say "Love" and "Peace." When we love our neighbor as ourselves, the neighborhood is peaceable. When we love our enemies, hostility turns to hospitality. When we employ agricultural tools rather than weapons of war, disarmament leads to peace. These three creatures express their joy and surprise that a world of edgy hostility on the verge of violence can be otherwise. The otherwise is because the God of love breaks the vicious cycles and invites our continuing work in love that works peace.

In verse 6 the creatures as children know the God of homecoming and so sing "Joy" and "Home." It is this God who turns our time and every time to joy, so that we may "rejoice in the Lord always" (Phil. 4:4). The world without God is ultimately alienated. The reliable restorative presence of God in the world ends the alienation and makes homecoming possible:

> Father of orphans and protector of widows
>   is God in his holy habitation.
> God gives the desolate a home to live in;
>   he leads out the prisoners to prosperity.
>   Ps. 68:5–6

We now live in a world of displaced persons, not only the refugees who must flee violence in their own "homelands" but also white males in our society who have lost their long-term advantage and sense their displacement. While socioeconomic, political redress is urgent, in the end it is the generosity of the creator, enacted through generous creatures, that will permit homecoming beyond violence.

This remarkable catalogue of songs to sing and petitions to cry provides an inventory of possible and essential transactions between creator and creatures. The hymn is one long question, and we may be grateful that this lyrical Missouri Synod pastor did not try to give answers; that would be too difficult for poetic embrace. The questions, however, operate with a crucial theological assumption, namely, that the creatures do indeed speak to the creator. What they say is all covenantal speech because life with the creator is one of relationality. Thus the agenda of awe, praise, woe, salvation, grace, thanks, care, life, love, peace, joy, and finally home is the proper discourse of covenantal life. We are not told and we do not know how an earthquake can cry, "Save," or how a pruning hook says, "Peace." But we know that these creatures (along with us), do their creaturely work with faithful regularity.

The intent of the hymn, after we are dazzled by creatureliness, is that it speaks directly to the creator and to our own human, creaturely work of the complete agenda from "awe" to "home." In the process the world is redefined away from the rat race of commodities to the real thing, the bottomless mystery of relatedness. Every rabbit and carrot knows this. And when we sing this hymn, we stand with sparrows in faith, joy, and awe.

SOMEONE ASKED THE QUESTION
(WHY WE SING)
Kirk Franklin, 1994

1 Someone asked the question
"Why do we sing?
When we lift our hands to Jesus
what do we really mean?"
Someone may be wondering
when we sing our song,
at times we may be crying
and nothing's really wrong.

Refrain:
I sing because I'm happy!
I sing because I'm free!
God's eye is on the sparrow
That's the reason why I sing.
Glory hallelujah!
You're the reason why I sing.
Glory hallelujah!
You're the reason why I sing.
Glory hallelujah!
I give the praises to you.
Glory hallelujah!
You're the reason why I sing.

2 When the song is over,
we've all said, "Amen,"
and your heart just keeps on singing
and the song will never end.
And if somebody asks you,
"Was it just a show?"
lift your hands and be a witness
and tell the whole the whole world "No!" (*Refrain*)

3 When we cross that river
to study war no more,
we will sing our song to Jesus,
the One whom we adore! (*Refrain*)

The Faith We Sing (2001), no. 2144

Chapter 19

Sparrow Song Three:
Someone Asked the Question

Kirk Franklin is a contemporary songwriter who offers "Christian love music" of a popular kind. This song, written in 1994, is a riff on "God's eye is on the sparrow," which we have previously considered. It is a riff, however, that opens up new awareness of our vocation of singing songs to God. Franklin's affirmation in this song is in the wake of his own childhood experience of abandonment. The hymn is happily self-conscious about our singing, and it poses exactly the question of our larger study: "Why do we sing?" The words of the hymn are an answer to that question.

Verse 1 is the voice of someone at the back of the church who observes as the congregation sings. When we reflect, as we do here, on congregational singing, we must admit that such singing is an odd practice, even if a most familiar one. Thus an observer might ask,

- Why do they sing?
- Why do they raise their hands in praise to Jesus?
- Why do they cry in singing when they are already deeply well off?

The hymn's refrain is a response to those questions. Our singing is an expression of our happiness (or as the children would say in our last hymn, "Joy"). That joy is grounded in freedom, so that all our singing is an echo of the African American mantra "Free at last; free at last; thank God almighty, free at last."

We sing in freedom—freedom from fear, freedom from alienation, freedom from threat, freedom from every bondage. The emancipatory reality is that our creatureliness is under God's sustained, reliable watchfulness. We know freedom through the teaching of Jesus that defined the watchfulness of God we have already cited: God's eye is on the sparrow, enough of an assurance to imagine that birds know that there is enough food and enough safety to "wing it." It is a remarkable connection to affirm that *we sing because sparrows are safe.* That is how Jesus has reassured us:

> "Consider the ravens; they neither sow nor reap, they have neither storehouse nor barn, and yet God feeds them. Of how much more value are you than the birds!"[1] (Luke 12:24)

How much more indeed! This is a blatantly anthropocentric affirmation. The "how much more" is a human-centered claim that is characteristic of the Bible, the claim to be God's most cherished creature. We might imagine that Jesus, if and when he addresses sparrows and ravens as did St. Francis, might have said to them, "How much more of value are you to me than humankind." This may be like a parent reassuring each child, one at a time, that he or she is of special value and the special object of love. But since Jesus is addressing humankind, we get this most welcome verdict of assurance, "How much more!"

From that sequence of "happy," "free," "sparrow," "sing," the hymn is to the "You" of the creator. Now we are done with explanation or justification. Now it is all praise to God. Finally, *You* are the reason I sing. Now the deep secret of faithful hymnody is disclosed. We sing because of God. God evokes celebrative honesty about our true life before God. For that celebrative honesty God requires poetic imagery. God evokes glad unself-conscious self-abandonment into figurative images on our tongues, sometimes hands raised in gladness, sometimes feet tapping in rhythm, sometimes bodies moving in dance, all acts of yielding willingly to the God of joy and freedom.

Verse 2 recognizes that the end of many of our hymns is a vigorous, confirming "Amen." We close our hymnals. But the song does not end. It never ends, because the joy is deep and durable, and the freedom is precious. This verse dares to imagine that our life in faith is one long, unending doxology. All of that doxology is a yielding to the creator-emancipator God whose very reality gives the lie to a flat, closed, low-ceiled existence. The refrain tells why the song is unending. It is because of "You." The faithful, at our best, never move out of the sphere of this Holy One but are always yielding themselves gladly back to God. On the "You" of God, Martin Buber can write,

> Through every single You the basic word addresses the eternal You. The mediatorship of the You of all beings accounts for the fullness of our relationships to them—and for the lack of fulfillment. The innate You is actualized each time without ever being perfected. It attains perfection solely in the immediate relationship to the You that in accordance with its nature cannot become an It.[2]

We take it for granted, but it is nonetheless astonishing, that we, God's creatures, have the capacity and the freedom to address God directly as "You." The creator God is accessible and welcomes such daring address. The appropriate address to this awesome creator God is "glory," a glad honoring of a regal figure to whom belongs "the kingdom, the power, and the glory, forever and ever." The *Hallal* of "Hallelujah" translates to "praise" or even "boasting." In our singing we shamelessly brag about God; such an act moves us out of the center of our own lives and permits us to acknowledge the true center of our existence, namely, the God who gives us life.

In verse 3 the words look ahead to a different time when we "cross that river." It is likely that this metaphor refers to death; if so, the phrase implies that until death we are fated to "study war," and death will relieve us of that sorry compulsion. It is possible, however, that the phrase might alternatively refer to an authentic conversion whereby we may "live a godly, righteous, and sober life,"[3] not unlike the prodigal son who "came to himself" (Luke 15:17). We may then be no longer in the grip of such a fearful compulsion as to mistakenly imagine that our lives may be secured by force of might. Either way, at death or in conversion, we will be in a new place of freedom and joy. In that new venue the singing will continue, because our life in that new locus is still from God and back to God:

> We do not live to ourselves, and we do not die to ourselves. If we live, we live to the Lord, and if we die, we die to the Lord; so then, whether we live or whether we die, we are the Lord's. For to this end Christ died and lived again, so that he might be Lord of both the dead and the living. (Rom. 14:7–9)

Thus Franklin sees clearly the truth of Paul's affirmation. Either way, we belong to God. Or as the Heidelberg Catechism has it,

> My only comfort, in life and in death, is that I belong—body and soul, in life and in death—not to myself but to my faithful Savior, Jesus Christ.[4]

Singing to "You" is the glad acceptance that we do not belong to ourselves. This affirmation has always contradicted the easy assumption of being self-made and self-sufficient. But it is acutely pertinent now to our modern world after René Descartes and John Locke:

> The difficulties of modern liberal-democratic theory lie deeper than had been thought, that the original seventeenth-century individualism contained the central difficulty, which lay in its possessive quality. Its possessive quality is found in its conception of the individual as essentially the proprietor of his own person or capacities, owing nothing to society for them. The individual was seen neither as a moral whole, or as a part of a larger social whole, but as an owner of himself.[5]

This illusion of self-possession, receiving nothing from God or neighbor and owing nothing to God or neighbor, has come to full expression in fantasies of self-realization and in predatory economics that are antineighborly in readiness to confiscate and usurp. Such an assumption inevitably generates greedy anxiety that insists on having more and anxiety about not having enough, and it eventuates in violence as a means of getting more from the neighbor, a Thou now reduced to a commodified "it."

In the face of that forceful mistaken ideology, we sing! We are not our own. We belong to another who is the source of our freedom, joy, and well-being. Thus our singing is a mighty affirmation; it is, moreover, a mighty protest against "normal" assumptions of self-possession. "Glory" belongs to God and will not be otherwise shared, not with money, not with the nation-state, not with youth or beauty, not with virility or machismo, not with any of the idols that most tempt us (see Isa. 42:8; 48:11). And so we sing. We sing "glory." We sing "Hallelujah." We sing alongside the sparrow whose daily singing is under the happy watchful surveillance of the creator God. The song does not end because that watchfulness of God never tires of caring for us and for the birds. As a result, Jesus assures us,

> "And do not keep striving for what you are to eat and what you are to drink. . . . Your father knows that you need them." (Luke 12:30)

Then Jesus summons us:

> "Strive for his kingdom, and these things will be given to you as well." (Luke 12:31)

Now we know! Alongside sparrows, we sing gladness and freedom.

WE ARE MARCHING IN THE LIGHT OF GOD

Translator: Gracia Grindal, 1984

We are marching in the light of God;
we are marching in the light of God.
We are marching in the light of God;
we are marching in the light of God.

Refrain:
We are marching, marching,
we are marching, marching,
we are marching in the light of God.

Additional stanzas ad lib.:
We are dancing . . .
We are praying . . .
We are singing . . .

Glory to God (2013), no. 853

Chapter 20

We Are Marching in the Light of God

This hymn is a marching song. Its lyric does not develop much because its purpose is to mark the cadence of feet moving together. It was a folk song of the Zulu/Xhosa tribes in South Africa and was formulated as we have it by a Methodist young men's group in order to protest against the oppression of the apartheid regime in that country. The lyric is simple and repetitious because the march to justice is slow and requires constancy and solidarity, with feet moving together. The simple cadence includes four elements:

The first element is "We"—the song is sung by those who are moving their bodies in the service of freedom. Specifically the "we" are the freedom movement of blacks in South Africa who not only resisted apartheid but who insisted that the policy must be changed and dismantled. Of course, the marching "we" can be extended and expanded to every community that moves for freedom.

Second, the singers are "marching." The song has an almost martial beat suitable for many feet in uniform cadence. Marching amounts to actual bodily energy that is invested at some risk in the face of the authorities who are or who appear to be threatening. In contrast to the marchers, the authorities (often the police and sheriffs, but supported by the courts and the government) are unmoved and immovable. This marching is the contest between an irresistible force in the face of an immovable object. The bet is that the irresistible force will defeat the immovable object.

Third, the marching is under the durable surveillance of the emancipatory God. We the marchers are convinced beyond doubt of the right and legitimacy of the cause for which we are marching. Thus the march is not only a political event. It is also a holy event invested with divine authority that readily challenges the authority of the oppressive regime. The linkage of "we" to "God" gives assurance, energy, and courage to the marchers who know themselves to be at risk in their marching.

The fourth element is "light": The glow of God's presence in which the march is conducted contrasts with the "dark" of the oppressive regime: "The light shines in the darkness, and the darkness did not overcome it" (John 1:4). The darkness cannot overcome the power of the light! Thus the psalmist can declare,

> The LORD is my light and my salvation;
>   whom shall I fear?
> The LORD is the stronghold of my life;
>   of whom shall I be afraid?
>   Ps. 27:1

Without that light, there is cause for fear. But the light in which we walk is "the light of God." The phrasing intends to counter the fear that is appropriate to the venue of marching, for that venue is regularly filled with dogs, guns, and threats of violence that are designed to intimidate.

These four elements together, over and over, indicate that the singing, while marching, is an acknowledgment that the journey is one of risk; the marchers, however, are undeterred by the risk because they do not walk alone. The singing makes palpable that the Lord of freedom is marching in, with, and under the marchers.

It is impossible to overstate the barbarism of South African apartheid that evoked the marching and the singing. Apartheid was a legal system in which all instruments of government were openly rigged to assure that a tiny white minority would in perpetuity sustain privilege over the large company of blacks whose land South Africa was and is. In the face of the rigged legal system, oppressed blacks had few levers of power or resources. What they did have was their bodies. The march was the deployment of their bodies, their only ample resource. Thus, in their suffering and energy they exposed the rigged legal system of apartheid as empty of moral authority and therefore unsustainable.

The singing itself does not voice arrival at a destination. It envisions a march that will not stop or be terminated. But obviously the marchers had in purview a destination of full justice. That goal may have been, on the ground, somewhat unrealistic, because actual social change is very slow. But we know the outcome of that march. We know that the apparatus of apartheid was eventually dismantled without violence. And we know that the sane and humane Truth and Reconciliation Commission, for all its complexity and false turns, provided a way beyond what might have been an endless escalation of violence and responding violence.

Many of us well remember that awesome day when Nelson Mandela was released from prison. That release came because of a complex of factors, including the courage and wisdom of Mandela and his prison mates. But it was the reverberating sound of the march that showed the regime that its claims were empty of moral authority and unsustainable. The light of God, in that moment, did indeed prevail over the darkness of apartheid. The marchers knew the truth and did the truth with their bodies.

"Marching" is the bet that the moral authority of pained bodies put at active risk can prevail against unjust established authority. It is a conviction of the marchers who have no other resource but who can no longer bear their pain of suffering, oppression, and humiliation. Since this marching song was originally given force in the midst of apartheid by a Methodist young men's group, it is proper to understand the song in the context of the biblical tradition. Given such a perspective, the exodus is the paradigmatic march that has in its long history featured many replications.

The exodus was an action taken against the predatory oppressive regime of Pharaoh. In Pharaoh's Egypt the Hebrew slaves had no resources or capacity for resistance. The Exodus narrative features four elements that belong, since that ancient action, to all such walks of emancipation. First and foremost, the triggering action of the exodus is *the public voicing of unbearable pain and suffering:*

> After a long time the king of Egypt died. The Israelites groaned under their slavery, and cried out. Out of the slavery their cry for help rose up to God. (Exod. 2:23)

It was a risk to bring such pain to speech. When it was brought to speech, however, it turned to relentless energy. The march depends on getting in honest touch with bodily pain and accepting that such bodily pain has intrinsic moral authority that cannot be denied or silenced by the coercion of the regime. When there is no articulation of bodily pain with its moral legitimacy, there will not be sustainable marching.

Second, it was the voiced pain of the Hebrew slaves that evoked the attention and participation of YHWH, the holy God of emancipation:

> God heard their groaning, and God remembered his covenant with Abraham, Isaac, and Jacob. God looked upon the Israelites, and God took notice of them. . . .
> Then the LORD said, "I have observed the misery of my people who are in Egypt; I have heard their cry on account of their taskmasters. Indeed, I know their sufferings, and I have come down to deliver them from the Egyptians, and to bring them up out of that land to a good and broad land, a land flowing with milk and honey. . . . The cry of the Israelites has now come to me; I have also seen how the Egyptians oppress them." (Exod. 2:24–25; 3:7–9)

The way of the narrative is that God came second to the march. God did not initiate the march but responded to and took seriously the voiced pain of the slaves. God's response promised active advocacy on behalf of the oppressed.

Third, the march thus became God-endorsed and managed. Israel came to see itself walking *under the aegis of God's guidance and protection*, that is, in "the light of God":

> The LORD went in front of them in a pillar of cloud by day, to lead them along the way, and in a pillar of fire by night, to give them light, so that they might travel by day and by night. Neither the pillar of cloud by day nor the pillar or fire by night left its place in front of the people. (Exod. 13:21–22; see 14:19; Num. 14:14)

The narrative attests that God's resolved, protective presence was continually with the marchers without stoppage, day and night.

Fourth, the march depended on the protective "light of God." But finally God could not do all the work of emancipation. *Freedom requires human agency;* God dispatched Moses to Pharaoh. We have, moreover, a detailed account of the ways in which Moses sought to refuse the mandate of God. Moses made all the excuses for himself that he could imagine (Exod. 3:11–4:17). God, however, was relentlessly insistent about the mandate to freedom; finally Moses had to stand before Pharaoh (5:1). This confrontation of Moses before Pharaoh is a paradigmatic drama of truth (the truth of God's light) standing exposed and vulnerable before power (the arrogance of Pharaoh). This encounter is the pivotal moment of the march, truth before power. That dramatic moment was inescapably filled with risk and fear. That is why the marchers must sing, because singing is a way of transforming fear into courage and energy, a transformation essential to such a confrontation. This meeting is occupied by the God of freedom, who is present with and for the marchers. It is the light of this emancipatory God that redefines the encounter with the brutalizing darkness of oppression.

The march of the exodus is paradigmatic and has many reperformances. Indeed, it is the work of the Jewish Passover to remember and reiterate that march against Pharaoh in the light of God. The Passover in contemporary practice is highly ritualized for purposes of reiteration and for socialization of each new generation of Jews into the march. But beyond that ritual reperformance, there are innumerable historical reiterations of that march. Michael Walzer, in his fine book *Exodus and Revolution*, avers,

> I have found the Exodus almost everywhere. . . . It is possible to trace a continuous history from the Exodus to the radical politics of our own time.[1]

Walzer, moreover, sees messianic politics in the modern world and notices that it shows up in contemporary Zionism:

> Exodus politics and political messianism are radically entangled in Zionist thought.[2]

On the world scene one could notice as well the march to the sea of Gandhi in India that finally defeated the British Empire, or the "Long March" of Mao Zedong in China that transformed Chinese politics and economics.

Bruce Feiler (*America's Prophet*), moreover, has traced the way in which Moses and the Exodus narrative have given shape and substance to U.S. identity.[3] As early as Cotton Mather, the Puritan theologian, the white-European occupation of "America" was cast as a reiteration of the Exodus narrative. As recently as March 21, 2017, David Brooks has judged that the Exodus narrative is the "organizing national myth" of the United States:

> It should be possible to revive the Exodus template, to see Americans as a single people trekking through a landscape of broken institutions. What's needed is an act of imagination, somebody who can tell us what our goal is, and offer an ideal vision of what the country and the world should be.[4]

Of course, the appeal to the Exodus narrative that is most vivid to our generation of U.S. citizens is the work of Martin Luther King Jr. Speaking of King's "Dream Speech," Feiler can write,

> In what is arguably the most famous speech by an American since the Gettysburg Address, Martin Luther King fused together Jefferson and Lincoln, pilgrim and slave, Emma Lazarus and the Old State House bell, to set up his defining message from that "old Negro spiritual" that Zora Neale Hurston had put into the mouths of the Israelites as they set out for the Promised Land: "Free at last! Free at last! Thank God Almighty we are free at last!"[5]

It should not be forgotten that King's primary strategy that eventuated in the important civil rights legislation of the 1960s was marching. The march from Selma to Montgomery, only the most famous of his many marches, was surely a reiteration of the Exodus narrative. It was a march that decisively altered the character of American politics. It was of course the case that such a gain from marching requires constant vigilance, for we are able to see the counterpressure that works ceaselessly to revoke the gains. Thus the march is never finished. The slaves must keep singing, must keep marching, and must keep counting on the light of God.

This marching song from South Africa is now in our hymnals, and congregations in the United States sing it. That congregational singing is more than a little removed from the initial risky singing in Pretoria and Capetown, but the echoes of that singing reverberate. There is, to be sure, a possible seduction in such congregational singing, for it can be an act of nostalgia by well-meaning church members who themselves have no intention of actually marching as truth to power.

It could be, however, that when we pay attention and sing ourselves into solidarity with those brave Africans, we will become aware that more is required and more is possible than nostalgia or remote solidarity. There is a compelling contemporaneity to such singing, and when we let our feet and our bodies identify with the marching cadence of the song, we might move beyond singing in the sanctuary to singing in the street. What the song knows and what the original singers knew is that every circumstance is a potential venue for marching.

Every socioeconomic matrix is freighted with injustice and inequality that requires redress. Every such circumstance permits the bearers of unbearable injustice to march against exploitative authority, wherein the bearers of injustice have no resource or leverage except their bodies. Every singing of this marching song constitutes an opportunity to do an inventory of the bodies that carry pain in the face of oppression, unjust practice, and unjust law. These bodies are the subject of the march. In our recent time we have seen, in sequence, the mobilization of the hurting, demeaned bodies of women, of blacks and of gays, and always of Native Americans. One might imagine that it is the bodies of endangered immigrants that now evoke such marching, because we currently live under a regime that relentlessly invades homes and cynically breaks up families in order to cater to the xenophobic adrenaline of a feckless body politic. The marching may remind us that social well-being is not a given to be received passively. It is rather a task to be engaged endlessly. The forces of coercion would as soon have us be passive couch potatoes of complacency and indifference rather than to notice and be in solidarity with hurting bodies. The cadence of the marching song may nevertheless continue to disturb the numbing force of consumerism, which is in the interest of injustice and inequality that want to dissolve the common good. The marching song, whenever we hear its cadences, is a summons to inconvenient action that may spill over into risk.

The marchers know that the march of justice is always marked by inconvenience and potential risk. As a result we may expect and anticipate that when congregations sing this marching hymn in memory of and in solidarity with South African blacks, it will spill over into our own risk. In the light of God, such marchers always trust that "[they] shall overcome." It is for good reason that Walzer can in conclusion voice the relentless contemporaneity of the old Exodus narrative:

> We still believe, or many of us do, what the Exodus first taught, or what it has commonly been taken to teach, about the meaning and possibility of politics and about its proper form:
>   first, that wherever you live, it is probably Egypt;
>   second, that there is better place, a world more attractive, a promised land;
>   and third, that "the way to the land is through the wilderness."
>   There is no way to get from here to there except by joining together and marching.[6]

Conclusion

The Covenantal Fidelity of the Psalms

It is impossible to make any generalization about the book of Psalms because it speaks in many voices from and into many circumstances. Nevertheless, I will risk a generalization without needing to force everything into it: I ask, "Why is it that the Psalter has such durable power among us?" I will answer that question by giving attention to three particular psalms.

The durable power and authority of the Psalter is that it concerns covenantal fidelity, surely the deepest urge and hunger that is elemental to our humanness. The critical term in Hebrew for that covenantal fidelity is *hesed*, variously translated as "loving-kindness" or "steadfast love." I prefer to translate it as "tenacious solidarity." It is the witness of the scriptural tradition and of the Psalms in particular that God is an agent and character of tenacious solidarity who has pledged abiding fidelity to Israel and then, through Jesus, to the church, and ultimately to creation. This means that the Bible is cast in relational categories that finally resist our efforts to reduce its claim to logical, syllogistic, or "reasonable" articulation, even though we continue to try to make such reductions. God is witnessed through this script, in the life of Israel and the church, as one who is ready and able to be in solidarity with us and as one who makes promises, issues directives, and keeps faith. Humanity, by way of Israel, is identified as and summoned to be creatures of solidarity, both in solidarity with God through love as obedience and solidarity with our neighbor through mercy, compassion, and justice. That solidarity, as partner to God and to neighbor, is one of deep tenacity. It is for that reason that the Bible, in poetic idiom, often drifts toward marital imagery, because it is in marital relationships or with that imagery that we speak most urgently about solidarity "for better, for worse, in sickness and in health."

But like all honest relational solidarity, the tenacity witnessed in the book of Psalms is acutely dialogical: it is an open, dynamic, ongoing, risky interaction that refuses settlement or closure, one that is always moving into new circumstances to new crises and new possibilities. The dynamic quality of this interaction of tenacious fidelity indicates the following:

First, in Israel's prayers and songs there really is someone on the other end; this is real talk addressed to someone whom we claim to be listening attentively. It is our modern embarrassed propensity to want to reduce this theological interaction to psychological practice, so that the Psalms become a script for catharsis or wholeness. And surely the Psalms serve that purpose. But they cannot, in covenantal reckoning, be reduced to such a dimension. The marvel of this poetry is that we, after Israel, dare to affirm that this is real interaction with a seriously engaged partner.

But second, because it is genuinely dialogical, our frequent theological assumption of the priority of God is called into question. This is a theological transaction in which either party can take the lead. Thus in the great familiar hymns of the Psalter, God is high, lifted up, awesome, and powerful. In much of the Psalter, however, Israel in its laments assumes priority in the relationship, takes the initiative, and addresses God in imperatives, as though to command God; and God very often accepts that calculus. It is an interaction of playfulness, risk, and openness that violates our usual theological expectations.

And third, the doxological quality of this tradition concerning tenacious solidarity is not always affirmative. In the poems that we know and love best, such as Psalm 23, such solidarity is deeply confirmed. Thus "surely goodness and mercy shall follow me all the days of my life" (23:6). But of course it is not always so in our experience or in the Psalter. Because the drama is relational and both parties exercise freedom, life is often experienced and voiced as *hesed* violated. We are familiar with the prophetic statements that critique and condemn Israel for covenantal fickleness. We are less willingly attentive to Israel's vigorous accusation against God for God's failed fidelity. Israel discerns that God is free and is not an automaton of reliability. Thus in the dread Psalm 88 Israel can say,

> O Lord, God of my salvation,
>   when at night, I cry out in your presence,

let my prayer come before you;
   incline your ear to my cry. . . .

Every day I call on you, O LORD;
   I spread out my hands to you. . . .

But I, O LORD, cry out to you;
   in the morning my prayer comes before you.
                              vv. 1–2, 9, 13

And no answer! In the end Israel can threaten God:

Do the shades rise up to praise you?
Is your steadfast love declared in the grave,
   or your faithfulness in Abaddon?
                              vv. 10–11

That is, dead people do not celebrate God, and if you let me die, there will be one less singer of your praise. In Psalm 89 the psalmist in deep pathos can ask,

Lord, where is your steadfast love of old,
   which by your faithfulness you swore to David?
                              v. 49

Israel knows, as God's *hesed* fails, that solidarity from God is much less than tenacious.

Since God has invited Israel into sustained dialogical engagement, even Israel's experience of God's unfaithfulness can be brought to speech and written into Israel's hymnal! (It is worth noting that in the Psalms the complaint of Israel is left unanswered.) Thus I am able to note four features of this dialogue of fidelity that gives staying power:

First, the Psalter is *an exercise in emotional extremity* that defies ordering through restraint. This is talk in which no secret is hid; nothing is held back. Those who speak are permitted to give voice to the full range of unrestrained emotion. Thus the great hymns of the Psalter soar in praise and thanks and ecstasy. The extreme example, I suppose, is Psalm 150, which dissolves in self-abandonment before God; the speaker summons the temple orchestra, instrument by instrument, to do the glad work of praise. Or alternatively, in Psalm 148 the singer summons angels, sun and moon, sea monsters, snow and wind, creeping things, and kings and young women to join the praise because our tongues are not adequate to what must be sung. Can you imagine all of creation dissolving into glad doxology before the holy one with nothing of the restraint of ecclesial propriety?

But the Psalter knows the counterpoint of negativity in which *hesed* is violated by God or by neighbor. And all of that violation by God and by neighbor, all that guilt and shame, anger and rage and vengeance, alienation and abandonment, is brought to speech. Because the Psalter understood, even before Freud, that we are speech creatures, and our full humanity, all of it, must be brought to speech.

Second, while we know about such emotional freedom in a therapeutic culture, what strikes us in this emotive exercise of extremity is that it is all *uttered in the presence of God.* Interaction with the God of covenant is not reduced to the strictures of obedience and deferential praise as some authoritarian forms of faith would have it. It is, rather, assured and affirmed that this dialogic practice with God concerns the full scale of our life, positive as praise and negative as complaint. The result is that life is all before God, the one who not only speaks to command but who listens even when put at risk by our utterance.

But more than that, this emotive exercise that has transformative impact is done *in the midst of the congregation.* Thus Israel is pledged to praise God "in the great congregation." It is contested and less clear that the negative voicings were so public. I judge that the articulations of lament, complaint, and protest were not done in private. Thus in the book of Job, Job utters his laments in the presence of his friends. Erhard Gerstenberger has proposed that there were "rituals of rehabilitation"—what we might call "therapeutic interventions"— by trusted members of the community who gathered to aid in the speech before God that would call God to account and summon God to engagement in circumstances of need.[1] Fredrik Lindstrom, moreover, has shown that in the psalms of lament there are no confessions of guilt because the one in need, in the presence of neighbors, did not grovel or even repent but spoke as one who had been victimized and was in need of succor.[2] The point was to insist that fidelity from elsewhere had failed and so there was need for restoration. Thus the famous accusation of Psalm 22:1, "My God, my God, why have you forsaken me?" was enough in public that it could be remembered and quoted and used again when divine fidelity had failed. The neighborhood calls God back to fidelity.

Fourth, and finally, this dialogue of fidelity, in which Israel speaks before God and neighbor in emotional extremity, is *highly artistic in its casting.* We do not know the origin of the Psalms, but we know that they arose in the practice of the community and were used and reused, treasured, refined, and transmitted, so that over time they became the reliable codes of articulation for the community of covenant. They became the readily recognized forms through which Israel spoke and sang its most urgent truth. We may identify two elements in such artistry that are worthy of the artistry of the St. John's Bible. The first is termed by scholars "genre."[3] That is, these recurring utterances and modes of expression were found to be reliable over time in the most urgent dimensions of life. In such awesome and demanding moments, we did not have to start fresh and reinvent the wheel because we already knew what to say and how to say it in this community of self-aware voicing. In any community that survives through time, reliable, trusted utterance is required, so we rehearse old patterns of speech at birth, at weddings, at death, at departure, and at arrival. We still say, "I love you" as time goes by. Indeed, such occasions do not require clever or innovative speech but reliable speech, of knowing ahead of time what to say and how to say it. Belonging to the community means to know and trust the codes. That is why in any mixed marriage it can be difficult because one does not know the codes of the in-laws. When we do not know the "how" of speech, we are likely to misconstrue the "what" of speech. Thus we can identify the patterns of speech that recur from psalm to psalm in the same genre; we can guess at the circumstances out of which they came and to which they bear witness. And we can readily transfer that pattern of speech to our own like circumstance. We do it all the time and do not notice that we do it. Modernity places the accent on innovation, but our deepest moments do not require new speech but old trusted speech that sounds the cadences of the community in its incessant practice of risk and assurance.

The second artistic point is that Hebrew poetry is characteristically expressed in poetic parallelism so that the same statement is offered twice or thrice, each time in different terms. Robert Alter, moreover, has shown that the second line of poetry often intensifies and deepens the claim of the first line.[4]

These two artistic features—highly stylized patterns and double or triple parallel lines—abetted by a rich field of venturesome images and metaphors, permit the articulation of profound emotional extremity in highly stylized ways. This means that the poetry not only lets human reality come to speech; it brings it to speech in a way that is formed according to the long-term wisdom of the community. "Formed" expression means that each time we utilize a psalm we participate in a long-recurring artistic gesture whereby our particular speech is joined with and reiterates the cadences of the community that has long been speaking its most intense emotional extremity before God in the midst of the congregation. In this way Israel not only knows *what* to say in every circumstance. It knows *how* to say it in a way that joins the ongoing dialogue over the generations. The use of the complete repertoire of the Psalter schools us in dialogic practice and permits us to join the conversation about fidelity, which is the most important conversation in town. The artistic forms are known and treasured by many mothers and fathers before us who share with us the recurring crises in the practice of fidelity. These forms, moreover, draw God into the ongoing crisis as well, so that the very recital of a psalm is something of a sacramental act, an act whereby the presence of God as listener and respondent is mediated to us.

In what follows I have selected three psalms that I take to be fairly representative of that covenant interaction in which we may participate. I have selected them because they give evidence of that fidelity (*hesed*) as tenacious solidarity as the subject of our deepest interaction with God and neighbor.

PSALM 103

Psalm 103 is a familiar and greatly beloved psalm because it offers to us wondrous assurance. It is unfortunate, in my judgment, that in liturgic use we line out a psalm, line after line, as though it were a single, continuous, repetitious, monotonous note. In fact, Psalm 103, or any psalm, cannot be well read in such a way because it flattens the rhetoric. It is much preferable, I suggest, to recognize that a psalm is a series of rhetorical riffs or poetic clusters that are not well served by our usual liturgic renditions. In Psalm 103 I propose that there are four such rhetorical riffs, over each of which liturgic attention might be given by repetition of its cadence or by expansive imagination that extrapolates.

As discussed in chapter 15 regarding the hymn "Praise, My Soul, the King of Heaven," the psalm is framed by a double imperative at the beginning, "Bless . . . ," "Bless . . ." (vv. 1–2) and by a four-fold imperative, "Bless . . . ," Bless . . . ," "Bless . . . ," "Bless . . ." at the conclusion (vv. 20–22). The imperative verbs suggest that the singing community can, in a rhetorical gesture, "bless" (that is, enhance) the character of God. The object of the verbs, in all cases, is "the LORD," the creator and the one who covenants with Israel. Those summoned by the imperatives include not only the "self," at the beginning and the end, but also angels, mighty ones, God's troops (hosts), ministers (ambassadors), all creatures, and then finally "me." The speaker has so much eagerness to enhance YHWH that he or she is unable to do it all; one needs the community to join the praise. One needs not only all earthly creatures, but all the inhabitants of the heavenly court and company of God. The psalm mobilizes all reality in the magnification of God.

The body of the psalm provides four reasons, each expressed in a rhetorical riff or poetic cluster, why heaven and earth are summoned to praise YHWH. Such extravagance is clearly a performance of emotional extremity, an exuberance and passion that go beyond reason. This is a response to the tenacious solidarity of YHWH.

The first rhetorical riff in verses 3–5 features five participles that assert YHWH's characteristic and recurring activity. It is YHWH, none other, who "forgives," "heals," "redeems," "crowns," and "satisfies." In this remarkable recital, Israel summarizes its entire awareness of YHWH, the one who does the pastoral work of forgiveness and healing, the one who does the emancipatory work of delivery, and the one who does the creation work of satiation. At the center of the recital is our term *hesed*, the one who crowns with steadfast love and mercy. The conclusion is that being young is not chronological; it is covenantal. The "young," the ones with vigor, energy, and daring, are those who are on the receiving end of God's participles. What better than to soar as an eagle!

> Even youths will faint and be weary,
>   and the young will fall exhausted;

but those who wait for the LORD shall renew their strength,
    they shall mount up with wings like eagles,
they shall run and not be weary,
    they shall walk and not faint.

Isa. 40:30–31

They shall run to bless the Lord!

**The second riff in verses 6–8 alludes back to the exodus, already signaled
in the third participle, "redeem."** The reference is explicitly to Moses; verse
6 voices an awareness, with another participle, that the exodus work of the
emancipation of the oppressed is work that YHWH does all of the time. Thus
this sixth participle could have been attached to the first five, but it is placed as
the beginning of a new riff.

Beyond the Mosaic deliverance in verse 6 is the Mosaic instruction of verse
7. This is a reference to the negotiation that YHWH and Moses conducted after
the violation with the golden calf. Finally, exasperated by recalcitrant Israel,
YHWH in Exodus 34 can just blurt out YHWH's own true identity:[5]

"The LORD, the LORD,
a God merciful and gracious,
    slow to anger,
and abounding in *steadfast love* and faithfulness,
keeping *steadfast love* for the thousandth generation,
forgiving iniquity and transgression and sin."

vv. 6–7, emphasis added

The center of that ancient declaration is the double use of *hesed*: "abounding in *hesed*, keeping *hesed* for the thousandth generation" (v. 7, au. trans.).
The psalmist knows the Exodus narrative and this self-assertion by YHWH.
The psalmist need not reiterate the entire statement from that tradition,
only the usable part of it. As a result, verse 8 in our psalm is a reiteration of
ancient disclosure; YHWH is marked, as Israel does not doubt, by mercy,
graciousness, patience, and *hesed*. Thus this second riff, again with *hesed*, gives
ample reason to bless YHWH.

**In the third riff of verses 9–14 the psalmist takes up one of the two deepest
human issues, namely, guilt and alienation.** The reality of sin and alienation
is recognized but not dwelt on. Indeed the church has used much more energy
on sin than does the psalmist. Instead what we have is a glad assurance of God's
generous response to human sin. It is no wonder that it was in the study of the
Psalms that Luther received his great insight about the grace of God.

The news is that God does not stay angry because of God's tenacious solidarity as stated in verse 8. Thus verses 9–10 break out of any quid pro quo calculus;
God will not be captive to anger and retaliation. Two images are mobilized to
declare divine generosity. The first is an appeal to the spaciousness of creation.
The heavens are high above the earth. The east is far distant from the west. The

spaciousness is almost unimaginable, certainly to the ancients, but even to us as we know more about space, even beyond Pluto. The speaker is dazzled by this distance beyond measure, which becomes a way to express the distance between human sin and God's inclination. Too bad that moralism has imagined that God is preoccupied with our guilt and failure, such a small God who is not inured to *hesed*.

The second image concerns a father-son relationship expressed in patriar-chal fashion, an anticipation of Jesus' parable of a lost son and a lost father. The father God is marked by a womb of compassion, so that this father acts like a tender mother. We get a double use of "compassion," an echo of the poetry of Isaiah:

> Can a mother forget her nursing child,
>   or show no compassion for the child of her womb?
> Even these may forget,
>   yet I will not forget you.
> See, I have inscribed you on the palms of my hands.
>   Isa. 49:15–16

This father God is like a mother God who will nurse the baby, who has written the baby's name on her sleeve, who will not be separated from her baby.

But then, in verse 14, it is as though the familial imagery is too small. Now the poet returns to creation with an allusion to Genesis 2, humankind from dust. The creator remembers that we are dust and need not expect so much of us. The father-mother remembers the fragile baby, the feeble irresolute teenager. Lower expectation from the parent is the order of the day because the parent God shows *hesed*, not because of us but because of God who is the final bearer of *hesed*. This is the God who forgives all our iniquities and who heals all of our diseases. Our chosen alienation is overcome by the wide embrace of the God of all *hesed*. We are embraced dust!

The fourth rhetorical riff of verses 15–18 takes up the second great human crisis, mortality. Indeed, Ernest Becker has seen that our denial of death is the central preoccupation of our human life.[6] It is because of our fear of death that we want more military strength and more guns. It is because of our fear of death that we want to keep others from having access to our store of material blessings from God. It is because of our fear of death that we act in abusive ways toward one another and toward ourselves. It is because of that same fear that we have an inordinate need to be right in ways that excommunicate the other.

The psalmist is honest about his life and ours. Yes, we are mortal. Yes, we will die. Yes, we are like a flower that fades. Yes, we are like grass that turns brown. Yes, we are blown away; for the most part we are not remembered or bothered with, leaving no trace in the sand. No denial here. No pretense. No strategy for survival. No mad science to preserve our bodies or our sperm or our special brains. If we look back to verse 14, we are all about dust. It turns out that our passion for longevity is a hoax. We will not stay young by the right drug or the right exercise or the right cosmetic surgery. Which of you by being anxious can add a millisecond to your life? Thus the faithful acknowledge,

> For all our days pass away under your wrath;
> our years come to an end like a sigh.
> The days of our life are seventy years,
> or perhaps eighty, if we are strong.
> Ps. 90:9–10

The acknowledgment is followed by a prayer:

> So teach us to count our days
> that we may gain a wise heart. . . .
>
> Let the favor of the Lord our God be upon us,
> and prosper for us the work of our hands—
> O prosper the work of our hands!
> Ps. 90:12, 17

It is a prayer and a ready recognition, not a denial.

But then Psalm 103 turns in verse 17 with a disjunctive proposition: "But . . ."! To counter the reality of mortality we get "But the *hesed* of YHWH is for always" (au. trans.). *Hesed* from YHWH does not cancel death. It persists in and through and beyond death. And that is enough for the psalmist.

If I have rightly discerned four rhetorical riffs along with the introduction and the conclusion, each of the four clusters pivots on the *hesed* of YHWH (au. trans.):

- "Who crowns you with *hesed* and mercy" (v. 4).
- "YHWH is slow to anger and abounding in *hesed*" (v. 8).
- "So great is his *hesed* toward those who fear him" (v. 11).
- "But the *hesed* of YHWH is forever" (v. 17).

It is no accident that this term keeps turning up in this rhetoric. It is Israel's best word concerning the ongoing dialogue with YHWH. Over time Israel has learned that this is the defining mark of YHWH. Over time Israel has learned that this is how we talk, this is how we know what to say, this is how we live.

One can imagine, in ancient Israel or in a contemporary congregation, a four-year-old standing alongside parents reciting this psalm. The four-year-old does not know Hebrew, does not know the word *hesed*, but says it anyway. Because that is what Mom or Dad say. That is how we speak; that is how we talk. That is what we say. When we talk this way, we advance the dialogue with God and neighbor. When we talk this way, we mark a territory of fidelity. The four-year-old does not ask if this is true. It is a drama of the way Mom or

Dad treats me, in my unexpressed guilt and in the fearfulness of danger I keep unspoken. I know about guilt and fear. But we talk this way, and then we act this way, and *hesed* becomes the world we inhabit.

Or one can imagine a teenager, sullen in church, if in church at all, head down, not reciting the psalm but vigorously and ostentatiously resisting the word of Mom or Dad, not for a minute believing this babble about *hesed*. Except after church, counting heavily on this *hesed* for the grace of the day. Or maybe dismayed because the *hesed* of Mom or Dad is not really reliable, but having in reserve the cadences of *hesed* that remain behind the fragile *hesed* of Mom or Dad. Maybe signing on for it; maybe refusing it and believing that it is a fraud; but being haunted by the cadence, partly yearning, partly knowing better, but in any case haunted. The psalm plants *hesed* at the center of our guilt and our mortality. No wonder the voices of heaven and earth must be mobilized in gladness.

PSALM 86

The dialogue concerning tenacious solidarity continues in Psalm 86 in a very different way. In contrast to the hymn of Psalm 103, Psalm 86 is a fairly conventional lament psalm in which the subject is not the wonder of YHWH, Lord of *hesed*, but the urgent situation of the speaker. Like other psalms that utilize the code of lament, the speaker addresses YHWH in an attempt to receive the attention of YHWH and, from that, the positive intervention of YHWH in the vexed life of the speaker. We may see that this psalm is segmented into three rhetorical clusters, though the delineation of these subclusters is not completely clear.

In the first rhetorical cluster of verses 1–7, we see the primary features of this code. The pattern consists in a series of imperatives followed and reinforced by a series of "motivations." The imperatives include the following:

- Incline
- Preserve
- Save
- Gladden
- Give ear

The speaker does not hesitate to address YHWH with imperatives on the assumption that the covenantal dialogue works in both directions, and the speaker has a right to make these appeals.

It is as though in some bewilderment or indifference YHWH hears the imperatives but is not moved by them. We can imagine that YHWH, high and holy, asks, "Now why would I obey your imperatives?" The question is not asked but implied. And the speaker responds with a series of motivations, reasons that God should act in response. The motivations are often introduced by the word "for":

- "For I am poor and needy" (v. 1)
- "For I am devoted to you" (v. 2)
- "For to you do I cry all day long" (v. 3)
- "For to you, O Lord, I lift up my soul" (v. 4)
- "For you, O Lord, are good and forgiving, abounding in steadfast love to all who call on you" (v. 5)

The reasons characteristically concern both the speaker's desperation and the identity of YHWH. The motivation in verse 5 is of special interest. It is as though YHWH had forgotten that YHWH is pledged to *hesed,* goodness, and forgiveness, pledged since the declaration of Exodus 34. Now YHWH is forcibly reminded of YHWH's true covenantal identity, with the expectation that, once remembered, YHWH will act accordingly. In this rhetorical cluster, that reminder to YHWH in the final petition likely turns out to be more powerful than the earlier motivations that focus on the speaker's need.

In the second rhetorical cluster of verses 8–13, there is a departure from the normal code of lament. These verses begin with a doxology in verses 8–10 asserting that YHWH is incomparable; no other god does what YHWH does; for good reason all nations will worship and glorify only YHWH. The purpose of the doxology is to call YHWH out, to remind YHWH of YHWH's singular identity and vocation. There is no other god bound in covenant like this one. There is no other god who acts covenantally like this one. Indeed, there is no other god like this one bound to *hesed,* committed to tenacious solidarity. The doxology in verse 10 refers to YHWH's "wondrous things," a term that concerns the miracles that YHWH has performed on behalf of Israel. Thus for all the claim of universalism in verse 9, the particularity of covenant is accented in verse 10.

In verse 11 the speaker voices two imperatives: "teach" and "give." These imperatives, however, are not like those in verses 1–6. Here they are an application to be properly instructed as a witness to the wonder of YHWH. Give me a heart to conform to your character, to walk in your way, and to honor your reputation (name). The imperatives of verse 11 are followed in verse 12 with a pledge to be wholly committed to YHWH. The verb looks ahead: "I will give you thanks . . . after you teach and lead me" (au. trans). The rhetorical unit concludes with a motivational doxology that matches the opening doxology of verses 8–10. The basis of the entire interaction is "Great is your steadfast love." Thus we can see that in this unit from 8 forward, the poetry is moving toward the statement about YHWH's *hesed* that is evidenced in the "wondrous things" and that is to be acknowledged in glad praise by the speaker. It is as though the speaker has been brought out of the needfulness of verses 1–6 and now relishes the goodness of life amid that *hesed.*

In the third cluster of verses 14–17, we are introduced to a different motif of lament, namely, the description for God of the trouble out of which the lament arises. The speaker has previously said that he is "poor and needy" (v. 1) and is in a "day of . . . trouble" (v. 7). But now we get more specificity in verse 14. Notice the abrupt address: " O God." That is, "Listen up!" Listen up to my trouble:

> O God, the insolent rise up against me;
> a band of ruffians seeks my life,
> and they do not set you before them.

I am surrounded by thugs. This most likely does not mean street violence. Most often it seems to refer to careless, slanderous people in the village who abuse one's reputation. In a shame culture such speech is immensely damaging, and one is helpless before it: My reputation and therefore my future are being put at risk. It is especially interesting that in the third line of the verse, it is asserted that the ruffians not only damage me, but they do not treat you, YHWH, very well either. The laments characteristically seek a way to show God that there is something at stake in all of the trouble for God as well as for the speaker. The trouble not only jeopardizes me; it puts you, YHWH, at risk as well, and therefore you should act. Act for your name's sake!

There is an abrupt move from "a band of ruffians" in verse 14 to "you" in verse 15. The two verses provide a sharp contrast to show how YHWH is quite unlike the insolent ruffians. Unlike them, YHWH is merciful, gracious, abounding in *hesed* and faithfulness. The insolent ruffians know nothing of mercy, grace, *hesed,* or faithfulness. The psalmist repeats the classic mantra from Exodus 34 that we have seen already in Psalm 103:8. This sequence of terms asserts YHWH's character and YHWH's covenantal responsibility.

It is on the basis of this doxology (that contrasts YHWH with the trouble-makers) that the psalm ends in a new series of imperatives (vv. 16–17):

- "Turn"
- "Be gracious"
- "Give"
- "Save"
- "Show"

These requested actions will demonstrate YHWH's true character, will honor covenant, and will expose the insolent ruffians as nobodies. The psalm concludes with two statements of completed action:

- You have helped.
- You have comforted me.

It is as good as done. It is done! The speaker has complete confidence that YHWH can be relied on to honor covenant and to restore what has been lost to insolent ruffians. The restoration concerns a good name (reputation) and a good future.

When we put the three rhetorical clusters together we can see that the dramatic movement of the entire psalm is from the initial "poor and needy" (v. 1) to "helped" and "comforted" (v. 17). This dramatic movement is accomplished according to the reliable *hesed* of YHWH that is mobilized through this psalm. But the trigger for that dramatic movement is the daring, demanding self-announcement of the speaker, who is willing to risk insistent imperatives in the presence of the God before whom all the nations bow down. The sweeping doxologies to YHWH are only a supporting role for the real action that concerns the desperate and helpless speaker. We should notice two important points that contradict conventional assumptions. First is the assumption here that God can be indifferent and unengaged and has to be persuaded to act. Such persuasion, moreover, takes the form of a doxological reminder that seeks to flatter YHWH into action. Second is the recognition that the speaker need not be excessively deferential before YHWH but has some right to assert and has a legitimate insistence to make. YHWH is pledged to tenacious solidarity. The speaker is entitled to tenacious solidarity. But it requires some liturgic *chutzpah* to move the drama of YHWH's pledge and Israel's entitlement.

Perhaps you will have noticed that in each of these three subclusters of the psalm *hesed* is pivotal. In the first subcluster of verses 1–7, the speaker in verse 5 repeats the old formula of *hesed* that asserts who God is and how God should act. In the second subcluster of verses 8–13, which has a more didactic tone, the opening doxology of verses 8–10 is matched by the concluding assertion of *hesed* in verse 13. In that verse, as in verse 17, the speaker uses a statement of completed action: "You have delivered." In the third subcluster of verses 14–17, YHWH, unlike the insolent ruffians, is a *God of hesed*. Thus in verse 5 in the first cluster, in verse 13 in the second cluster, and in verse 15 in the third cluster, it is all about *God's hesed*. This repeated accent on *hesed*, however, is not a witness to others. It is addressed to YHWH, as though to insist on God's *hesed*, about which YHWH has, until now, been negligent.

This dialogical poetry addresses YHWH, covenantal partner, with great insistence. This is especially clear in a rhetorical element in the Hebrew that is not recognizable in our translations. In Hebrew, the second-person-singular pronoun "you" is most often attached as part of the verb. But Hebrew also has an independent second-person-singular pronoun that stands apart from the verb. It is often used for special emphasis. It does not occur often, but when it is used, it often comes along with the pronoun attached to the verb so that we get a double "you, you." In this psalm, unlike any other that I know, we get six uses of the independent pronoun for purposes of accent that suggests the great intensity of this articulation:

- You are my God (v. 2).
- You are good and forgiving (v. 5).
- You are great (v. 10).
- You are our God (v. 10).
- You are a God merciful and gracious (v. 15).
- Because you, YHWH, have helped (v. 17).

The independent pronoun is used in some of these cases because there is no finite verb to which to attach the pronoun. Nonetheless, the sum of these uses is a voicing of great intensity. The repeated uses call attention to the bold, direct address to YHWH that is in part affirmation of YHWH but in part summons to YHWH, that is, a calling out of YHWH.

We can imagine this psalm in liturgy, even though we do not often use it so. It is all imperative and motivation, in conventional context reason enough to avoid it. But when we are bold enough to use such a prayer in our assemblage, the routine is interrupted by urgent contemporaneity. This poetic imagery, if we pay attention, invites us to connect our utterance to our life experience. Mostly we live in a world that is without God. In that world, it is all rough-and-tumble thrust and rush that run toward violence. The inventory of insolent ruffians can reach all the way from an unkind coworker or colleague to an unbearable older sibling, from street assault to rumors and realities of terrorism before which we are left helpless and desperate.

In the face of such ruffians we know about being helpless. We are, however, not helpless when we are adequately schooled in this strident rhetoric of insistence. This lament psalm, along with many others, does not suggest that we engage in doxological denial to pretend there is no danger. Nor do such psalms suggest that we shrink away in cowardice. Rather the lament psalms suggest that as tenured members of covenant we take the initiative on the basis of our entitlement. We have been invited into tenacious solidarity, and now we insist on it. A by-product of such speech is the recovery of nerve, courage, and freedom enough to announce ourselves. The central point, however, is that God can be summoned back to God's true self and to God's proper covenantal work. We have here, in this psalm, a script for such daring summons whereby we also become our true selves and may return to our proper work.

PSALM 109

Psalm 109 is a poignant poetic piece that should be held in reserve for very special circumstances. In it the unidentified speaker makes two extended statements, one that concerns the failure of a neighbor and one that looks to God as an alternative.

The psalm is divided into three unequal parts. In the first part, verses

1–4, the poem is introduced as an address to God and a petition that God should intervene into the speaker's vexed life. Verses 2–3 describe for God the jeopardized circumstance of his life with an accusation against those who are his adversaries. They are labeled as "wicked" and sound like the "insolent ruffians" of Psalm 86. They have broken faith by speaking destructive slander that will destroy even a good person in a social circumstance where a good reputation counts for all. Even more, the speaker describes himself as one who has "loved" his adversaries, that is, acted as a good neighbor (as in "Love thy neighbor"). For his good actions toward them, however, they have returned evil. Their evil destructiveness is gratuitous. Nothing the speaker has done merits such a negative response. As a result of their action, his life is at risk; for that reason he speaks to God with intensity and urgency.

In the extended second part of the psalm, verses 5–20, we have a long address to God in which the speaker proposes to God the kind of punishment that should be meted out to his adversaries. Note at the outset that our translations regularly introduce this part of the psalm with "They say," putting the violent rhetoric that follows into the mouth of the adversary, as though the speaker were quoting them. (Or alternatively, these verses are put in quotes, a move that accomplishes the same thing, as though it is all a quote from his enemy.) But in fact there is nothing in the Hebrew that justifies "They say," or quotation marks. This is not a quote whereby the violent rhetoric can be transferred to another. This is the speech of the initial speaker. And while we, in our modern nicety, might be offended by such rhetoric and wish it had not been said, it is probable that the speaker intended every syllable of it and is not embarrassed at all by voicing such deep emotion.

These verses propose (a) that God should appoint a "wicked man," that is, a "hanging judge" to try those whom he accuses; (b) that a guilty verdict be brought against them; and (c) that a detailed punishment should be inflicted on them. Like many victims of violence, this speaker knows ahead of time how the trial should come out.

What follows is a series of jussive verbs that are commendations to the hanging judge in the hope that the judge will be as severe as possible with the accused, so grave is the affront of the offender. In verses 8–13, we are offered the most vigorous extended wish for vengeance in all of Scripture, a thirst for vengeance that fills out the wish of Lamech in Genesis 4:24:

> "If Cain is avenged sevenfold,
>   truly Lamech
>   seventy-sevenfold."

Seventy-sevenfold will be sufficient, but not less than that; the rhetoric sounds familiar to us from contemporary witnesses who often say after an execution, "At least justice was done." This is a cry for justice in confidence that God and the judge appointed by God are committed to such justice. It is all a death sentence: few days of life remaining; wife left a widow; children become orphans; property forfeited; family line cut off (vv. 8–13).

In verses 18–19 the speaker imagines that the curse, the imposition of death upon another, is like oil that soaks in or like clothing that envelops him. The offender is both inside and outside a carrier of curse. We may notice in particular the wish of verse 12 (emphasis added):

> May there be no one to do him a *kindness*,
> nor anyone to pity his orphaned children.

This term "kindness" is a weak translation of our word *hesed*. May no neighbor show him *hesed*; may none do tenacious solidarity toward him. And the reason for this wish is that he himself "did not remember to show kindness" (v. 16). That is the sum of this affront. He was no good neighbor. He was incapable of neighborly solidarity; for that reason all of these wishes constitute hope that he in turn will be denied such neighborly solidarity. Indeed his lack of *hesed* led him to pursue "the poor and needy and the brokenhearted to their death" (v. 16).

In verse 20 this plea for retaliation has been exhausted. It ends in this verse with a reference back to the initial charge of verse 5 ("They reward me evil for good"): ". . . who speak evil against me." The speaker has exhausted human possibility and knows there is no hope for *hesed* from such human neighbors.

But then, in the third part of the poem, verses 21–31, the mood and the address shift abruptly: But you, Lord YHWH! The turn is from human failure to divine possibility. Now the speaker, so filled with vengeance, dares to address God with an imperative petition: Act for me! Act for me because no neighbor will. The petition bids God to act for the sake of God's reputation ("name's sake"). You, God, want to be known for solidarity, so show me solidarity. And the second line of the parallelism is ". . . because your steadfast love is good, deliver me." On the basis of your tenacious solidarity (*hesed*), deliver me! Deliver me from a hopeless social circumstance of slander. This second imperative, "deliver me," is followed by an extended motivation:

> For am I poor and needy [see v. 16],
> and my heart is pierced within me.
> I am like a shadow at evening;
> I am shaken off like a locust.
> My knees are weak through fasting;
> my body has become gaunt.
> I am an object of scorn to my accusers;
> when they see me, they shake their heads.
> vv. 22–25

The speaker has no resources or possibility. It is all up to God.

In verse 26 we get more imperative petitions: "Help . . . save . . . according to your steadfast love." In verses 27–29 we get a return to jussive wishes that bid God to reverse the threat and transpose it into a blessing for the speaker. The outcome that assumes the good response of the *hesed*-performing God is well-being. God will save the needy whose lives are at risk (v. 31). And the speaker will give thanks and praise in the throng of those who trust YHWH and count on *hesed* (v. 30).

This third section begins in petition and ends in thanks, trusting that all will be restored because God is an agent of tenacious solidarity. Thus we get a complete contrast between the failed neighbor (vv. 5–20) and the blessing God (vv. 21–31). In the first sequence everything is deathly; but the turn to God, who will hear, act, and deliver, leads to new life.

It occurs to me that this psalm pivots on the four uses of *hesed*, two in each of the two speeches. In the first, the wish is for no *hesed* for the adversary (v. 16) because he had shown no *hesed* (v. 12). This is a world so filled with enmity that it is without *hesed*. The alternative world occupied by YHWH is one saturated with *hesed*. For that reason, the petition appeals to God's *hesed*:

- Because of your *hesed* deliver me (v. 21).
- Save me according to your *hesed* (v. 26).

It matters decisively in the world of the Psalms that the *hesed*-doing God is a character in the drama of creation. The conviction of the Psalter is that this God of *hesed* can indeed be summoned into the world by urgent petition. This psalm does not say so, but I imagine that because the Psalms are praxis and not only mere rhetoric, the performance of *hesed* is present in the life of the community that names the God of *hesed*.

I said at the outset that Psalm 109 should be reserved for special circumstances. This is no ordinary prayer, and for most of us it violates our sense of propriety. My standard pedagogical ploy in taking up a psalm is to ask, "Who is speaking here? Who would use this psalm and find it helpful?" Certainly it is not my psalm. and I would not say it because my life has sufficient *hesed* in it that I can manage. I asked this question of this psalm once in class, and my student Linda answered promptly. She said, "This is the statement voiced by a woman who has been raped." (I learned later that Linda herself had been violated in that way.) Her response would not have occurred to me, but she knew beyond a shadow of a doubt about a world of violence void of *hesed*. She knew about being abandoned without any advocate. This was her special circumstance, and she found this prayer to be compellingly appropriate. She knew about the authenticity of rage before God, and she knew about the turn to the God of *hesed*, but only after the vengeance had been given full voice.

So I thought about other such special circumstances:

- I could imagine a mother in Iraq just as her son had his head blown off by a bomb.

- I could imagine a poor black person in our economy amid the endur-
  ing legacy of slavery that has dropped him into despairing poverty
  and incarceration.
- I could imagine Jeremiah Wright, on behalf of many African Americans, saying, "God damn America."
- I could imagine a cry of the vulnerable against exploitative institutions
  of all kinds that render one helpless without an advocate.

This is emotional extremity addressed to God. This is emotional extremity
voiced in the congregation of those who are engaged in the work of *hesed*. This
is such extremity artistically expressed by a series of jussives that pivots abruptly
to "But you, Lord YHWH." This is not everyday talk, but we keep it in reserve
for the times when we are left exposed without *hesed*. We may be glad that the
psalm does not end with verse 19. It ends with thanks (v. 30), that the *hesed* of
YHWH stands at the right hand of the needy (v. 31).

CONCLUDING REMARKS

Everywhere in these three extended psalms we have found the rhetoric of
hesed, its reliability, its absence, its failure, and it capacity to summon. In
Psalm 103 we have seen *hesed* at every turn, repeating the old mantra from
Sinai, operative in the midst of our guilt and our mortality. In Psalm 86 we
have seen a bid for *hesed* in the midst of tribulation, when God must be called
out, again with the old formula. And in Psalm 109 we have seen a turn from
failed human *hesed* in the neighborhood to the ultimate source of reliable
hesed in YHWH. Such overt preoccupation with *hesed* is not everywhere
evident in the Psalter; nevertheless, I dare suggest that *hesed* is everywhere the
subtext of the Psalter, because it is the deepest need of the human heart, the
deepest desire of the human community, and the deepest mark of the God
who occupies this poetry. The book of Psalms is our most elemental script
for the ongoing work of *hesed* that is both our proper rhetorical practice and
our proper bodily investment. We, in the image of this God, are intended for
tenacious solidarity.

I perhaps do not need to say, in conclusion, that the continuation of this
dialogue about fidelity is an urgent task for the sake of the well-being and
future of our society. It is urgent because the dominant claims (and therefore
the dominant rhetoric) of our society are skewed away from matters of fidelity.
Indeed dominant modes of discourse and practice aggressively contradict such
a way of speaking and of living.

Among the markings of a way of speech and life that contradict the way of
hesed are the following:

- We are witnessing a *monetization of social relationships* and thereby a *reduction of relationships to commodity transactions*. The outcome is that human persons become tradable commodities. And in the midst of acute economic inequality, many vulnerable persons thereby become disposable and dispensable commodities.

- We are witnessing a reduction of bodily human reality to a series of *technological fixes*. Thus staying manly simply requires a drug for virility. Staying young simply requires cosmetic surgery. Managing high-energy children simply requires more screens to entertain them. The attractiveness of technological fixes for dense human reality is a denial of the organic truth of the human body and the body politic.

- We are witnessing a passion for individualism that sustains a market ideology that reduces our imagination and policy formation to *instrumental reasoning*, in which the thick and inscrutable human questions—questions of fidelity—are bracketed out as nonexistent. We settle for policy formation that is contained within the myopic world of monetization, commoditization, and technical reason. The erasure of liberal arts in our society is a sign and a measure of the way in which instrumental reason has displaced the complexity of the human body and the body politic.

In the face of these onslaughts of dehumanization, the continuation and maintenance of a dialogue about fidelity is an urgent task, for such dialogue generates futures, sustains neighborhoods, and holds the prospect for peace with justice. By way of reflection on these three psalms—a hymn, a lament, and a profound cry for vengeance—I mean to suggest that the book of Psalms is a primary script for a conversation that exposes the dominant claims of our society to be inadequate and finally false. The performance of this counterscript requires, to be sure, immense imagination. But it also evokes that imagination, as is evident in the long history of performance. The liturgical performance of the Psalms, such as hymn singing, is not simply an incident in liturgical sequence. It is a frontal act of resistance to dehumanization and the modeling of an alternative of interactive fidelity as a way in the world.

Hymn singing is *a bold act of resistance* against this triple threat that we face in our contemporary culture of

- monetization
- technological fixes
- instrumental reasoning

Hymn singing is, moreover, *the performance of an alternative*. In this alternative, we profess the following:

- That faithful relationships count more than monetization
- That dwelling in sacramental mystery counts more than technological fixes
- That claims of thick meaning count for more than the convenience of instrumental reasoning

We make these professions, often without awareness or acknowledgment. But with awareness or not, with acknowledgment or not, that is our work in hymn singing.

Set in this context of resistance and alternative, we are able to see clearly *why we sing.* We sing in order to acknowledge and attest that the center of our daily life is in the deep reality of faithful relationships, sacramental mystery, and thick meanings. When we do not sing regularly in the company of the baptized community (that is, "sealed as Christ's own forever"), we are easily talked out of these realities, and we settle for what is cheap, thin, and convenient, which is so much on offer among us. That is why we sing!

Set in this context of resistance and alternative, we are also able to see clearly *what we sing.* We do not sing vacuously with the elevator music of the consumer economy. Rather we sing out of the thickness of Scripture that concerns the creator God who generously gives life, the emancipatory God who opens futures, the commanding God who summons to particular obedience. That is, we sing particularly and specifically because we know the narrative plot of faith that pivots on the name, history, and promise of this God. Even though our artistic sensibility requires a rich variety of images and metaphors to voice the plentitude of the God of the gospel (not unlike Scripture!), we are not in doubt concerning the particularity of our history, our future, and our obedience. *That is what we sing!*

The why and what of hymn singing summon us into poetic cadence and imagery because the thickness of the why and what we sing cannot be reduced to one-dimensional propositions of certitude. In singing we host a very different world, one that draws us to the wonder of God and to the reality of our humanness in the image of that God.

Acknowledgments

Notes

Foreword

1. "The Heidelberg Catechism," in *Book of Confessions, Study Edition* (Louisville, KY: Westminster John Knox Press, 2017), 57.

Preface

1. *Glory to God: Hymns, Psalms, and Spiritual Songs* (Louisville, KY: Westminster John Knox Press, 2013).
2. Peter C. Ho, "The Design of the MT Psalter: A Macrostructural Analysis," a dissertation submitted to the University of Gloucester, 2016, 93–99.
3. See Lewis Hyde, *The Gift: Creativity and the Artist in the Modern World* (New York: Vintage Books, 2007), 218–20.
4. Ibid., 218. The narrative account is from Hyde, who in turn quotes Chauncy. Chauncy was directly involved in the formation of New England Unitarianism.
5. Ibid., 220.

Part One: Why We Sing

1. See Peter L. Berger and Thomas Luckmann, *The Social Construction of Reality: A Treatise in the Sociology of Knowledge* (Anchor Books; Garden City: Doubleday & Co., 1967), and Walter Brueggemann, *Israel's Praise: Doxology against Idolatry and Ideology* (Philadelphia: Fortress Press, 1988), ch. 1.
2. Gerhard von Rad, *Old Testament Theology*, vol. 1 (New York: Harper & Brothers, 1962), 356–70.

Chapter 1: Psalm 104

1. See Walter Brueggemann, *From Whom No Secrets Are Hid: Introducing the Psalms*, ed. Brent A. Strawn (Louisville, KY: Westminster John Knox Press, 2014), 56–79.
2. See William P. Brown, *Sacred Sense: Discovering the Wonder of God's Word and World* (Grand Rapids: Eerdmans, 2015).

3. *Glory to God: The Presbyterian Hymnal* (Louisville, KY: Westminster John Knox Press, 2013), 10.
4. Jon D. Levenson, *Creation and the Persistence of Evil: The Jewish Drama of Divine Omnipotence* (San Francisco: Harper & Row, 1988), 17; Levenson attributes "rubber duckey" to a student.
5. See Walter Brueggemann, "Why Are You Talking about Having No Bread?" in *What Did Jesus Ask? Christian Leaders Reflect on His Questions of Faith* (New York: Time Books, 2015), 110–15.
6. John Calvin, *Institutes of the Christian Religion*, vol. 1, ed. John T. McNeill, trans. Ford Lewis Battles, LCC 20 (Philadelphia: Westminster Press, 1960), 35, 37; see James Barr, *Biblical Faith and Natural Theology: The Gifford Lectures for 1991* (Oxford: Clarendon Press, 1993).
7. Francis of Assisi, "All Creatures of Our God and King," *Glory to God*, no. 15.
8. Tilly Lubis, "Hallelujah! Sing Praise to Your Creator," trans. David Diephouse, ibid., no. 18.

Chapter 2: Psalm 107

1. Harvey H. Guthrie Jr., *Theology as Thanksgiving: From Israel's Psalms to the Church's Eucharist* (New York: Seabury Press, 1981), 18.
2. Erhard S. Gerstenberger, *Theologies of the Old Testament* (Minneapolis: Fortress Press, 2002).
3. Claus Westermann, *The Praise of God in the Psalms* (Richmond, VA: John Knox Press, 1965), 27–28.
4. See Claus Westermann, *What Does the Old Testament Say about God?* (Atlanta: John Knox Press, 1979). Westermann has shown the way in which the themes of "blessing" (creation) and "deliverance" (history) constitute a defining interface for Old Testament imagination. Our psalm keeps both themes in purview.
5. Claus Westermann, in *The Psalms: Structure, Content & Message* (Minneapolis: Augsburg Publishing House, 1980), 73–83, identifies songs of thanks as "Individual Psalms of Narrative Praise." The accent is on narrative because such psalms, as in 107, tell the entire story of being in trouble, lamenting to God and being delivered, and finishing with praise and thanks to God; the genre requires the entire narrative recital.
6. *The New Century Hymnal* (Cleveland: Pilgrim Press, 1995), 5.
7. Such "progressive" reductionism is exemplified by a response of a recent hospital chaplain who was asked by the parent of a desperately sick child to pray for a miracle: "I don't pray for miracles." The next day the parent asked the office of chaplains, "Do not send me a chaplain who cannot pray for miracles."
8. Karl Barth, *Church Dogmatics* III/3 (Edinburgh: T. & T. Clark, 1961).
9. Martin Buber, *Moses: The Revelation and the Covenant* (Atlanta Highlands, NJ: Humanities Press International, 1946), 75. See Walter Brueggemann, *Abiding Astonishment: Psalms, Modernity, and the Making of History* (Louisville, KY: Westminster John Knox Press, 1991).
10. Michelle Alexander, *The New Jim Crow: Mass Incarceration in the Age of Colorblindness* (New York: New Press, 2012).
11. On the vexed linkage of sin and suffering, see Frederick J. Gaiser, *Healing in the Bible: Theological Insight for Christian Ministry* (Grand Rapids: Baker Books, 2010), 198–99, and his citation of Gerhard von Rad and Samuel Balentine. More programmatically, see Fredrik Lindstrom, *Suffering and*

Sin: Interpretations of Illness in the Individual Complaint Psalms (Stockholm: Almqvist & Wiksell International, 1994).

12. Guthrie, *Theology as Thanksgiving*, 45.
13. Ibid., 69.
14. Isaac Watts, "When I Survey the Wondrous Cross," *Glory to God: The Presbyterian Hymnal* (Louisville, KY: Westminster John Knox Press, 2013), no. 223.
15. Howard B. Grose, "Give of Your Best to the Master," in *Hymns of Faith* (Carole Stream, IL: Tabernacle Publishing Co., 1980), 501.
16. George Stroup, *Before God* (Grand Rapids: Eerdmans, 2004), 146–47.
17. Martin Rinkart, "Now Thank We All Our God," trans. Catherine Winkworth, *Glory to God*, no. 643.
18. David Gambrell, "A Grateful Heart," ibid., no. 652.

Chapter 3: Psalm 105

1. Gerhard von Rad, "The Form-Critical Problem of the Hexateuch," *The Problem of the Hexateuch and Other Essays* (New York: McGraw-Hill, 1966), 1–78.
2. See Arthur C. Cochrane, *The Church's Confession under Hitler* (Philadelphia: Westminster Press, 1962).
3. "Good Christian Friends, Rejoice," trans. John Mason Neale, *Glory to God: The Presbyterian Hymnal* (Louisville, KY: Westminster John Knox Press, 2013), no. 132 (emphasis added).
4. Charles Wesley, "Christ the Lord Is Risen Today!" ibid., no. 245 (emphasis added).
5. Gerhard von Rad, *Old Testament Theology*, vol. 1, *The Theology of Israel's Historical Tradition* (New York: Harper & Brothers, 1962), 108.
6. See Walter Brueggemann, *Chosen? Reading the Bible amid the Israeli-Palestinian Conflict* (Louisville, KY: Westminster John Knox Press, 2015).
7. Martin Luther King Jr., "How Long? Not Long," public speech delivered in Montgomery, Alabama, March 25, 1965. See Martin Luther King Jr., *A Testament of Hope: The Essential Writings of Martin Luther King Jr.*, ed. James M. Washington (New York: HarperCollins Publishers, 1986), 227–30.
8. See Patrick D. Miller, "Deuteronomy and the Psalter: Evoking a Biblical Conversation," in *Israelite Religion and Biblical Theology: Collected Essays*, JSOT Supp. 267 (Sheffield: Sheffield Academic Press, 2000), 318–27. On Psalm 1 and Deuteronomy, see specifically 329. See also Frank Crüsemann, *The Torah: Theology and Social History of Old Testament Law* (Edinburgh: T. & T. Clark, 1996), 234–75.
9. See George W. Stroup, *Before God* (Grand Rapids, Eerdmans, 2104), 155–61. Stroup comments on "saying grace" before meals as a quintessential act of gratitude: "The cost [of giving up the practice of saying grace] may be far higher than anyone has calculated. If children (and other Christians) do not understand their daily bread to be a gracious gift from God, then it may not be surprising that consciously or unconsciously they draw a different conclusion—namely, that their 'bread' belongs to them. It is provided by the 'family breadwinners,' and therefore is the family's personal property. If it is 'theirs,' then there is really no reason to give thanks to God for it. And daily bread may be only the first in a long list of entitlements that make up 'the American way of life' which children are taught are possessions and not gifts from God" (161).
10. Katherine Hankey, "I Love to Tell the Story," *Glory to God*, no. 462.
11. Jean Janzen, "I Long for Your Commandments," *Glory to God*, no. 64.

Chapter 4: Psalm 106

1. See James Wallis, *America's Original Sin: Racism, White Privilege, and the Bridge to a New America* (Grand Rapids: Brazos Press, 2016).
2. See James Cone, *The Cross and the Lynching Tree* (Maryknoll, NY: Orbis Books, 2011).
3. Taizé Community, "Jesus, Remember Me," in *Glory to God: The Presbyterian Hymnal* (Louisville, KY: Westminster John Knox Press, 2013), no. 227.
4. See Terence E. Fretheim, *The Suffering of God: An Old Testament Perspective*, Overtures to Biblical Theology (Philadelphia: Fortress Press, 1984), 144.
5. Charlotte Elliott, "Just as I Am, without One Plea," *Glory to God*, no. 442.
6. Martin E. Leckebusch, "Your Endless Love, Your Mighty Acts," ibid., no. 60.
7. Francis of Assisi, "All Creatures of Our God and King," ibid., no. 15.
8. Martin Rinkart, "Now Thank We All Our God," trans. Catherine Winkworth, ibid., 643.
9. George W. Stroup, *Before God* (Grand Rapids: Eerdmans, 2004),146–47.
10. Ibid., 149–50.

Part Two: What We Sing

1. For some of the contextual data for these hymns I have relied on *The New Century Hymnal Companion: A Guide to the Hymns*, edited by Kristen L. Forman (Cleveland: Pilgrim Press, 1998).

Chapter 5: Blest Be the Tie That Binds

1. "Proper 22," *The Book of Common Prayer* (New York: Seabury Press, 1979), 182.
2. Karl Barth, *Church Dogmatics* III/3 (Edinburgh: T. & T. Clark, 1961), 268.

Chapter 6: God of Grace and God of Glory

1. Fred Shapiro, "Who Wrote the Serenity Prayer," *The Chronicle of Higher Education*, April 28, 2014, https://www.chronicle.com/article/Who-Wrote-the-Serenity-Prayer-/146159.
2. Abraham J. Heschel, *Who Is Man?* (Redwood City, CA: Stanford University Press, 1965), 113.

Chapter 7: He Who Would Valiant Be

1. John Bunyan, *The Pilgrim's Progress* (New York: Signet Classics, 2009), 283.
2. Ibid., st. 2, l. 5.
3. Ibid., st. 3, lines 1–4.
4. Ibid., st, 3, l. 5.
5. John Bew, *Citizen Clem: A Biography of Attlee* (London: Riverrun Press, 2016).

Chapter 8: Holy, Holy, Holy

1. Isaac Watts, "Before Jehovah's Awful Throne," in *The Evangelical Hymnal* (St. Louis: Eden Publishing House, 1922), 64.
2. Ronald E. Clements, "Patterns in the Prophetic Canon," in *Canon and Authority: Essays in Old Testament Religion and Theology*, ed. George W. Coats and Burke O. Long (Philadelphia: Fortress Press, 1977), 53.
3. Herbert Frederick Brokering, "Earth and All Stars!" *Glory to God: The*

Presbyterian Hymnal (Louisville, KY: Westminster John Knox Press, 2013), no. 26.

4. Francis of Assisi, "All Creatures of Our God and King," ibid., no. 15.

5. See Cameron Wybrow, *The Bible, Baconianism, and Mastery over Nature: The Old Testament and Its Modern Misreading* (New York: Peter Lang, 1991); and A. McGrath, *The Reenchantment of Nature: The Denial of Religion and the Ecological Crisis* (New York: Doubleday, 2002).

6. Daniel W. Hardy and David F. Ford, *Praising and Knowing God* (Philadelphia: Westminster Press, 1985), 50–56.

Chapter 9: I Sing the Mighty Power of God

1. See William P. Brown, *The Seven Pillars of Creation: The Bible, Science, and the Ecology of Wonder* (Oxford: Oxford University Press, 2010), 161–76. My discussion is much indebted to that of Brown.

2. The translation "master worker" is somewhat speculative, but it is the best we have.

3. Brown, *Seven Pillars*, 167–68.

4. Ibid., 169–70.

5. Martin Buber, *Moses: The Revelation and the Covenant* (Atlantic Highlands, NJ: Humanities Press International, 1946; 1988), 75.

6. On this text Gerhard von Rad (*Wisdom in Israel* [Nashville: Abingdon Press, 1972], 34) comments, "This is a fine, wide-ranging sentence which can set one's thoughts moving in many different directions. It speaks of the king's glory in investigation (at that time the king was the foremost champion and promoter of all search after wisdom); but before this there stands the saying about God, whose glory lies in concealing, whose secrets, therefore, are to be worshiped by men. God conceals, kings discover—to both, glory is due. What a profound knowledge of God and of men is encompassed by this handful of words. . . . God and king stand opposite each other, once again characterized by secrecy and revelation."

7. E. O. Wilson, *Half-Earth: Our Planet's Fight for Life* (New York: Norton, 2016).

8. On the use of the term, see Jürgen Moltmann, *God in Creation: A New Theology of Creation and the Spirit of God* (Minneapolis: Fortress Press, 1993). For a different casting see Richard Kearny, *Anatheism: Return to God after God* (New York: Columbia University Press, 2010).

9. John Barton, *Understanding Old Testament Ethics* (Louisville, KY: Westminster John Knox Press, 2003), 39.

10. Karl Barth, *Church Dogmatics: The Doctrine of Creation,* III/3 (Edinburgh: T. & T. Clark, 1960), 13.

11. See Cameron Wybrow, *The Bible, Baconianism, and Mastery over Nature: The Old Testament and Its Modern Misreading* (New York: Peter Lang, 1991).

Chapter 12: O for a Closer Walk with God

1. Austin Miles, "In the Garden," in *The Chalice Hymnal* (St. Louis: Chalice Press, 1995), 227. Miles offers this sugar-sweet reflection on the narrative of John 20:11–18 concerning Jesus' resurrection appearance to Mary Magdalene. Because Austin's rendering is quite privatized, it moves in a very different direction from our hymn.

2. Anonymous, "Just a Closer Walk with Thee," in *The Chalice Hymnal* (St. Louis: Chalice Press, 1995), 557. The origin of the gospel song is unknown but has many popular renderings.

Chapter 13: O Master, Let Me Walk with Thee

1. Dietrich Bonhoeffer, *The Cost of Discipleship* (New York: Macmillan, 1955), 37.
2. *The New Century Hymnal* (Cleveland: Pilgrim Press, 1995), 885.

Chapter 15: Praise, My Soul, the King of Heaven

1. Of the three hymnals with which I am regularly working, the Episcopal hymnal retains the unexpurgated gender-exclusive language of Lyte's original; the Presbyterian hymnal presents the original language as well as a more gender-inclusive rendering (see no. 619). The *New Century Hymnal* of the United Church of Christ oddly omits the hymn completely.
2. This usage of self-addressing self reflects the "many selves of the self," on which see Roy Schafer, *Retelling a Life: Narration and Dialogue in Psychoanalysis* (New York: Basic Books, 1992), 21–35 passim.
3. See Nathan C. Lane, *The Compassionate but Punishing God: A Canonical Analysis of Exodus 34:6–7* (Eugene, OR: Pickwick Publications, 2010).

Chapter 16: Sparrows as Models of Faith

1. *The Heidelberg Catechism* (Philadelphia: United Church Press, 1962), 9.

Chapter 17: Sparrow Song One: God's Eye Is on the Sparrow

1. Melissa Florer-Bixler, "Sparrow, Swallow, and Us," *Christian Century* 134, no. 17 (August 16, 2017):12–13.

Chapter 18: Sparrow Two: God of the Sparrow

1. William P. Brown, *The Seven Pillars of Creation: The Bible, Science, and the Ecology of Wonder* (Oxford: Oxford University Press, 2010), 4.
2. On the "fundamental relational character" of creation, see Terence E. Fretheim, *God and World in the Old Testament* (Nashville: Abingdon Press, 2005), 13–22. Fretheim, also a Lutheran who understands this best of all, cites Samuel Balentine, Douglas John Hall, Martin Buber, and Keith Ward as eloquent support for his thesis (298, n. 61). George Steiner (*Grammars of Creation Originating in the Gifford Lectures for 1990* [New Haven, CT: Yale University Press, 2001], 62) suggests the same dialogic quality concerning God and the world: "Primary to the Old Testament and Talmudic reading of the necessities and consequences of creation is the notion that God cannot, in some sense, be Himself if He does not incur the perils of alienation, of contamination entailed by the making of matter and of man. . . . There is in the Torah a theme of interdependence between God and man."
3. "Jesus, Thou Joy of Loving Hearts," trans. Ray Palmer, *Glory to God: The Presbyterian Hymnal* (Louisville, KY: Westminster John Knox Press, 2013), no. 494.

Chapter 19: Sparrow Three: Someone Asked the Question

1. While a crow is not a sparrow, attention may be given to the research of Kaeli Swift, "What a Crow Knows," *The Week*, July 21, 2017, 36–37, who reports on the emotive reaction of crows; she goes so far as to suggest that crows "mourn their dead and hold 'funerals.'"

2. Martin Buber, *I and Thou*, trans. Walter Kaufmann (New York: Charles Scribner's Sons, 1970), 75.
3. *Book of Common Prayer* (New York: Church Publishing, 1979), 63.
4. *The Heidelberg Catechism* (Philadelphia: United Church Press, 1962), 9.
5. C. B. MacPherson, *The Political Theory of Possessive Individualism: Hobbes to Locke* (Oxford: Oxford University Press, 1962), 3.

Chapter 20: We Are Marching in the Light of God

1. Michael Walzer, *Exodus and Revolution* (New York: Basic Books, 1984), 4, 25.
2. Ibid., 136.
3. Bruce Feiler, *America's Prophet: Moses and the American Story* (New York: William Morrow, 2009).
4. "The Unifying American Story," *New York Times*, March 21, 2017, A25.
5. Feiler, *America's Prophet*, 252.
6. Walzer, *Exodus and Revolution*, 149.

Conclusion

1. Erhard S. Gerstenberger, *Bittritual u. Klageleid d. Einzelnen im Alten Testament* (Neukirchen-Vluyn: Neukirchener Verlag, 1980).
2. Fredrik Lindstrom, *Suffering and Sin: Interpretations of Illness in the Individual Complaint Psalms*, Coniectanea Biblica Old Testament Series 37 (Stockholm: Almqvist & Wiksell International, 1994).
3. See Erhard S. Gerstenberger, "Psalms," in *Old Testament Form Criticism*, ed. John H. Hayes (San Antonio: Trinity University Press, 1974), 179–223; and Barbara Green, *How Are the Mighty Fallen? A Dialogical Study of King Saul in 1 Samuel*, JSOT Supp. 365 (Sheffield: Sheffield Academic Press, 2003), 55–115.
4. Robert Alter, *The Art of Biblical Poetry* (New York: Basic Books, 1985).
5. See Nathan C. Lane, *The Compassionate but Punishing God: A Canonical Analysis of Exodus 34:6–7* (Eugene, OR: Wipf & Stock, 2010).
6. Ernest Becker, *The Denial of Death* (New York: Free Press, 1973).

Index of Scripture

Index of Hymns